To my friends
Ralph and Shirley Varker
From
Janet Little (pg 191)
and
Jennifer Little Steves (pg 179)

FORTUNE

BUILDERS

FORTUNE
BUILDERS

by David A. Chodack

IMPACT
PUBLISHING CO.
1601 OAK PARK BLVD., PLEASANT HILL, CA. 94523
(415) 935-4370

Book design by Marian Hartsough
Cover design by Dennis Kiernan of Epop Productions, Inc.
Typesetting by Turner, Brown & Yeoman
Printing & Binding by Fairfield Graphics

Fortune Builders

IMPACT
PUBLISHING CO.
1601 OAK PARK BLVD., PLEASANT HILL, CA. 94523
(415) 935-4370

Dedication

I would like to dedicate this book to all the wonderful people featured in these pages. They took time out of their busy schedules to open up their lives to a total stranger, and without them, this book would not have been possible. I would like to take this opportunity to publicly say, "Thank you."

Acknowledgments

I would like to thank Dave Glubetich, Publisher, and Judy Moretz, Senior Editor, at Impact Publishing, who gave me the chance to do this book, and then gave me all the help and encouragement I could ask for. Also my thanks to Roger Blewett, Marketing Director, Ron Jackson, and all the other fine people at Impact Publishing who have contributed to this book.

I would also like to thank Betty Crouse, who typed most of the manuscript and caught most of my mistakes before they got any further, my mother, Jean Chodack, who also helped out with the typing chores, and my wife Fran and my children, Julian and Annie, who had to put up with me while this book was taking shape.

Contents

Forward   *xi*

Introduction   *xiii*

STEP I
Starting on Their First Million

1 *Opportunities are Where You Find Them*   3
   Matthew and Marion Toller*

2 *It All Comes Down to the Numbers*   15
   Don Joseph*

3 *A Rewarding Pastime*   21
   Rachel Gunther Cabarrubias

4 *Don't Sell When You Can Rent*   29
   Gene Allen

5 *The Sweet Song of Success*   35
   Wayne Phillips

6 *Starting Over in a Small Town*   53
   Roger and Karen Hett

7 *Broke and In Debt*   65
   John Broadfoot

8 *Off to a Flying Start*   71
   Roland and Mayme Voise

9 *$9 to $9,000,000 in 900 Days*   81
   Phil Drummond

STEP II
Paper Millionaires

10   *An Unemployed Widow with Small Children Makes Good*   89
          Lucille and Bland Giddings

11   *Ballplayer Hits a Homerun with Housing*   103
          Randy L. Green

12   *Business Success Pyramids Wealth*   111
          *Irwin Kief**

STEP III
Living Like Millionaires

13   *A Poor Credit Risk*   127
          Carl Crouch

14   *Salesman Profits by Buying*   135
          Nick Koon

15   *Interest Rates Don't Matter*   145
          Charles Hughes

16   *The College of Hard Knocks and Big Bucks*   155
          *Bill Felix**

17   *The Bankrupt's Road to Riches*   161
          Elbert Lee

18   *Buying Low in a Seller's Market*   165
          *Simon Lantzer**

19   *Millions from Rentals and Wrap-arounds*   175
          Charles Carrithers

20   *Success and the Single Woman*   179
          Jennifer Steves

21   *Pets and Children Welcome*   191
          Janet Little

22   *Share the Wealth*   197
          Paul Simon

Definitions   209
References   217
For More Information   219

*A few of the subjects asked to keep their identities confidential for personal reasons. Their names are marked by an asterisk.

Foreword

There is an enormous chasm separating the wealth builders described in these pages and the rest of us. On one side of the chasm are those who have dreams. On the other side are those who have dreams and the courage to make them come true. These are the modern day pioneers. They forge into unknown territory, risking all to be free. They don't fight Indians and wild animals. They fight the myths of conventional wisdom. They don't conquer a rough and untamed wilderness. They conquer the unexplored reaches of their own souls. The financial barriers they overcome are no less an adversary than the Rocky Mountains were to our forefathers.

In centuries to come, the wealth builders of today, these few who dare, will be revered as much as we revere those brave ones who opened up a new continent in the early days of America.

This book tells the stories of 22 such wealth builders. They are ordinary people with extra-ordinary commitments to do great things. I take my hat off to them.

Robert G. Allen

Introduction

There are many fine books about real estate investing, but this book is not about investing, it is about investors—those who are just starting out, hustling, working and struggling to achieve financial independence; those who are well on their way; and those who have already made it.

Most of them have a lot in common. They are all bright, energetic, hard working people with a basic belief in themselves and their own ability to make it, to accomplish things and to control their own destinies. None of them started out rich, and most of them had no background in real estate until they began investing. Since then, most of them have read every real estate book and newsletter and attended every investment seminar they could find out about.

In talking to these successful investors, the same names kept coming up: Lowry and Nickerson, Robert Allen, Bill Greene, Dave Glubetich, Miller and Schaub, Mark Haroldsen. These are the authors and seminar leaders most frequently mentioned as the important influences who helped people get started and inspired them to succeed. But even though many of these investors have taken the same seminars and read the same books, they do not necessarily all do things the same way.

They have taken what they learned and added some new things of their own. They often combined techniques and philosophies from the different seminars they attended and adapted them to fit their own personalities and/or local conditions.

Each place is different, just as no two investors are exactly the same, and what works for Don Joseph in Cleveland, Ohio, and has helped him to earn over $100,000 tax-free dollars in the past year, would never suit self-made millionaires Carl Crouch in Riverside, California, or Charles Carrithers of Newport News, Virginia.

Charles Hughes, of High Point, North Carolina, makes a substantial positive cash flow on his three hundred single family homes, but he wants to move into larger properties because he hasn't got enough depreciation left to shelter all his income from taxes. Wayne Phillips of Baltimore, Maryland, has so much depreciation on the four hundred plus units he owns in partnership with his brother Richard, that they are moving into syndications and limited partnerships so they can sell some of that excess tax shelter to high income investors and generate some more tax-free cash for themselves.

Millionaire real estate agent and investor Randy L. Greene of Long Beach, California, believes in 100 percent financing, and will not buy property if he has to put up any money of his own, while millionaire broker and investor Nick Koon of Westerville, Ohio, goes on TV to tell people he will buy their houses for cash.

Millionaires Bland and Lucille Giddings of Mesa, Arizona, have built their fortune over the last few years investing only in nice middle class areas where they rent to solid, working adults; Midwestern millionaire Bill Felix rents almost exclusively to college students who usually turn his apartments into instant slums.

And millionaire Simon Lantzer of Oakland, California, has made his money buying in the ghetto and renting to people in the government subsidized housing program known as Section 8.

By reading about these people you will learn how and why they have become successful, how and why they are doing things the way they are. Some of them have developed unique and effective methods for managing property, others are experts at acquiring properties for less than they are worth and/or at various forms of creative financing.

All of them have been more than generous with their time and their hard-earned secrets of success. In their own words, they have gone into detail about their general philosophies of investing, as well as individual deals, so that beginning investors will be able to learn from them and duplicate their success.

The book has affected me even as I was writing it. My own background in real estate is primarily as an agent and a small-time investor, renovating properties and then turning them over for an immediate profit. I also do basic, introductory seminars for buyers and sellers.

I always knew there was money to be made in buying property and holding it for rental—prices in the San Francisco Bay Area, where I live and sell property, have tripled in the last five years. All I have heard in that period of time is that "prices can't go any higher because nobody can afford to buy anymore," and, of course, people keep buying anyway.

But I am one of those people who hates managing property and dealing with tenants, so except for my home and one piece of income property, I had never held anything I bought for more than six months.

I had never heard of half the gimmicks and techniques for making money that are outlined in this book, and many of those I was aware of seemed too farfetched to work. Until very recently, it has been a strong seller's market in my area, and as an agent, I preferred to work with sellers rather than buyers. So I have always approached many creative techniques from a negative perspective. I have been surprised and contemptuous that some agent or buyer was wasting my time and my seller's time. Everyone knew that sellers, not buyers, dictated the terms in our area, since many properties attracted multiple offers and sold for more than the asking price.

Then things changed. Interest rates went sky high, and sellers became more anxious to deal. About that time, in early 1981, I began doing the research for this book. I suddenly realized that while I was finding reasons why various deals wouldn't work in my area, other people—like Simon Lantzer—were operating in my area, or comparable locations with similar market conditions and building a fortune by making the same kind of deals work.

I have already put to use some of the information I gathered while interviewing the people in this book. I recently wrapped up a deal in which we had a willing buyer and seller who were in perfect agreement on the terms of the sale, but a note holder who was determined to hold out for ridiculous concessions or sabotage the deal. He wanted $15,000 cash paid off on a $30,000 note, and an interest increase from 10 percent to 18½ percent on the balance. The buyers, who were already giving the seller about $12,000 cash as a down payment, offered the note holder $10,000 cash and an increase to 12½ percent interest, but the note holder said "No." He went to an attorney and threatened to foreclose on the grounds that the seller was endangering the property by leaving it vacant.

The buyer's attorney advised that even a land contract, where the seller retained title to the property, could leave everyone open to a law suit if the seller really pressed the "due-on-sale" clause and insisted that the entire loan be paid off at once. So we worked out a complicated lease option designed to run for the length of the note (four and a half years), at which time the buyer would have to refinance the property anyway.

Once I am done with this book I am looking forward to jumping into real estate investments with new enthusiasm, knowing now that what I always thought couldn't be done *can* be done and *is* being done by people all across the country. For me, reading books of theory—even if they are based on one person's actual experience—is interesting; but talking to and/or reading about dozens of people who are putting all the theories into everyday practice brings it into the real world and makes it seem possible for me, too.

No matter who you are—young, old, black, white, high school dropout or Ph.D., there should be at least one person, one story in this book, that you can personally relate to. These people come from all walks of life and all parts of the country. The only thing they all had in common when they got into real estate was a will to succeed and to make their lives better, fuller, richer in every sense of the word.

I would love to be able to write this book as a Cinderella story, a real-life fairytale where everyone lives happily ever after and never makes any mistakes or has any regrets about anything they have done. But, unfortunately, life doesn't work that way, and neither does real estate. It is the safest, easiest way I know for ordinary people to make it in this world, but it is not foolproof.

To claim that real estate investing is a panacea, a lazy man's way to riches, and ignore the pitfalls, or gloss over them, would be dishonest at best. It is important to know what not to do when you are investing, so I have included some brief remarks on what happens when an investor makes mistakes.

Beyond learning from this book, I hope you will find it entertaining, too. For myself, I quickly found that in addition to wanting to learn *from* these successsful investors, I also wanted to learn *about* them. They are not just models of success, they are unique, interesting individuals, each with their own stories to tell. I got great pleasure from hearing those stories and writing them down. I hope you will enjoy them, too.

FORTUNE
BUILDERS

STEP I

Starting on Their First Million

1

Opportunities Are Where You Find Them
Matthew and Marion Toller

"Real estate is dead. The market is going to crash. Interest rates are too high. Nobody can buy. Nobody can sell. The bottom is about to fall out. Real estate was hot a couple of years ago, but if you didn't make it then you never will. Now it's just too late." Pessimists have been spreading remarks like this since late 1979, and a lot of uninformed people believe them.

Matthew and Marion Toller missed the great real estate boom of the late 1970s, but they don't waste time looking back and bemoaning any lack of opportunities in these days of tight money and high prices. They believe opportunities always exist if you really look for them.

"Bad times are the best times to make money," says Matthew. "Smart people make money when times are bad because sellers are desperate, so you can find more sellers who are willing to accept creative terms and carry some of the financing. We work at finding good deals. We start at seven in the morning, and sometimes we're still on the phone at eleven o'clock at night, or even later. And when we're not on the phone, we're combing the newspaper ads or the Multiple Listings Book, or going to seminars and workshops or meetings of investors' groups. We work at it full time."

And they reap the full time benefits. The Tollers have been involved in real estate since September, 1980, and as of August, 1981, they owned over a million dollars' worth of property in joint ventures. They have built up a net worth of over $250,000, and they bought twenty-four houses with little or nothing down between June and August,

1981. Not half bad for a pair of ex-student activists who never would have dreamed of being real estate investors or landlords only two or three years ago, and who didn't even own their own home before September, 1980.

"At that time we weren't interested in making money," Matthew says. "We wanted to save the world, but after a while, we just burned ourselves out. I even wound up in the hospital with an ulcer because I was taking it all so seriously. That's when I knew it was time to get out of politics and into the real world.

"Eventually we both got good jobs selling cars, and we began living the good life, making a lot of money, spending a lot of money, partying a lot. It was a welcome change after our poor, serious, striving student days, but after awhile that wore thin, too.

"We got tired of our jobs and tired of the way we were living. We felt we weren't really doing anything with our lives, but we were in an earning-spending rut, and it was hard to break out of it.

"Then the interest rates went up, and car sales went straight down. We had been earning $40,000 to $50,000 a year selling cars, and that dropped to almost nothing, so we decided it was time to make the change. We were selling expensive cars—Porsches—to clients who had money, and it seemed like a lot of them had made it in real estate. From talking to them, we began to get ideas. So we began reading all the real estate investment books we could get our hands on. We had a little bit of money saved, and a lot of time on our hands, so we also began attending real estate seminars taught by people like Robert Allen, Jack Miller and John Schaub, Jimmy Napier, Pete Fortunato and Jay Turner, to learn all we could about buying and managing property.

"Then we just started looking at properties and making offers. We got a lot of *No!'s*, but a few owners gave us options on their property, or agreed to sell to us outright at really favorable prices and/or terms. We would negotiate with the sellers first and tie up the properties, and then we would go out and find investors to buy them.

"A couple of times we have lined up deals and have not been able to come up with the money, but for the most part we haven't had that problem. Right now we've got more investors than we know what to do with. One person finds they can trust us, and they tell all their friends.

Finding Investors

"We found our original investors mostly by going to seminars and investment groups and speaking out a lot, making ourselves known. We knew how to grab a crowd's attention and hold it from our activist days. It's just salesmanship. If you're a salesman, you know how to sell yourself. That's what we did."

"We found a lot of people who attend these seminars don't want to be involved in managing property," says Marion. "They want to invest their money, not their time. So we decided to invest our time instead of our money. Between us, we've been to every major seminar at least once; we stand up and ask a lot of questions, meet a lot of people, and tell them about all the no-money-down deals we have tied up.

"Not all of our deals are no money down. Sometimes we'll find a house that's selling below market value and requires some cash down payment, but in those cases we always find someone else, a partner, and let them put the money down in return for half ownership.

"Almost all our no-money-down deals involve negative cash flow —so there, too, we find investors who are willing to put up the money. Then we find the property, buy it, and manage it.

"We have written agreements with all our investors, specifying how long we are going to maintain the joint venture. Usually these agreements are drawn up to last for three to five years, but it depends on the circumstances. At the end of the agreed time period, each of us has the right to buy the other out, or we put the property on the market, sell it to a third party, and split the profits equally.

"People trust us because we try to be honest and open with them. We take the time to get to know the people we deal with and to let them get to know us. It takes a little longer that way—we don't always wrap up our deals all in one day—but it pays off in the end; not only with investors, but with sellers, too. Sellers will definitely give you a better deal if they like you and feel comfortable with you—especially when it's also a good deal for them, when they're getting what they want, too."

"I'm a promoter," says Matthew, "a salesman. I like people, and I like dealing with them. I like helping everybody get what they want out of a deal—my family are traders in the commodities market, so it's in my blood—and that's how I get what I want: money. The buyer and seller don't have to be at each other's throats. They don't have to be enemies. If you look at the whole picture—taxes and everything else— then it's usually possible to structure a deal so that everybody will be happy in the end.

"For instance, we've had deals where the seller carried back two notes instead of one so he could sell one note and get some immediate cash that way. Let's say the house is selling for $50,000 and the seller is willing to carry a loan for $40,000 at 10 percent interest, but he wants $10,000 cash. We give him two notes, one for $38,000 at 10 percent interest, and a second one for $12,000 at, say, 17 percent or 18 percent interest. Then he takes the second note and sells it for $10,000 and he has the cash he wants. He holds on to the first note for $38,000, and we get the property with no money down.

"Other times we have had to get a second mortgage through a

mortgage broker and use that as our down payment. That's when the seller insisted on full price and didn't want to be bothered with discounted notes (i.e., selling a $12,000 note for $10,000 cash). For instance, if that $50,000 house had a $35,000 assumable loan, we would get the seller to take out a second loan on it for another $15,000, and then we would just assume both loans when we took title to the property. That way the seller would get the $15,000 cash, and again, we would get in with no money down."

"Of course, the easiest way is when we can just get the second ourselves," Marion adds, "or get a new first to cover the entire purchase price. But that means one; finding a property which will appraise for more than we are paying, and two; a seller who won't balk and try to back out of the deal when he realizes he has sold too cheaply. So those are hard to find.

"We have occasionally had sellers carry notes secured by other properties we own, but only when the price was exceptional and we intended to resell the property right away. If a property ever goes bad on us—becomes more trouble than we're prepared to handle—and we have to just give up and walk away from it, we're not going to lose everything else we've built up, too."

They Never Get in Too Deep

For this reason, one thing the Tollers never do—even short term—is to put up a personal note as collateral. Everything they borrow is secured by liens on specific pieces of property—usually the property they are borrowing the money to buy—so that if anything ever does go wrong, no creditor will have a general claim against them or their assets. Having started with almost nothing, Matthew and Marion are extremely careful about holding on to what they've got, which they have worked so hard to obtain—especially since they have gotten so much of it by profiting from other people's mistakes.

"There are so many people in this business who get in over their heads," Matthew says, "and then, when they realize they're drowning, they drag everything they own down with them. Marion and I have deals blow up on us, but by insulating ourselves we've been able to contain the damage and keep on going. We never put our own money into a deal, and we put in as little of our investors' money as possible. We try to structure our deals so that any money we need to buy a property comes from that property itself and is secured by that particular property. That way, if we've made a mistake and it turns out to be a loser, we've only put in time and effort—no cash, except for closing costs and any negative cash flow.

"Whenever possible, we insulate ourselves even further by trying to control properties without even taking title. Many of the properties we have tied up are on lease options. We put up a nominal deposit—anywhere from one hundred to five hundred dollars—and in return, the owner agrees to sell us the house at some future time, anywhere from three months to five years down the road, at a mutually agreed on price. This is usually about five percent more than the house is actually worth at the time we sign the lease option, so of course we are hoping the value of the house will go up more than five percent before the time comes for us to actually buy the house. That's why we try to get the longest possible option we can. The longer the time period, the more the house is likely to go up in value.

"For instance, someone has their house on the market for $60,000 with no offers, and they need to get rid of it. They bought another house, and can't afford the double payments, or they are just sick and tired of dealing with tenants, or whatever. They are impatient, and anxious to be rid of the property. So we sign a five year lease option to purchase the house for $65,000 in five years, and to rent it for $400 a month until then.

"We then take overall responsibility for the house. We find the tenants, screen them, do the credit check and collect the rent each month—usually $450 to $500 if we are paying the owner $400—and the owner doesn't have to deal with any of it anymore. On the other hand, he still holds title to the house, so he *is* getting all the tax benefits: interest and depreciation write-offs, etc.

Inflation Works for Them

"It's just another type of 'Don't Wanter' situation. We're doing the owners a favor, performing a service, by taking the management off their hands, finding good tenants, making it up out of our own pockets when the rent is late . . . naturally, we expect to get paid for doing all this, wouldn't you? So we collect our pay when we either exercise the option or sell it to someone else at a profit. It takes awhile, but we figure that as long as there's inflation, we'll make out okay in the end.

"The way it works is like this. We agree to pay the owner $65,000 for his house *if and when we decide to buy it.* We have five years to make up our minds. If we decide not to buy the place, we can sell the option to someone else at a profit—assuming the house is worth more than $65,000 by then—or we can just walk away from it if we decide the house is a total loser. It's sort of a one-sided contract. The seller has to sell it to us for $65,000 if we decide to exercise our option any time before the five years is up, but we don't have to buy it if we change our minds. All we have to do is keep up with the maintenance and pay him his $400 each month until the five-year lease runs out.

"Ideally, with only 10 percent interest a year, that property which is worth $60,000 today will be worth about $95,000 five years from now, so by purchasing it for $65,000 we will make $30,000 profit, or $6,000 a year for managing the place. Here's how it breaks down:

Starting Value:		$60,000	
Plus 10%		6,000	
	New Value	66,000	End of year one
Plus 10%		6,600	
	New Value	72,600	End of year two
Plus 10%		7,260	
	New Value	79,860	End of year three
Plus 10%		7,986	
	New Value	87,846	End of year four
Plus 10%		8,784	
	New Value	96,620	End of year five

So we make our profit in the end, and in the meantime it gives us good experience in managing properties.

"Don't Wanters," people who are tired of owning a piece of property, are the cornerstone of Matthew and Marion's business. Don't Wanters are the ones who are ready to offer the best prices and terms. They are the ones who will consider no-money-down or lease option deals. They are the ones who have money, but don't want the headaches which come with wheeling and dealing and managing property.

How do you find Don't Wanters?

"You make a lot of offers, low offers with all the terms set to benefit you, the buyer, and you wait to get one accepted. Sometimes you will make offers every day and only get one or two properties a month. Other times you will be deluged with good properties and have to hustle to get investors to buy them. You have to have patience, stamina and perseverance," says Marion.

Matthew and Marion have learned to develop all three. "It's an up and down business," Marion says, "and many people give up too easily. Sometimes it will take us several days to wrap up a deal, or even months. It gets nerve-wracking at times, but it's worth it. Anybody can buy at full market value."

Involvement Leads to Success

One deal has led to another as their empire has rapidly grown. Once word gets around that you can put together deals—that you can get buyers and that you can find good properties for little or no money down—you start hearing about things through the investor's grapevine, and people start hearing about you. Then the work begins.

"People who want to get rid of their property will come up to me at seminars and workshops and offer it to me on a lease option or offer me a finder's fee if I can get them a buyer," Matthew says. "I make some occasional money that way, but we prefer working directly with investors, buying property and managing it. I have a real estate license, but I don't really want to be an agent working for commissions. I'm sure I could sell three or four million dollars' worth of property easily and make a good living that way, but I wouldn't be building up equity or contacts the way I am now."

Matthew and Marion also make extra money by doing an occasional "double escrow." As soon as they buy a piece of property that is really underpriced, at perhaps $60,000, they turn around and sell it for an immediate profit, say $65,000, before they even take title. They arrange for the two escrows to close simultaneously so the money is automatically transferred from one to the other. Their buyer puts up all the money to pay off the seller, and Matthew and Marion keep the difference: $5,000 minus the escrow fees of a thousand dollars or so.

To avoid conflict of interest, Matthew and Marion never sell anything to one of their investors, but do everything on a strict partnership basis. Doing extra deals on their own allows them to concentrate on real estate full time without having to charge an hourly fee for management services (which would then reduce or eliminate their equity in the properties they manage), or having to take outside jobs or sell off any partnership properties in order to get money to live on. As rents go up, positive cash flow from the properties should eliminate this problem entirely. In the meantime, they get by comfortably, if not lavishly, as they build for the future.

And their involvement in real estate grows deeper with each seminar they attend. The more they learn, the more they want to learn. And the more they learn, the more they find ways to make money for themselves and their investors. Fourteen months and they are still at it: learning and making money, making money and learning. They have subscribed to *Impact Reports* for over a year, and in addition to attending seminars and reading *The Monopoly Game* and *Double Your Money In Real Estate Every 2 Years*, and other books on real estate investing, they act on the advice they read and hear.

Matthew uses his real estate license to attend Realtors tours and open houses, as well as exchange groups where properties are traded among investors.

If a "deal" comes on the market, he and Marion will know of it through hard work and a network of contacts. If a new idea comes along for financing or purchasing distress properties with little or no down payment, they will go to a class or a lecture to find out all about it.

Since they don't like to put their own money into the properties they buy, Matthew and Marion have to use their knowledge and skill instead.

They approach real estate investing as a profession, not a hobby. They have a definite service to offer their investor-partners, and through their half of the appreciation they are very well paid while remaining independent.

Cutting Management Problems

The main thing, the most valuable thing they have learned from all the seminars they have taken is how to cut management problems down to a minimum. That is how they are able to manage so many properties at once and accumulate equity so quickly. By using a good tight lease agreement, stringent credit checks and their own intuition, they are able to scare off potentially troublesome tenants and stop problems before they begin.

"All of our properties are single family homes in decent working class and middle class areas," Marion says, "and we get them rented without any trouble—usually to couples with both of them working. If they have children or pets, they have to put up an extra security deposit and agree to be responsible for any damage; and the lease says we correct any major problems, but the tenant is responsible for minor repairs such as leaky faucets, etc."

They also have their own ideas about how to deal with people psychologically. "You have to come on hard at first," says Matthew, "and then you can ease up later. If you're too nice to tenants or sellers they'll walk all over you. If you come on like a hard-nosed S.O.B. at first, and then you suddenly do something nice for them, they'll love you and think you're great, but at the same time they'll respect you, too, and realize you can't be pushed around."

They use their own, modified version of a lease they got from Jack Miller and John Schaub, called a "discount lease." If they want $450 a month rent, they set it at $500 a month. Then, if the tenant pays on time, he/she gets a $50 "discount." If the rent is late, he/she pays the full amount. This eliminates the negative connotations of a late fee.

In spite of their seemingly hard attitude, Matthew and Marion agree that you get respect and fair treatment from tenants by dealing with them the same way you deal with sellers or investors: honestly and openly. "We can go to dinner at the home of just about everyone we've ever bought a house from or invested with—that's the kind of relationships we've developed, and we can visit most of our tenants, too," Marion says. "People like us. That's why they trust us with their money and their property, and we try hard not to let them down. We are professionals."

'Some of our old friends thought we were a little nuts," Matthew says, "but now most of them are starting to come around. They can see we're really building something. Sure, it takes up a lot of our time, but what are we supposed to do with that time, anyway? Sit around in the evenings and watch TV or get drunk and do drugs? We would rather work towards the future. Besides, it is a fantastic challenge. There is so much to learn, so much to do..."

The Trouble With Agents

Matthew and Marion do most of their looking on their own. Echoing the words of many professional investors, they say they are perfectly willing to work with agents, but they find that many agents are not creative and flexible enough to deal with them.

"Many of them seem to be afraid of creative deals," Marion says, "and worried about their own possible liability. They tell us that their broker would never let them present an offer like that, or they can't do it because there is no security for the seller. We don't have much problem with sellers once we explain to them what we're talking about. Not all of them will go for it, but most of them will at least listen. The agents are the ones who don't seem to understand what we're trying to do. I mean, by law they're supposed to present any and all offers, but what can you do? I suppose we could complain to the local real estate board, but it's just not worth it."

Instead, the Tollers work independently, going through the newspaper ads line by line. When they see something that looks like a possibility, they get in touch with the owner and talk terms. If the property looks like a good bet, they drive by and then set up an appointment to see the inside, usually with an offer already written up.

They walk the streets in neighborhoods they especially like, cultivating store owners, hairdressers, anyone who comes in contact with a lot of people. They offer referral fees and also find other ways of repaying favors in a constant effort to find out about divorces, pending foreclosures and defaults, tenant-landlord disputes, anything which might cause a property owner to become a prospective seller. It is hard work, but so far they say they love every minute of it. Will it pay off in the long run? All indications seem good

Right now, Matthew and Marion seem to be doing just fine. Their management program is going well, and they are having no trouble handling success. Tomorrow? Who knows? They take it one step at a time.

Setbacks Are Temporary

They have suffered their share of setbacks, too. In the spring of 1981 they thought they had it made. A deal was in the works to buy over 200 houses from one seller—20 or 30 a month over a period of several months. The seller was willing and anxious, they had an investor lined up; all they had to do was tie up a few loose ends. Then the roof caved in.

"Our original investors backed out at the last minute," Matthew says, "so we went searching around for some new ones, since this was a terrific deal, too good to just pass up like that. We began dealing with a broker who had been recommended to us, and he thought he might have some people who would be interested, and he did. The only trouble was, they wound up maneuvering us right out of the deal. Most people we deal with are honest, but every once in a while something like that happens, and we wind up putting in a lot of time and effort and getting nothing out of it. That's just the way it is. We pick up the pieces and go on to the next deal."

For Matthew and Marion, that meant transferring their operations from a San Francisco suburb where prices and negative cash flow were just too high, to Tucson, Arizona, where the opportunities are greater.

"It's just great down here!" Matthew exults. "Everything is so much slower than the Bay Area, and that works in our favor. There, everyone is too super-sophisticated and negative. Here, I can go to seminars, learn these new techniques, and when I try them out, they work! There is a huge backlog of unsold homes here, so sellers are more open to creative deals.

"We've picked up twenty-four houses in the last couple of months and haven't had to put any money down on any of them. Most of them work like this: a $50,000 house with a $30,000 mortgage at 9½ percent, for instance, payable at $252.26 a month. We assume that, get a second mortgage for $10,000 at 18 percent, payable at $161.05 a month for 15 years, and then we get the seller to carry a third for the remaining $10,000 for three to five years at 10 percent, payable at about $80 a month, interest only, for a total payment of $493.31 plus taxes and insurance. It will rent for $350 to $400, so we're averaging $150 to $200 a month negative cash flow. We handle that by getting investors who pick that up in exchange for a half interest in the house, or tenants who agree to live there for three to five years and cover all the payments and maintenance in exchange for half ownership.

"With investors, we charge them $3,000 up front. $2,000 is a loan which we have to pay back when the house is sold, in three to five years—that way it is tax free, because it is not income—and $1,000 is a management fee.

"With tenants, we charge a $1,500 processing fee, and then we set the whole deal up through a title company. They pay their money directly to the title company each month, and it goes into a special account. When they have made their 36th, 48th, or 60th payment, depending on the length of the original contract, the title company files a signed grant deed which we have left with them, and the tenants automatically go on title as half owners. If they are fifteen days late with any payment, the title company sends them a notice that the agreement is null and void and they have to move out.

"This way, it is all nice and formal and impersonal; Marion and I aren't even involved. The title company does it all. At the end of three to five years—whenever the third note to the seller is due and payable—we go through the same procedure, whether the other person is an investor or a tenant. We have the place appraised, and then either one party buys the other out at the appraised price, or we just put the property up for sale on the open market and split the profits equally.

"Right now, we're negotiating with a builder who has about 80 unsold houses, and we may take those on and sell them for him on an equity sharing basis. We're even thinking of opening a brokerage business that will list houses and sell them that way. With high interest, high prices, and houses sitting unsold, that seems to be the wave of the future, and we intend to ride it for all it's worth."

2

It All Comes Down to the Numbers
Don Joseph

"Help Wanted! No previous experience necessary. Motivated self-starter. Hard working, creative thinker who values independence. No guaranteed salary, but commissions and bonuses equal to approximately $400,000 after first year—half in tax-free cash payments and half in tax deferred, long term retirement benefits—for right person."

This is not exactly the type of Help Wanted ad you're used to seeing in your local newspaper, is it? In fact, it probably sounds made up, which it is, and too good to be true, which it is *not*. This ad never appeared in any newspaper, and it is unlikely that it ever will. But it's not too good to be true; it is true. The promises it makes are real. They can come true, and they have come true for Don Joseph of Cleveland, Ohio.

In June of 1979, when he took the Lowry-Nickerson seminar, Don had no experience with real estate. He had a successful business manufacturing and selling a new type of dress pattern for hard to fit women. He had a patent on his own idea, and was going around the country giving workshops for groups of women, showing them how to use his patterns.

He had built the company from the ground up, and it was starting to take off. Business was booming. He was in demand, and so were his patterns. But then he got a new idea:

"I had met all the challenges in my business," he says, "and I really wasn't all that crazy about sewing for a living. I knew nothing about real estate, but it seemed intriguing. And I knew you could make a lot of money."

Cranking Out the Cash

Like $300,000 in the twelve months between April of 1980 and April, 1981; and $130,000 or so of that was cash in his pocket. It was tax free, because it was not income, but *borrowed* money, nontaxable money. It was taken out of the loans he obtained on properties he bought far below market prices. Another $185,000 or so represents the equity he has left in his properties, above and beyond what he paid for them, even after taking out the $130,000 in cash.

Of course, some of it did have to go back into the properties to pay for repairs and improvements—maybe half of the $230,000 total. But after all, Don is just getting started, and he doesn't expect to become a millionaire overnight. He expects it will take him at least another couple of years.

"The Lowry-Nickerson seminar was the greatest experience I've ever had," he says. "It took me about six months to get going. I didn't really get started until around January, but it turned my life around. If I had taken that seminar five years ago, I know I would be worth at least $5 million today. Especially since it was so easy then. Now it's gotten harder, with the high interest rates and all."

How does he get around that? How has he managed to prosper in the midst of hard times, in a business that was brand new to him just two years ago? By finding "Don't Wanter" owners and distress properties that he can snap up for far less than they are worth. And by being smart enough to realize that 15 percent, 15½ percent, or even 16 percent or 16½ percent interest is worth paying as long as the return on the money still comes out right. If a property will still crank out a positive cash flow, even with a first mortgage at 16½ percent and/or a second at 18 percent or 20 percent, why worry about the interest?

Common sense told Don early in the game that almost any interest rate the banks and mortgage lenders could throw at him was okay, as long as he could get property at the right price. If the sellers weren't willing to sell at a price that made sense to him, then they would have to carry the loan themselves at a low interest rate which would keep the payments down to the amount Don was willing to pay.

For example, Don bought four buildings—two duplexes (two-unit buildings) and two triplexes (three-unit buildings) as a package, all for $35,000. He made an agreement to give the seller $15,000 cash as a down payment, on two conditions: the seller had to permit Don to take title to one of the buildings before any money changed hands; the seller also had to agree to carry a $5,000 mortgage on each of the four properties, for a total of $20,000, the remainder of the $35,000 purchase price, and to agree to subordinate those loans—to take junior position, i.e., hold them as a second mortgage, as opposed to a first—to any new loans Don might obtain. The seller agreed.

Don took title to the first property and immediately went out and got a $20,000 first mortgage against it. He paid the seller $15,000 cash, took title to the other three properties, and then took out loans against those properties, totalling another $50,000. He now has $90,000 in loans against four properties which he just bought for a total of $35,000. He has already gotten $55,000 in cash out of the properties; plus, he is getting another $400 per month in positive cash flow from the rents.

With another property, Don was able to buy it for $7,500, with $2,500 down and the seller carrying a $5,000 second for 20 years at 10 percent interest. But Don didn't want to put up $2,500 of his own money—not on a property like that—so again he got title before he had to hand over the money. This time, he got a $15,000 mortgage from the bank and pocketed $12,500, after giving the seller his $2,500 down payment.

With a third property, Don got the seller to agree to a $20,000 purchase price with a $4,999 cash rebate to the buyer after the close of escrow. Don got a $16,000 first mortgage on the property from a bank, and the seller agreed to carry back a $5,000 second mortgage. Then, after the close of escrow, the seller discounted the second mortgage from $5,000 to $1, and sold it back to Don at that discounted price. So, in effect, the bank financed 100 percent of the purchase price. Don didn't walk away with much cash in hand, but his mortgage payments are only $260 a month, while the rents are $526.

Making Deals that Pay

As you have probably guessed by now, Don is not buying choice properties in prime areas. "Just plain ugly," is how he describes some of his properties; but he isn't out for pride of ownership. He will buy anything anywhere in the Cleveland area, he says, as long as he can crank out some cash.

Don doesn't care what type of property it is, suburban tracts or inner city ghettoes, as long as it makes sense on paper. The numbers, it all comes down to the numbers. Either they add up, or they don't. Don figures in: price; terms; amount of work to be done; time and cost involved; potential for upgrading rents; potential for upgrading value. They are all interrelated, and they are all important. Everything has to be considered.

For instance, a building was for sale because the seller was sick of it and didn't want to deal with it any more. It was a headache. There were 16 units, but only 10 were producing any rent. On the other hand, the mortgage payment was only $207 per month, so Don took it off the owner's hands, with nothing down. He now has 12 of the units rented for a total of $2,100 a month, and he expects to have the last four rented out soon for an additional $500 a month.

How does he find all these people who want to throw money and property at him? By looking for them. And by creating them. Not every seller starts off as a Don't Wanter. Some of them start off feeling casual—if they get their price and terms, they will sell; if not, it's no big deal. But then, after a few months, their attitude changes as they begin to lose faith in their properties.

Take the sellers who put their 28-unit building, including six stores and a library, on the market for $125,000. Don negotiated with them on and off for six months before he got the building for $70,000. This is the only deal Don has been involved in which has required any substantial amount of cash. The sellers demanded $20,000 in cash as a down payment, but in return, they agreed to carry the remaining $50,000 of the purchase at 9 percent interest for 30 years, so Don decided it was worth it. Especially since the $20,000 was not coming out of his pocket anyway.

Rather than cough up $20,000 in hard-earned cash, Don took in a partner and let him put up the money. Don agreed that he would manage the building and supervise the necessary renovations and improvements, and they would split any profits when the building was sold.

Don began negotiating with the sellers in October of 1979 but didn't reach an agreement with them until May of 1980, and then the deal didn't close until July. Now Don expects to put the building on the market around July of 1981 and sell it for about $150,000. The renovations have all been paid for out of the positive cash flow . . . over $4,000 a month as of July 1981.

Not only did Don have no experience with real estate when he started, he also knew nothing about building or remodeling. He is active in the local Lowry-Nickerson group, and so he found workmen through recommendations of other members or by word of mouth. Everything he knows, he has learned in the last two years, most of it by hard experience.

"I can't even hammer a nail straight," he says, "so I hire the work out, and I've really gotten an education in dealing with contractors and workmen, most of it in the school of hard knocks. I don't give anybody money in advance and tell them to go to work, anymore. I've done that and then never seen them again.

"I also make sure anybody I deal with has insurance, including workmen's compensation that covers any sub-contractors, too. And I make them sign a release when they finish the job, saying they won't file any mechanic's liens."

Everything Matters

Don believes that attention to the paperwork, the legal side of buying and renovating property, is just as important as doing a good job with the management and renovations. He doesn't believe in going to a Realtor, letting him/her write up the offers and contracts and then sitting back passively. In the beginning, he did go to attorneys and let them draw up documents, but gradually, he began synthesizing all the knowledge he gained from the attorneys he dealt with and putting it all together to suit his own tastes.

Now he uses forms he has designed himself. He has made up his own notes, offer forms, contracts, etc. He takes them to a lawyer to get them approved and polished before he uses them, but he designs them himself.

"My standard offer form is six pages long," he says. "It's got two pages of weasel clauses alone, things I can throw out when we're negotiating so it looks as though I'm really giving up something.

"For instance, I always break my offer down into three categories. I put a value on the land, on the improvements (the building itself), and a value on the personal property, like stoves and refrigerators. Now, if I'm buying an apartment building, the seller is going to get nervous if he has never paid personal property taxes and he thinks that suddenly I'm going to; I'll take that out of there, but then he's got to do something for me. I mean, it only makes sense, right? If I'm giving up something, then he should give up something, too. Believe me, what I give with my right hand, I take back with my left.

"So with over 30 of these obnoxious clauses in there, I can usually wear them down until I get at least the price or the interest rate I want."

The average property Don buys has been on the market at least three months, so the sellers have already had a chance to get discouraged before Don ever gets to them. And then he works them over some more, pointing out the problems with the property and showing how it only makes sense at the price and terms he has in mind, take it or leave it.

In the beginning, he had to hunt for properties; now people call him with deals all the time, both owners and agents. He still puts in about sixty to seventy hours a week, but now more of that time is spent supervising crews and attending to administrative details.

"I don't just do one house, or one property at a time," he says. "I may have five or six projects going on at any one time."

Aside from the one property he owns with a partner, Don owns and manages all his other properties (about $450,000 worth, as of May, 1981) himself, and that's the way he likes it. He prefers doing it all his own way, without having to consult anyone else.

"I'm really lucky," he says. "I've got a great partner. A lot of people I know have had terrible luck with partnerships, but I can't complain about that. I just find I can go further and faster on my own. I'm interested in possible limited partnerships, where I would be the general partner, and the other, limited partners would be strictly passive investors; they would have no say in anything. They would merely put up their money and get part of the profits when the place was sold."

For now, though, Don is concentrating on investing on his own and on expanding the Lowry-Nickerson group, bringing in more members so that they will all benefit by helping each other. Right now, they buy materials, paint, carpeting, etc. in quantity and at big discounts, and Don is working on a group insurance plan that he estimates will save about $1,200 per year, just on his own properties.

He has even found a lawyer he enjoys working with, so Don's future seems bright. There's only one slight cloud on the horizon: no, not the high interest rates, those don't bother him in the least. His problem is that he has still got about $250,000 worth of inventory from his old business sitting there gathering dust in a warehouse, and he has been so busy—and so happy—with real estate investing, that he has not had a chance to sell it.

So, if anyone out there likes dressmaking and wants a business of their own . . .

3

A Rewarding Pastime
Rachel Gunther Cabarrubias

Maybe there's something in the sea air around Long Beach, California, which breeds ambitious young real estate millionaires, or maybe it's just coincidence. In any case, Long Beach is home not only to 28-year-old Randy Green, profiled in chapter 11, but also to Rachel Gunther Cabarrubias, another up and coming creative investor.

Actually, Rachel's not really in the millionaire class yet. She does own over $1 million worth of property, but she keeps it well leveraged, and she estimates her net worth is probably not much more than $400,000 or so. Then again, Rachel is only 23 years old, and has been investing in real estate for just about a year and a half. She started doing it as a hobby.

Rachel lived at home with her family and worked full time as a microbiologist in the Quality Control Department at CalCan Dog Food Co., so she wasn't looking for either a career or a place to live when she stumbled into real estate; it just seemed like an interesting way to pass some of her spare time. She was working towards a Master's Degree in Microbiology at Cal State, Long Beach, but that particular semester there were no courses she wanted. Then she saw an advertisement for the Robert Allen Nothing Down seminar, and decided to go.

She knew nothing about real estate before that. Her mother owned one rental house, but Rachel's own background was in science, not business. She registered for the seminar and charged the $400 cost on her MasterCard, hoping her mother would never find out she had done something so crazy.

Doing Her Homework

The seminar lasted all weekend. By the end of it, Rachel was very excited, but she didn't feel ready to buy anything yet, because she needed time to learn and memorize all the terminology and feel comfortable about writing an offer on anything. So she kept studying the manual she had gotten at the seminar, and started going through the newspaper "For Sale" ads and making phone calls, trying to find good properties she could get with no money down.

Rachel tried to make at least ten phone calls a day just to get basic information on properties and eliminate the ones she knew she would not be interested in. Then she did additional work, following up on the ones which sounded promising by going to see the property in person, talking to the owner, and then, if she was still interested, making an offer. Finally, after six months, she bought her first property.

She found a duplex selling for $102,000; she was convinced it was underpriced, so even though the deal required $15,000 in cash, Rachel wasn't worried. She talked the seller into taking out a second mortgage on the house, and Rachel agreed to cover the $250-a-month payments and all closing costs and loan fees.

In the last six months she has bought a dozen properties—three single family homes, the rest duplexes or multi-unit buildings—and she hasn't put any of her own money in. In fact, more often than not, Rachel can take a little money out when she buys something. Her typical transaction goes something like this:

John and Jane Doe have their house advertised for sale in the paper. It's a nice, clean, three-bedroom, two bath place in a comfortable, but not luxurious, area. They are anxious to sell, because: A) The property is a rental and has become a nuisance to them. B) They are moving out of the area and need it sold fast. C) They are getting divorced.

Rachel sees the house and likes it. She talks to the Does, finds out what their situation is, why they are selling, etc. They are asking one hundred thousand dollars, which Rachel considers fair, so she makes them an offer. She will pay full price, but only if they will meet her terms.

There is a $50,000 mortgage which Rachel wants to assume, because it is at 9 percent interest, but that leaves $50,000 more to meet the asking price. Rachel doesn't have $50,000, so she asks the Does what is the smallest amount of cash they could accept. They would like at least $25,000, but agree to settle for $20,000 cash and take a note for the remaining $30,000. Then Rachel shows them how to go and get an assumable second mortgage for $25,000 from a mortgage company, based on their $50,000 equity in the house, and she agrees to make all payments and pay the closing costs and loan fees. John and Jane then give $5,000 of the $25,000 they get from the mortgage company to

Rachel, and sign the property over to her in exchange for a $30,000 note.

Rachel now owns a $100,000 house which will rent for about $550 to $700 a month. The payments on the 9 percent first mortgage are $402.32, the payments on the second are $376.78, and taxes and insurance add another $100 a month, so she's got $879 going out each month. The third note, held by the seller, is a straight note, all due in five years with ten percent interest and no payments in the meantime, so Rachel has to come up with anywhere from $179 to $329 per month to meet the negative cash flow.

This is where the $5,000 comes in. It will cover all the negative cash flow for at least one or two years. At the end of that time, the property will be worth more, and Rachel can take out a larger second to keep covering the negative cash flow; plus, she can raise the rents.

At the end of five years—assuming only a ten percent inflation rate—the house will be worth $160,000:

> $110,000 after one year
> $121,000 after two years
> $133,000 after three years
> $146,000 after four years
> $160,000 after five years

Rachel will owe the sellers $45,000 ($30,000 note at 10 percent interest for five years=$15,000 interest). She owes $48,850 on the $50,000 first mortgage, and $35,000 on the refinanced second, for a total of $128,850. So, using none of her own money, she has a profit of over $30,000.

In addition, she got to write all that negative cash flow (including the $15,000 interest paid to the seller) off her income tax, and took depreciation benefits as well. That should add at least $10,000 to $15,000 more over 5 years in terms of real, after-tax benefits, for a total of $40,000 to $45,000.

If you assume that inflation in housing prices will average 15 percent over the next five years, then the house will be worth $198,000:

> $115,000 after one year
> $130,500 after two years
> $150,000 after three years
> $172,500 after four years
> $198,000 after five years

and Rachel will have about $80,000 profit, overall. Not bad, for a hobby!

Not all of Rachel's properties have a negative cash flow, even with none of her own money in the deal. Whenever possible, she gets the seller to carry a large enough note at a low enough interest rate, or with no payments until it is all due, so that the property will at least break even. Some of them even have a positive cash flow, which helps to offset the negative cash flow on some of the others.

Moving Up

Rachel manages to do all this without buying any slum properties or fixers. She doesn't mind doing a little cleaning or painting just to spruce a place up, but generally she likes attractive, liveable properties in decent areas, properties which the sellers don't want for reasons of their own. A typical (?) example:

"My girlfriend saw this ad in the *Wall Street Journal* for a condominium complex in Washington, so she called me. It said right in the ad, 'Don't Wanter.' I mean, what a thing to put in the ad!! So we called up and the woman had owned it for 20 years and she was tired of the property, tired of dealing with it, and she wanted out. So we helped her refinance the property, first of all. That way she got the cash she needed, we got $150,000 cash for taking the property off her hands, and she's carrying a straight note for the balance, with no payments until it is due.

"Of course, most of that $150,000 went back into the property to cover the negative cash flow, maintenance, etc. We only kept $15,000 each for ourselves. But still, I was excited. Before that, I had never taken out more than about $5,000 in cash when I bought a property. The best part is that we got the property for only $1.3 million, and it was appraised for $1.5 million last year. So, we figure we'll keep it for about a year, and then sell it for a nice profit and see what else we can buy."

How does she do it? Just by trying. "The Robert Allen seminar showed me how to do it," she says. "It's all there in the course and the workbook, and then, once I got started, I've been taking all sorts of other courses and reading other books, trying to expand my knowledge. I don't really spend that much time looking for properties any more. Now I have agents calling me to offer me deals they think I would be interested in."

Making Management Easy

Rachel has also found she prefers buying property to managing it, so she looks for properties which already have management, like the condo complex, and uses a variety of creative techniques to minimize problems when she does have to manage a property herself.

Sometimes she will give the tenants a lease option, but a very special type of lease option, one which gives the tenant the first right to buy the property, if and when Rachel gets ready to sell it, but specifies no time limit and no prearranged price. All the contract says is that someday, when Rachel gets ready to sell, she and the tenant will get an independent appraisal done on the property and then the tenant will have the option to buy it for the appraised price, at favorable, low-down-payment terms.

In the meantime, Rachel charges more than the normal rent and applies the difference towards the eventual purchase. This way she finds the tenants take care of the house, since they expect to own it some day, and she attracts a better, more ambitious and responsible type of tenant to begin with.

In other cases, where the tenants are not interested in a lease option, Rachel charges a rent that is slightly lower than the average rent for the area, and writes a clause into the lease stating that the tenant will be responsible for any repairs under $200. This way she doesn't get phone calls in the middle of the night complaining of leaking faucets or whatever.

And, last but not least, Rachel chooses her tenants and her neighborhoods with care. She likes solid residential neighborhoods which people will consider their home and not a place to move away from as soon as possible. She tries to make her rentals clean and attractive, and then she looks for working people, the type who know how to fix things themselves and don't mind doing it. Since she is neither handy nor rich—yet—she can't be bothered by tenants who expect the landlord to pamper or baby them. Between rental agencies where the tenant pays the fee, and newspaper ads, she has little trouble finding the type of tenants she wants, and she insists on solid references from banks, employers, and previous landlords.

The ease with which she has been able to buy and manage property, starting with almost nothing, excites Rachel. She enjoys real estate investing and says if it wasn't fun, she wouldn't do it. The money is nice, but that's secondary.

The Hobby that Grows

She is basically a bright young scientist, investing in real estate because it fascinates her, not because she is consumed by a need to get rich. Originally, she said she wanted to keep real estate as a hobby. Biology was her main love and her main career, and she had no intention to pursue real estate full time. Now, that is starting to change.

She can't even remember exactly how many properties she owns... thirteen... fourteen... She has so many that she started putting some of them into her sister's name. Her sister is only 19 and still in college, so she is not actively involved with Rachel's properties, but it helps her to build up a credit rating, and Rachel hopes eventually she will get interested in investing on her own.

Now that she has accumulated so many properties and agents call her to tell her about new ones, Rachel can relax a little.

In the beginning, she spent a lot of time just writing offers. Back then, only one out of five or six would be accepted—and that was after Rachel had pre-screened them on the phone. Now that people bring her deals, the percentage is much higher because the agents know what she's looking for, and they don't even call her unless the owner is ready to negotiate.

"When I buy," Rachel says, "it's either my price and their terms, or their price and my terms. I will pay full price if I get it on my terms, with no money down. But if I have to put up cash, then I expect to get the property at a discount. I don't pay full price and put up cash unless it's priced under the market value to begin with.

Rachel's success has already won her a trip to Bermuda where she was on a TV program called "Making It," which was sponsored by Robert Allen and taped for later showing in the U.S. The show is about self-made people making it in the world on their own efforts, starting with little and gradually amassing a lot. That is the story of Rachel Gunther Cabarrubias, all the way. If she is not a millionaire well before she is thirty, it will probably be because she decided to give it all away . . and she's doing it all in her spare time. But that may soon change, too.

"First I changed my major from Microbiology to Business," she says, "because I realized I didn't want to be stuck in a lab all the time. I love people and want to work with people, so my supervisor suggested I get an M.B.A. and move into management. Then I got so busy with real estate that I haven't had time for school, so I've decided to take off for a while.

"I love real estate investing. The more I do, the more excited I get. I got married a couple of months ago, and I even bought property while we were on our honeymoon. We were in Mexico, and we both liked it, so I bought a time-share condominium.

"Now my husband is urging me to quit my job so I'll have more time for investing, and still be able to spend some time with him in the evenings. Bruce is an electrician, and he doesn't get involved in the buying, selling or financing aspects of investing, but he does enjoy fixing up properties, and he supports my interest in investing. It helps keep the relationship interesting and gives us something to talk about. He even goes to RAND group meetings sometimes.

"I have started to think about becoming a full-time investor and quitting my job. Right now there are so many fantastic opportunities it is just unbelievable. I was elected Chairman of the Orange County RAND group (Robert Allen Nothing Down; the followup to Robert Allen's 'Nothing Down' seminars, an on-going group of graduate investors who meet once a month to trade ideas, listen to speakers and try to help each other find good buys), and so I learn of many opportunities that way. Sometimes members have more deals going than they can handle, or they don't think a particular deal is right for them because of their own personality or personal situation, but they know it is a good deal, so they will tell other members about it.

Borrowing that Pays Off

"I have been buying houses all over Southern California, in Colton, Riverside, San Diego—I'm buying six condos in Palm Springs—most of them brand new ones which I'm buying from builders who are going belly up. Most of these houses have already been appraised, but they aren't selling, so I'm getting them for as much as 40 percent below the appraised value. Then I get new FNMA loans (Federal National Mortgage Association, or 'Fannie Mae,' a semi-private government-backed corporation which buys mortgages from banks and savings and loans), for 80 percent of that appraised value and walk away with money in my pocket which will more than cover my negative cash flow."

It works like this: Rachel buys ten $100,000 houses from the builder for $60,000 each. (To do this successfully, she's found she has to bid on blocks of houses. Builders who need cash and can't wait to sell each house individually, are the only ones who will give such favorable discounts.) She then gets a loan on each of them for $80,000—80 percent of the appraised value—and walks away with $20,000. Her payments on the houses are about $1,250 a month each, and she can rent them for maybe $750, so she has a negative cash flow of $500 a month, or $6,000 a year. At the end of two years she has paid out $12,000.

But . . . she has the $20,000 she first took out of the house. If she just puts $12,000 aside to cover the negative cash flow for two years, she still has $8,000 in cash to spend elsewhere. If she puts the $20,000 into a money market fund and pays out five hundred each month to feed the house while earning interest on the rest, she will have at least $10,000 left out of her original $20,000. Each house will be worth at least the $100,000 it would be worth today if she bought only one house instead of ten, so ideally she will make between $48,000 and $50,000 on each house. If prices go up even ten percent a year, the houses will each be worth more than $120,000, and Rachel will make even more money.

"I'm always looking for people with a good income and good credit rating who will co-sign with me on some of the big loans I'm going after. I either pay them a flat fee, or give them a piece of the property, so they can share in the equity and appreciation.

"I'm trying to buy ten houses in Sacramento, and some townhouses—200 of them—in Tucson, Arizona. I'm not afraid of big deals any more. Big numbers don't scare me. It's just a couple of extra zeros. People in the RAND group have been coming to me lately and asking me to help them put deals together, offering to take me in as a partner. I seem to have an aptitude for real estate.

"My job takes up a lot of my time, and beyond that, it's exhausting, because they change my schedule every month. I go on different shifts—daytime, swing shift, or graveyard,—and sometimes it's hard keeping up with everything else I do. Right now I'm working hard because I want to support my mother. I want her to be able to retire and live comfortably.

"Someday I may quit my job, but not until I have enough cash flow from my properties to be financially secure. Security is very important to me. That's one reason I invest in real estate.

"I also like the people I meet. The RAND group has gotten to be just like one big family. People will call each other up and say, 'I'm having a problem with some kind of deal, or some kind of property, what do I do?' It's really great.

"I feel I owe a lot of my success to Robert Allen. He got me started, and he's really helped me. I used to call him when I had problems, and he would listen and give me advice. And the way the market is now, it's just fantastic. It's a wonderful time to buy real estate. I'm trying to buy all I can, while it's cheap.

"The opportunities are there for the asking. You just have to get out there and talk to people and start making offers. I've been able to apply so many of the things I learned at the seminar. It's amazing what you can get from people if you just ask."

4

Don't Sell When You Can Rent
Gene Allen

FBI men are taught to be slow and methodical. They don't rush into things. They believe in careful and patient investigation. That's how it was for Gene Allen of Clearwater, Florida. He took his time and pursued his main career, first as an FBI agent, and later as a private security specialist. But once he got a chance to really investigate the possibilities, he knew real estate investing was what he wanted to do.

"I had been fooling around with real estate since 1962," he says. "But the Robert Allen Nothing Down seminar is what really got me going. I had a general idea of how real estate worked, but I knew nothing about creative techniques for negotiating or for financing properties. The seminar helped me to understand how sellers are likely to think and how to deal with them. Now I don't just take 'No!' for an answer any more."

Gene got started when he was transferred, and he found he couldn't sell his house. No one was buying, so he rented it instead. When he was transferred again, he did the same thing. After a couple of moves, he was a landlord, with two rental houses. He found that inflation and kids were working together to eat up his paycheck, but now he had property that was building up equity. It was like silent income that was building up untouched.

But Gene was too busy to take real estate very seriously. It was strictly a part-time thing; almost a hobby with him (especially since his properties were out of town and he didn't even have to deal with them on a regular basis). He spent nine years with the Bureau, and then worked in private industry for a few more.

While he was in Chicago, he bought some run down storefronts and converted them to offices. He did none of the work himself. He contracted it all out, but still he made money.

Then he moved to Florida, bought a run-down duplex, and converted that to offices. He kept one for himself, and rented the other office to someone else.

People started coming around, asking him about the idea and how he did it, how others could do it, etc. A lot of people seemed to be interested in creating or leasing office space. There was obviously a good market out there, so Gene bought a small office building. He found commercial property easier to handle than residential property, and he was still getting a nice positive cash flow.

Gradually, he started spending more time on real estate and less time doing investigations and security consulting, and soon he was a full-time investor.

"My father was a contractor," he says, "so I know something about construction, but there is no way I would do the work. I hire it out. I get good workers by word of mouth, by talking to other investors in the RAND (Robert Allen Nothing Down) group, etc. That's what I did in Chicago, and that's what I did here, was to hire people and do all the coordinating and overseeing, tying up all the loose ends and making sure that everything runs smoothly.

"I think my FBI background helps me, because real estate requires patience and investigation. You can't expect deals to pop up every day, and you don't want to just jump at the first thing which comes along. There are a lot of variables to consider."

Evaluating the Property

Gene starts out by looking at the condition of the property. If it is run down, then what will it cost to put it in good shape? What will the benefits be?

Next, he comes to the question of changing the use of the property to see if he can increase the value that way. He looks for the Highest and Best Use for that particular property—the use which will give it maximum value and rental appeal. This may mean changing the property from residential to commercial. Or from industrial to residential, or one type of commercial usage to a better, more profitable type of commercial use.

The Highest and Best Use for any property is an individual matter, determined by the type of property involved and the location. Location, Location, Location. The three most important things to consider when you buy a piece of property, and the most important also when you are considering the Highest and Best Use. They are intimately tied together.

For instance, you would normally expect commercial property, offices and/or stores, to be the more valuable type of property. It brings in the most rent with the least trouble, and usually appreciates at least as fast as residential property. But there are some areas, or even certain locations, within any given area, that just will not do well as commercial locations, i.e., stores which are out in the middle of nowhere, away from any major population areas. Large shopping centers create their own audience, even if people need to travel to get to them, but this doesn't work for the smaller ones. They need to be where the people are. A vacant lot in the middle of a crowded city? What a waste of land if it's in a residential area; but if it's in among all those office buildings where there are thousands of people just looking for a place to park, you have a gold mine.

These are the types of decisions Gene has learned to capitalize on. He looks at a piece of property, and by examining all the possibilities from every angle, he sees things other people don't.

He sees hard-to-find office space in an area where stores are going begging. It's all a game of possibilities. For instance, as stores, they are selling for $40,000 for four of them. Fixed up, with a little paint, a little sparkle, they will rent for about $200 each, and the property will be worth about $50,000.

It will cost about $2,500 for labor and materials to get the places in nice condition, and then there are closing costs, taxes, etc., so a buyer will be lucky to pick up $5,000 equity as a reward for all his/her work; and if he sells it again right away, even that will be swept away by real estate commissions or advertising costs and taxes. But, if he/she converts the stores to offices which will rent for $400 per month, the building will be worth $80,000 to $100,000, because in that particular location offices, not stores, is the Highest and Best Possible Use for that building.

So Gene began to realize he was more than just an investor. Ordinary investing, buying properties which were already in good shape and being put to good use and merely keeping them rented out, was too passive for Gene. Even though he didn't want to do the physical work, Gene enjoyed the challenge of taking on conversion projects. He liked doing the planning himself, if not the execution, and he liked seeing his own ideas go into a project.

On the other hand, he doesn't like managing property, and decided he wanted to spend as little time on it as possible. He began getting rid of some of the residential properties he owned and looking around for another small office building to buy, and that's when he entered the latest and newest phase of his life.

Fresh Opportunities

"I couldn't find any office buildings to buy," he says. "Oh, I mean I found some and even put in a couple of offers, but they didn't get accepted because there was always somebody ready to pay more than I was. I couldn't find anything like the one I had, with a positive cash flow. So, I figured since there was such a demand, maybe I should go and build one."

Gene went out and found some land and evaluated the area and decided that yes, it was ripe for a new office building, and then he went looking for money. He had a track record as an investor, so he was able to get a bank loan for 80 percent of the costs, and three partners to put up the rest of the money, so that his own share is only one-fifth of the total cost of the building. It is his first joint venture.

"I am a developer more than an investor," he says. "I am a computer of numbers, a dispenser of funds, a personnel coordinator and a marketing specialist. I'm sort of a supercontractor while the project is going on, overseeing the General Contractor and all the subs. Then when the building is finished, I'll probably rent it out and manage it myself for an additional management fee, just the way I'm getting a separate fee—aside from my share of any positive cash flow—for developing the project. I'm not sure yet. We may hire one of the big commercial real estate firms to handle the leasing, and then I'll just manage it."

For awhile, Gene considered his out-of-town rental houses, his ex-homes, as a sort of savings account. He didn't find them to be much trouble, since he usually had friends and/or ex-neighbors looking after the places while he was gone. And after all, if you knew your landlord was an FBI agent, would you want to fool around and be late with the rent? But now he's in the process of getting rid of those. He prefers commercial property, and wants to get his money out of the houses and put it into his new projects.

In addition to the office building in Clearwater, Gene is looking ahead to the future. He bought an option for $10,000 on 500 acres of raw land near DisneyWorld in Orlando—a $3 million deal if he decides to exercise the option. Now he's trying to line up backers to help him develop it. If not, he can sell it at a substantial profit.

All told, Gene estimates he owns several million dollars' worth of property, and has a net worth on the order of 600 to 700 thousand dollars. He estimates his yearly income at around $60,000, most of it safely sheltered from taxes, and as Florida grows, he expects his business to grow with it.

"I tend to be conservative," he said, "so it took me awhile to really get into real estate, but once I did, I just knew it was for me. I think my background does help, because everyone around here knows I used to be with the FBI, and there's a lot of sharks out there, especially once you get into developing. Plus, it taught me how to dig into something carefully and get all the facts."

Such as all the possible ways to squeeze money out of a piece of property. When he bought the piece of land he is developing in Clearwater, it had a mobile home. That was of no use to Gene, so he sold it for $3,000 and immediately got some cash back on his investment.

The land was also covered by ferns. To many people that would be just a minor nuisance, one more thing to clear away before the property could be built on, but to Gene it was another chance to make money. He did some investigating and found he could sell the ferns to a wholesale plant dealer for about $2,000—more cash returned on his investment, more cash to put into the project.

It is this ability to find not only the Highest and Best Use for properties, but to also find new, unexpected ways to pull money out of them, that is making Gene a wealthy man. But money is not everything, and he also enjoys the challenges investing and developing present, and gets deep satisfaction from seeing his projects take shape.

5

The Sweet Song of Success
Wayne Phillips

Wayne Phillips of Baltimore, Maryland, is a determined young man and when he wants something, he's not afraid to work and dream and sweat and strain until he gets it.

"When I was a kid," he says, "I had a picture of a set of Ludwig drums I wanted; I put it on my wall so it was the first thing I saw when I got up in the morning and the last thing I saw at night. That way I was able to visualize those drums constantly in my mind, and I knew that someday I would have them.

"I worked after school, and on weekends and during the summer, cutting lawns at 25¢ apiece (of course, here in Baltimore, the lawns weren't very big, just little narrow strips of grass), and doing odd jobs for people, and finally I had saved enough money and I got those drums.

"My parents had always listened to big band music on the radio, so I was exposed to Harry James, Benny Goodman, and all of those, and somehow I just decided I was going to practice until I was good enough to become famous, and then play in front of large audiences and be a professional musician.

"When I finally got the drums, I practiced and practiced, and that was all I did—all I thought about—until I got out of high school. From the time I was eight or nine years old, that was all I really cared about, playing the drums. The neighbors used to complain, and the cops came by several times, because we lived in a second floor apartment.

That's when I decided that some day I would have my own house with a studio to practice in, where nobody would bother me. Playing the drums was all that mattered to me then. I didn't even discover girls until I was eighteen!"

Once Wayne got out of high school he began to make up for lost time in the romance department, but his dream of owning his own home had to wait. Right after high school he went on the road as a professional drummer, just as he had always seen himself doing. His reputation grew, and by 1973 he was living in L.A. and working primarily as a studio musician playing on jazz albums.

It was a good life while it lasted, but as Wayne says now:

"As a musician you are either on top of the world, or starving."

Jazz is not the music to play if you're after the big money, and Wayne found that in spite of his growing respect within the music world, it was hard to make ends meet. Fortunately, he knew someone who owned six apartment units that needed some work, and they were able to make a deal: Wayne would manage the building and spend some time helping to upgrade it in exchange for reduced rent.

It was a comfortable arrangement while it lasted, allowing Wayne to live cheaply and go on playing the music he enjoyed without having to give up eating. Then in late 1974, the owner decided he wanted to sell, and he advised Wayne to start looking for a new place to live.

Time to Buy

"At that time, there was a recession and a severe money crunch," Wayne says, "and a lot of people were losing their houses. There were VA houses which had been repossessed for sale all over town, and it seemed to me like it was a good time to buy, except that I didn't have any money. Then I got an idea.

"I had a friend named Bob who was a real estate broker and investor, and I told him that if he would help me find a house and put up his commission as the down payment, I would pay him back by working on one of the fixer houses he owned. He agreed to that, and he gave me a house to work on.

"Well, it took me six weeks of full-time work on that place just to paint it inside and out. I'd gotten myself in a little deeper than I'd anticipated, but I stuck it out, and when I was finished, we went looking for a house.

"I must have been to at least ten VA repos all over L.A. before I finally got one in the Tujunga-Sunland area in the foothills. My friend Bob put up his commission as the down payment, just as we had agreed, and I got the house for $21,665 and moved in in April, 1975.

"At that time I really knew nothing about real estate. I hadn't taken any seminars or read any books or anything, but I knew I wanted my own house, and I figured that if I could get one without having to put up any of my own money, there was no way I could really go wrong. Government loans—VA and FHA—were the only ones you could assume in those days, because that was before Wellenkamp."

(In 1978 a California Supreme Court ruling in the case of *Cynthia Wellenkamp versus the Bank of America* said that due-on-sale clauses, which were included in most bank and saving and loan mortgages, were an unfair restraint on trade, since they hampered the seller's ability to sell his property. These clauses were therefore declared unenforceable in California. This meant that any loan made by a state chartered institution—one without "Federal" in the name, as in First Federal Savings, etc.—was automatically assumable, just like government guaranteed VA and FHA loans. As of June, 1981, a bill is pending in the California legislature which would overturn the Wellenkamp decision and make buyers take out new loans at current interest rates each time a property changes hands, and the battle over assumable loans is going on in several other states as well.)

An assumable loan meant a lower interest rate and lower payments. Also, VA repos were readily available at low prices because most of them were bought with nothing down (VA finances one hundred per cent of the purchase price for qualified veterans, while FHA requires at least some money down), so the people didn't feel they were losing too much if they walked away from them when times got hard and they lost their jobs or whatever."

So Wayne Phillips was now a property owner. He finally owned his own home where he could practice on his drums and feel like his own man. He was 27 years old, and had been a professional musician for nine years.

The First Investment House

"In the summer of 1975, when I had finally gotten settled into my new house, my older brother, Richard, came to visit from Maryland. He didn't have any background in business or real estate either. He's a classical guitarist, and at that time he was playing with orchestras, doing eighteen to twenty concerts a year and making about nine or ten thousand dollars—even less than I was making.

"Well, he saw my house, which I had bought with no money, and he expressed interest in the house next door. It wasn't for sale at that time, but before he left, he let the owner know that if he ever wanted to sell, we would be interested.

"Well, a few months later, the owner did decide to sell, and he was asking $28,000 with an assumable VA mortgage of $19,000. Now this house was a bit nicer than mine, so we offered him $24,000. He turned it down and sold the house to someone else for a higher price, but then that deal fell through, and he was stuck. He'd already bought another house somewhere else, and so now he had to get this one sold in a hurry.

"So, I get a knock on my door early one morning and he's standing there saying 'I'll take your offer. You can have the house for $24,000.'

"So I hit him with the good news and the bad news. 'The good news,' I said to him, 'is that we still want to buy your house. The bad news is that you're going to have to help us buy it.'

"We worked out a deal where my broker friend, Bob, loaned us his commission for a down payment again, and then we assumed the VA loan and the seller carried back a second mortgage for the balance. The rent on the house paid off the first mortgage, and the second, and left us about fifty dollars a month to pay off Bob. (He had agreed to loan us his commission for up to eighteen months without interest.) That was in November of 1975, and it was the first piece of income property my brother or I had ever owned."

Wayne was excited and wanted to follow up on this first purchase by buying more property. He decided it might be a good idea to go and talk to some bankers to see if he could arrange to be prequalified for mortgage money (i.e., approved to borrow X amount of dollars whenever he found a suitable property) so he could move quickly if he saw any good deals and would not have to restrict himself to VA and FHA assumptions. He thought that owning two pieces of property, one in his own name, and one in partnership with his brother, would help establish his credit-worthiness, but it wasn't that easy.

"It was hard borrowing money from banks in those days," Wayne says now. "They would look at me and all they would see is that I was a musician; I had a beard and long hair, and they decided I was probably a flaky person, a drug addict, or who knows what.

Down Payments from the Credit Union

"Then a great thing happened in January of 1976. They passed a law saying credit unions could make mortgage loans. The manager of the Musician's Credit Union was a good friend of mine, and I'd done a lot of favors for him, so as soon as this law went into effect I went to him and told him I wanted to borrow some money."

As soon as he had a commitment from his credit union to loan him up to $40,000 cash, or 80 percent of the value of any property he might buy up to $50,000, Wayne called his friend Bob and told him to find any deal he could that would not involve any money down. Bob didn't think there were any deals like that to be had, but Wayne was not so easily discouraged.

Eventually, they found a nice duplex off Gower Street in Los Angeles, right near all the recording studios in an area Wayne knew well. The seller was asking $40,000, and Wayne agreed to pay full price—$32,000 from his credit union, and $8,000 down—but he wrote it into the offer that the seller was to refund $8,000 to him to cover the cost of repairs. The seller agreed.

"My friend Bob was going crazy by this point. He didn't believe me when I called him and told him I could borrow $40,000 just like that, any time I wanted to, and he certainly didn't believe I could get my down payment back right away. He told me it simply couldn't be done, but here I was, doing it, and he was getting his commission on a $40,000 sale, so he was happy, even if he couldn't believe it."

Then, in the spring of 1976, Wayne was invited to become the drummer for the Charlie Byrd Trio, a well-known jazz group. He moved back to Maryland and his real estate activities were put on the back burner for a while. By this time he was engaged to Kathy, who is now his wife. At that time she was a production manager at Arista Records, and she was living in Wayne's house in L.A. taking care of that, and also keeping an eye on the house next door and the duplex.

Wayne's brother, Richard, had his Maryland real estate license by then, but aside from helping Wayne find a condominium to live in and loaning him the commission to use as the down payment, he wasn't really using it. He was still making his living as a classical guitarist, while Wayne was working with Charlie Byrd. Real estate was strictly a part-time avocation for both of them, and they were both too busy to buy anything new.

Things went on that way until the summer of 1978 when Wayne got back to L.A. and found out that credit unions could now loan up to $100,000 per person for real estate deals. Since he and his brother were both members of the Musician's Credit Union, they could borrow $200,000 between them—minus the $32,000 loan they had already. So Wayne called his friend Bob again.

"We found fourteen units for $206,500 with a kickback of $60,000 for repairs. I borrowed the down payment of $44,000 from my friend Bob —he took out a second on his house, and then I paid him right back— and even after paying him, we still walked away with $16,000 cash after the close of escrow.

"Well, Bob was going crazy. I was really blowing his mind. He couldn't believe you could walk away with cash like that after buying something. He just wasn't used to doing things that way. But here he was, making a commission on $206,500.

"And, we had a positive cash flow besides.

"It was just about this time that I was on an airplane and I read an ad for Mark Haroldsen's book, *How To Wake Up the Financial Genius Within You*. So I sent for the book, and I read it and reread it, and I got excited. Here was a guy who had become a millionaire doing the same thing I had already been doing. So that made me want to do more. I

decided then that I wanted to be a millionaire, not someday, but fast—
within a year or two. I had grown up in a lower middle class family,
and I had a desire for some of the material things in life. I was tired of
doing everything second class and I wanted to move up and start going
first class. And also, my mother didn't have much, and I wanted to be
able to take care of her."

Setting a Goal

By this point, Wayne was also deciding that real estate, not music,
was the way to get where he wanted to go. He had recorded an album
with the Charlie Byrd Trio in the summer of 1978, and it was really
starting to climb the charts and take off as a hit. But all Wayne got out
of it was a couple of hundred dollars, union scale, for his time in the
studio. Wayne felt frustrated and unappreciated, and he decided it was
time to get out, make some changes, and have some more control over
his own destiny.

He and Kathy got married in October of 1978 and moved back to
Maryland. At first they rented out the house Kathy had occupied in
Los Angeles. Later, they sold it and used the money to buy more
property in Baltimore.

Wayne attended Mark Haroldsen's seminar, and through Haroldsen, he found out about Bill Greene from Mill Valley, California, who
also gave seminars on how to make a fortune in real estate. Wayne
took that seminar, too. By this point he was a self-confessed "book
junkie," reading anything he could get his hands on which had anything to do with investing in real estate.

Then Wayne set a goal. He, his wife, and his brother would buy at
least one million dollars' worth of property within the next four years.
Then the three of them set a much more immediate goal for themselves: they would make at least 5,000 offers on different properties in
the Baltimore area by the end of 1979.

"About this time, I started getting letters from real estate agents in
L.A. wanting to sell my house for me. They had me down on their lists
of out-of-town owners, so they were sending letters telling me my
house was probably worth a lot more than I realized, and I could get a
lot of money for it. When they told me it was worth around $60,000, I
got excited again. I knew I was on the right track.

"By this time (late 1978-early 1979) we had a solid credit rating, and
we were able to get money from banks, so we started making all-cash
offers on cheap properties. We would borrow from the bank on a short
term note, say ninety days, steal the place for a low price, go in there,
fix it up, refinance it for at least what we had put into it, and then pay
off the short term note.

"For instance, the first one we bought, we got for $17,000 and had to put almost $3,000 into it. Then we got it refinanced for $20,000 and walked away with about $100 in our pockets. Then, the second property we got was five units. The seller was asking $60,000, but the units were pretty run-down and had been on the market a long time, so we offered him $23,000 in cash, and he took it. We put about $4,000 into the property and refinanced it for $44,000. We walked away with about $17,000 in cash on that one. Then we picked up a duplex for $12,000 in cash and turned around and got a $15,000, fifteen-year mortgage without even doing a thing to it. After that, we decided to really go at it.

"How did we manage to write up and present so many offers? Well, for one thing, we decided to concentrate mainly on one area of Baltimore, known as Highland Town, where there are mostly brick row houses—duplexes where each apartment usually rented for $180 to $190 a month in early 1979. We studied the area and decided that $20,000 was a fair price for those properties, so $20,000 was what we decided to offer, no matter what the sellers were asking.

Making the Offers

"We had three standard offers we made up: the first called for the seller to carry an $8,000 second (40 percent of the $20,000 purchase price), and for us to get *at least* a 60 percent first. Ideally, we tried to get a first for around 75 percent, so we could walk away with some cash at the close of the deal. Second, we would offer all cash if the price was right, and then refinance the property as soon as we fixed it up. Third, and last, if the owner was going to carry the first, and that was the only way to get the property, we would put 25 percent down if it seemed like a really good deal.

"We would go through the MLS book, the newspaper, and just drive around and look for places. All our offers were made subject to inspection, but since we were making so many offers we didn't have time to look at them all. We'd just pick out places which seemed to be over- or underpriced, or had been sitting on the market for over three months, and we'd shoot off an offer.

"At first, we generated a lot of hostility, but not too many accepted offers—maybe one or two out of every hundred. People would get furious at us and throw us out of their offices. 'What have you got, X-ray vision?' they would say to us. 'How can you make offers on properties you've never even seen? What are you wasting our time for?' But even with only one or two percent getting accepted, when you make an average of 15 or 20 offers every working day you wind up buying an awful lot of property. When we sat back in early 1980 and added it all up, we realized we had made five thousand and twelve offers in 1979, and we'd already reached our goal—we had bought over a million dollars' worth of property.

"Now this was over a million dollars, going by our purchase price. But since everything we bought was at least 25 percent below market value, it was really worth a lot more than a million. The first thing I did to reward myself for reaching that goal was to go out and buy a brand new Jaguar."

Wayne also had something else to celebrate in 1979. On the basis of the album he had recorded with the Charlie Byrd Trio the previous summer, he was voted seventh best jazz drummer in the annual *Downbeat* magazine poll. Ironically though, this helped solidify his decision to abandon his career as a professional musician and concentrate full time on investing in real estate.

"Charlie Byrd had been around for a long time and was a fairly well-known jazz guitarist," Wayne says. "He had a few successful records in the 60's, but nothing like this one. This album which I played on in the summer of 1978 was by far the most successful album he had ever had, and I felt my drumming had at least partially contributed to that success, and I didn't feel I was properly acknowledged or rewarded.

"And I was tired of it all by that point, anyway. The last six months I had performed with the trio it wasn't really fun anymore, so I decided it was time to get out, and real estate seemed to offer the freedom and the financial independence I wanted."

Soon, the Phillipses had over one hundred units, and found they could no longer rely on their former haphazard style of contacts with contractors and handymen. They began to employ a full-time maintenance crew. To avoid all the problems of being "employers," they decided to pay their people on an independent contractor basis.

"I don't pay my people much," Wayne explains, "but instead, I'll tell a guy I'll give him, say, a quarter interest in one property if he'll help me with all my other properties, keeping them all in good repair. That way, he feels like he's part of what I'm doing, instead of just working for me. I know they're not going to rip me off too badly if they've got a share in it all. Besides, the people I hire are all people I've used before on individual jobs and/or have gotten on recommendations from other investors, so it works out pretty well.

"Then there are other, big jobs which we still have to contract out. For instance, we're buying seventy-one units which we're going to rehab, and we've got to get the place painted inside and out, so we had to get bids and we're going to get the whole job done for $18,000. Now, that's a fantastic price, and the way I got it was to go to some guys who had worked for us before, and I told them, 'You give me a good price on this job and I'll also let you do these fifty-two units we're also buying and anything else we get in the future.' We can throw a lot of work their way, so it's a good bargaining tool, and I do the same thing with the other contractors we deal with."

But actually, we've gotten slightly ahead of our story. It was not until the summer of 1980 that Wayne and his brother started buying larger properties.

Stepping Up the Tempo

"After awhile we found it was becoming too much trouble to keep track of so many individual properties. We've only sold one property that we bought here in Maryland, and that was a single family house about fifty miles away. It was a good deal; that's why we bought it in the first place, but it was too far away and too small to bother fooling around with, so we got rid of it.

"Then, in the summer of 1980, we started buying properties with twenty units and more. In the beginning we concentrated on small properties, because that was what we had to do to get started. It's pretty hard to start out by buying fifty units when you have no money! It's a lot harder to buy a large property like that with no money down, especially when you're just beginning. But once we got established, we decided we could buy a lot more property a lot faster by concentrating on larger units. Plus, there was no competition. Nobody else was buying these places. Some of them were on the market for months, and no one else had made offers on them.

"Besides us, there are only about four other investors in the Baltimore area buying properties over twenty units. I don't know why . . . I guess most people are scared of buying in low income white or black areas where a lot of these properties are located. So now (June, 1981), we've got four hundred units and seven full-time office and maintenance people working for us. We've got contracts to buy another two hundred units, and we would buy even more, except we can't find enough qualified people to help take care of them all, so that holds me back a little bit.

"I don't have any trouble finding good properties to buy. They're all over the place. Not only that, but the government is even giving us money to buy places and fix them up. It's a program called HUD (Department of Housing and Urban Development) 221 D-4."

HUD 221 D-4 is designed to encourage private investors to buy and rehabilitate low to moderate income housing units. Certain areas are designated as target areas, and usually specific goals are set, such as 8,000 units of rehabilitated housing for the city of Baltimore, usually within certain designated neighborhoods, rather than citywide; 5,000 for New York City; 1,200 for Philadelphia, etc. (Figures given are strictly hypothetical and are not meant to be taken as an accurate measure of the aid given to any city or area.)

Once the goals or quotas are set, announcements are placed in the local newspapers, in HUD offices, etc., inviting proposals from investors, contractors, and/or developers. Applicants have to find a property and then submit a preliminary proposal explaining what they intend to do to the property, how much they expect to spend, etc. They must have approval of this preliminary proposal before they can even submit a formal application for funds.

Once all the paperwork is completed—a process which can take up to a year, so you had better have a patient seller—and the plans approved, the applicant will receive a loan for up to 90 percent of the total cost of purchasing the building *and* rehabilitating it. This includes all the carrying costs while the work is being done and the units are vacant. HUD will even pay a ten percent general contractor's fee on top of it all.

In return for such generosity comes paperwork, reams and reams of it, and almost total government control of the financial side of the deal. HUD must approve the project. HUD must approve the property, the area, the purchase price, and the type and cost of repairs. And when the project is completed, the investor has to sign a 15-year lease with the local housing authority and rent all the apartments to people who qualify for assistance under the Section 8 subsidized housing program. To anyone who has ever been in the Army, or even just watched "M*A*S*H" on TV, Section 8 is a mental case, a discharge for psychiatric reasons. But this Section 8 program has nothing to do with that. It is simply a program to subsidize the rent of people whose income falls below a certain level set by the poverty experts in Washington.

The tenant pays up to 25 percent of his/her gross income, and HUD, through the local housing authority, pays the difference between that amount and the rent considered to be fair market rent for that particular unit.

Normally, fair market rents for Section 8 units are determined in advance before a tenant moves in and readjusted every year. Landlords who cooperate with the regular Section 8 program pick their own tenants from the pool of those eligible for Section 8 subsidized housing. An inspector then comes out, and a specific rent is agreed upon. A one-year contract is signed between the landlord and the housing authority. At the end of a year, the contract is renegotiated, and the rent raised according to a set formula. At the end of the second year, the process is repeated. (Usually three years is the limit for renewable, one-year contracts. For a further discussion of the Section 8 program, see Chapter 18 about Simon Lantzer of Oakland, California.)

With the HUD 221 D-4 program, rents are set in advance for the full fifteen year period. They go up each year, but they are not subject to reevaluation or negotiation. Once he signs the contract and accepts the government's money, the investor knows exactly how much rent he can charge for each unit for the next fifteen years.

Tax Breaks—and Unusual Problems

There is one additional feature of the HUD 221 D-4 program, and that is the tax advantages. The IRS lets investors who participate in the program depreciate the property over a five-year period instead of the fifteen year minimum they usually require for depreciation of residential property.

What this means to an investor is that he/she gets two to six times the amount of tax benefits he/she would normally get. For example, say Jane Smith buys a building worth $100,000 (exclusive of the value of the land, which cannot be depreciated). She has a taxable income, after all her other deductions, of $20,000 a year, so her prime motive for buying property is to get more tax write-offs and shelter as much of that $20,000 as possible. If she participates in the HUD 221 D-4 program and gets to depreciate the building in only five years, she gets a full $20,000 worth of write-offs each year, and pays no income tax at all.

Now, assume that Jane's income in search of a tax shelter is $200,000 per year, and that her building is worth $1 million, and you can see where the advantages of participating in the HUD 221 D-4 program can be quite significant. But things rarely work out the way they're supposed to, and for Wayne, Richard, and Kathy Phillips it created an unusual sort of problem, one that more of us should be stuck with.

"Our accountant told us we had too much depreciation and too many write-offs," Wayne says, "so we had to start generating more income to take advantage of it; otherwise, it was going to waste. So we decided to split the seventy-one unit project into twelve investment units. We're keeping two for ourselves and selling the other ten to investors who need more tax write-offs, for $25,000 apiece. Fifty thousand will go for expenses, and the other two hundred thousand is our fee for putting the whole thing together.

"There's a lot of bureaucratic red tape involved, and months and months of paperwork like you wouldn't believe, so a lot of people don't want to get involved in deals like this, but for two young guys like my brother and I who are hustling and trying to get somewhere, it's great. I mean, it's taking about nine months to get the whole thing approved and off the ground, but what the heck. I mean, I'll work for nine months to make a hundred thousand dollars. Wouldn't you?"

Yes. Especially when it's all tax free. But don't feel too sorry for Wayne and Richard Phillips trying to struggle along on only one hundred thousand tax-free dollars a year, because they also have a lot of other things going for themselves. That little house in Los Angeles they bought together for $24,000 in 1975 has been supplying them with a steady $250 a month over and above expenses (Wayne's broker friend, Bob, has been keeping an eye on it for them) and in May, 1981, it was appraised for $128,000, so they decided it was time to refinance.

The $97,000 they get out of the refinancing (80 percent of the appraised value minus expenses) is going into more property in the Baltimore area.

"It's going to cost me about $800 a month now in negative cash flow," Wayne says, "because I had to pay 16½ percent interest on the new loan; but the money I get out of it will generate about $4,000 a month in income once I put it into property here in Baltimore. So I'll spend $800 to make $4,000. Somehow that seems to make sense to me.

"Why don't I just sell it and avoid the negative cash flow entirely? Because I figure that in another five years it will be worth a quarter of a million. And all my other properties at least pay for themselves, so I can afford one $800-a-month negative property."

Branching Out

Like many other successful investors, the Phillips brothers have also branched out into seminars.

"Once I started going to a lot of seminars and attending a lot of local investment groups like the Lowry-Nickerson group," Wayne says, "my name got around and people were always calling me for advice. I was on the phone constantly, maybe four or five hours a day, trying to help other people solve their problems, and I barely had enough time any more for my own. I was charging one hundred dollars an hour for consultations, but it still wasn't worth it to me because my time is more valuable than that. But I didn't want to just cut people off. I enjoy helping other people, so that's when I hit on the idea of doing a seminar. We put ads in the local newspaper and then held three free lectures to help drum up interest, and then we gave an all-day seminar for $200. We got 93 people at the first one and took in about $10,000 after all our expenses, so that wasn't too bad for one day's work.

"We ran our first ad on Sunday, and then on Monday, Tuesday and Thursday we ran more ads and gave some free preview lectures. The following Saturday we held the seminar. We've done six of them so far, and now we charge $250, but that's not our main motivation.

"What we really get out of it is that every once in a while one of the people who take the seminars is going to get out there and do something. We show them how to get started, how to get money, and how to stay on top of management problems. Now, most people who take the seminar just sit on their tails and never do anything with what we teach them. But maybe one out of ten will actually do something, and then, when they run across a deal that's too big or too complex for them to handle alone and they're afraid of getting in over their heads, who are they going to come to? That's where we get our reward.

"We've got ten signals we teach people to look for that will tell them when an owner is really ready to sell. I don't want to give them all away because I'm working on a book of my own, but I'll give you a few ideas. One, which I got from Bill Greene, is to look for dirty windows. That tells you the owner and/or the tenants aren't taking care of the place. Another secret is to look for properties which have been around too long—more than three months on the market—or are overpriced. And, of course, any property you can get with no money down, even if you have to pay full market value.

"I've become an expert in the Baltimore area market because I'm out there hustling twelve to fourteen hours a day, six or seven days a week. I think I know values in this area as well as anybody around. You tell me where a property is and how many units it has, and I'll tell you what the rents should be and what that property is worth.

"I handle all the acquisitions and financing, etc., and my brother handles the maintenance. In the beginning, we had to do most of it ourselves, but now we have a full-time maintenance crew and full-time office staff to keep on top of it all. It's still a matter of keeping on people though, visiting the units periodically, supervising the maintenance crews to make sure they get on any problems as soon as they happen. With four hundred units, there's always something to be done, but it's not as hard as most people seem to think.

"I would say that our one week link is bookkeeping, just because there's so much of it. Like today, for instance, we must have gotten sixty-five different utility bills in the mails. You know, for the hallway lights and things like that. That's another reason we started moving into larger properties. With single family homes, each unit requires its own separate file, and that compounds the bookkeeping. Of course, that's not the only problem that ever comes up. There are others."

Tenant Relations

"For instance, we had this one tenant who got behind in his rent and we were too lenient with him and let him slide for awhile. Then when we finally decided to evict him, we came up in front of this judge who is very pro-tenant and anti-landlord, and when we won in court and got a $1,200 judgment against the tenant, the judge let him appeal. So the guy was putting his rent money into an escrow account all this time where we couldn't touch it until the case was resolved. We won again and he tried to appeal it a third time, but the judge in that case said he would have to put up a $1,000 appeal bond since he had already lost twice, and he finally got out. But it took six months of our time, and we only got $1,200 out of a total of about $1,600 he actually owed us.

So we went and filed a notice with the credit bureau, so now his credit is shot. In the end he hurt himself and other tenants, too, because now I'm not as easy going. I give them five days past the date when the rent is due and then I go down and file a rent notice. And now we check with the credit bureau before we rent to anybody.

"We also check with their former landlord, as well as their current one, because we've been burned that way, too. Sometimes if you've got a bad tenant on your hands you'll say anything just to get rid of him, but the former landlord has no reason to lie.

"One thing we never have any trouble with is finding tenants. There is a vacancy factor of only one percent in the Baltimore area. We usually run a small ad in the paper, and within a week the place is rented. In fact, I feel Baltimore is the best place in the whole country to invest right now because of all the spillover from Washington, D.C. Prices there have gotten so outrageous that a lot of people are commuting from Baltimore, since it's less than fifty miles away, and our prices are so much lower. The whole Washington-Maryland-Virginia area is booming. It's one of the largest metropolitan areas in the United States, with over 15 million people in a one hundred-square-mile area. Here in Baltimore, prices have doubled in the last three years, and even now, with sky-high interest rates, we're still getting appreciation of about one and a half percent a month."

Getting What He Wants

"But, of course, we try to go for owner financing anyway instead of paying those high interest rates. That's one very important thing I've learned, is to ask for what I want. When I ask sellers to carry a note at a low interest rate, they usually tell me the same old thing about how they can get better interest by putting their money in the bank. And I explain to them that that is true, but then they also get taxed up to 70 percent on unearned income. The deal I offer them is better for both of us.

"I'm willing to pay them more money for the property if I get the interest rate I want. For instance, the payments on $15,000 at 15 percent interest for 15 years are $209 a month, and the payments on $25,000 at 5 percent interest for 15 years are $196 a month, so which way do I come out better? That way the seller is only paying 40 percent on long term capital gains instead of the 70 percent tax on unearned income, and my capital gains are reduced by $10,000 when I go to sell the property a few years down the road.

"I've found you can even negotiate with the banks if you put it to them the right way. I even got one bank to give me a moratorium on payments for three months. They had let the seller get about nine months behind in his payments because they really didn't want to foreclose. The property was kind of a dump, and they didn't really want to get stuck with it. There were vacant units, and they didn't want to deal with it, but finally they couldn't put it off any more, and that's when I came into the picture.

"I went to the vice president of the bank and I just told him that if he foreclosed, he would have a hard time even getting back the money his bank had loaned on the property. He would probably wind up having to write part of it off as a loss, and that would look bad on his record—especially since the federal auditors happened to be auditing his bank at the time.

"On the other hand, if he let us put down $8,500, and gave us a moratorium on payments for three months, until we could get the property fixed up, and then half payments for another three months, we would gradually increase the payments until we were all caught up, and even pay off the nine payments the seller had missed. And then they would have a good, solid, well-managed building for collateral, instead of a run-down dump.

"We are problem solvers. We take over problem properties no one else wants to deal with and turn them around. For instance, I just found out about a castle that's coming up for sale. It's fifty years old, with seventeen rooms and seven bedrooms on five acres, and it's got to be worth at least $250,000, but the owner only owes $53,000 on it and it's coming up for foreclosure. It's owned by a doctor who's getting divorced, and apparently he deliberately stopped making the payments, just to spite his ex-wife. So I'm going to contact him and see if he'll take $20,000 cash. He just may do it, because half of whatever he gets out of the house goes to his ex-wife, and revenge seems to be more important to him than the money involved. Then I'll pay the bank off to get it out of foreclosure, and refinance it, and my wife and I can move in and live there."

But even if Wayne Phillips doesn't get his castle, he won't have too many complaints. He and his wife already have a lovely new house which they built for themselves in Towson, Maryland, a suburb just north of Baltimore; and a condominium in the Bahamas. And, yes, Wayne finally has his sound-proofed practice studio in the basement, just as he always dreamed he would. Does he have any advice for new investors?

Directions for Beginners

"Tell them it's easier to get started now than ever before. People are more sophisticated now, and more willing to deal. When we were starting three years ago, no one around here understood what we were doing, and they were really hostile. Now things are starting to change. My brother and I were kind of pioneers here in Baltimore, and now the market has opened up more. You have to read books, go to seminars, learn all you can. You never know when you're going to pick up something useful. For instance, I went to the Lowery-Nickerson seminar; for two days I sat there, bored, because I already knew most of what they were talking about. I already owned a lot of property by that point, and I was already doing just about everything they were teaching.

"But if I hadn't taken that seminar, I never would have found out about the FHA Title One Program. It's a federally guaranteed loan program administered through private lenders. You just tell them you want to put a new roof on your property, or make some other repairs or improvements, and you can borrow up to $7,500 against each property. You don't need any contractor's estimates or anything like that. Most of the lenders we dealt with didn't even put a new mortgage on the property. They simply lent us the money on our signatures. After all, the government is guaranteeing the loan, anyway.

"My brother and I were able to borrow about $125,000 that way, so it was worth it to me to spend $500 and sit through two days of a seminar which covered mostly what I already knew. Just that one idea made it all worthwhile.

"Also, tell them that rehabbing is the wave of the future. I honestly believe that. Rehabbing older, rundown properties is the way to get rich in the '80's. We've made a lot of money buying run-down old houses that wouldn't rent for much because they were on busy streets, and then fixing them up, getting the zoning changed and renting them out as doctor's or lawyer's offices.

"We also take buildings with central oil burning furnaces, where the landlord pays for the heat for the whole building, and convert them to gas heat with a separate furnace for each unit so the tenants pay for their own heat. You have to look for old, junker properties and then figure out how to improve them and make them more cost efficient. That's another sign I look for when I buy property. If the landlord's paying the heat, the total expenses shouldn't be more than 40 percent of the total rents, and if the tenants pay for their own heat, the expenses shouldn't be more than 25 percent. If expenses are higher than that, I know I can cut them down and increase the value of the property that way.

"I see a severe housing shortage coming up in this country, and that's going to drive rents and prices up. That's why the money is going to be in rehabbing older properties."

No Regrets

Wayne intends to cash in on that housing shortage by accumulating as much property as he can. With four hundred units as of June, 1981, he and his brother Richard have set a new goal for themselves of at least 1,000 units by 1984. Does Wayne ever have any regrets about giving up his career as a musician?

"No, not really. When I first started and I was painting that house for my friend Bob, back in L.A., some of my musician friends used to give me a hard time. They would come around and make fun of me because I was always all covered with paint. But today most of those guys are still starving, and I've got everything I want: a fine house, a good relationship with my wife, and the independence to do what I want.

"No, even if someone offered me a big recording contract tomorrow, I wouldn't take it.

" 'Keep your eye single,' that's what it says in the Bible. You can't have two different masters. I have what I call my Two Year Success Formula. I figure you have about a half million adult hours. About one-third of those will be spent sleeping, and then another third for recreation. It's that final third and what you do with it—whether you spend it just sitting around on your tail—which really determines how your life is going to go.

"Real estate isn't a career for me, it's a vehicle. It's one of the few ways left which can help you reach your goals and become financially independent.

"Basically, real estate is satisfying for me. I don't miss performing or being a professional musician. I've got a lovely studio downstairs whenever I want to play, and my drums are all set up down there. Some days are good and some days are bad. You catch me on an off day, and I might say I'm tired of real estate and I want to get out—for instance, when we got caught with a lot of deferred maintenance this past winter—but for the most part, I'm satisfied. I'm helping other people, giving them a decent place to live, and I'm helping myself, too.

"There's a guy here in Baltimore who is kind of a legendary landlord—he owns something like 15,000 units—and I told him, 'I don't want as many units as you have . . . only about half what you've got!! And then, my ultimate goal is to trade them all into one super luxury building with about four hundred units, and then, maybe go condo . . . But in the meantime, I'm keeping busy. We recently found 124 nice units for $1.2 million with a $600,000 loan at 6 percent interest, so I convinced the seller that for tax reasons, he was better off borrowing the $100,000 cash he wanted out of the property instead of taking a standard down payment. I got him to carry a loan for the entire $1.2 million at 6 percent, and then took him down to a mortgage company I know. They lent him $100,000 at 18 percent interest, using the $600,000 note for his equity in the property as collateral.

"This way, he got $100,000 cash, tax free, since it was a loan, not a down payment on the sale, and in his situation, that was equivalent to receiving $250,000 on which he would have had to pay taxes. Plus, the

$18,000 a year in interest is a tax write-off for him, and he's using that to offset the $36,000 a year in interest he's taking in (6 percent of $600,000). So now we've got 124 nice units with a low-interest loan and a positive cash flow, and the best part is that I think we're going to be able to turn them all into condos and sell them off at about $30,000 each right away."

6

Starting Over in a Small Town
Roger and Karen Hett

Edna, Texas, is a small town on the Gulf Coast, about 95 miles, or an hour and a half by freeway, from Houston. Offhand, it may not sound like the hot spot of the United States for investing in real estate, but Roger and Karen Hett find it suits them just fine.

Up until 1977, Roger and his brother ran a wholesale novelty goods business in Fort Worth. Then sudden and unexpected reverses wiped out the business and almost everything else they had. The brothers parted ways, and Roger and Karen wound up in Edna.

"We decided to move to a small town because it's a better place to raise children," says Karen Hett. "Before, we lived in what was probably the nicest, safest, most expensive suburb of Fort Worth, but still, if my children were going somewhere two blocks away, I wanted them to call me when they got there. Now they have a lot more freedom, and I don't worry about them as much because everyone knows everyone else in town and looks out for each other's kids.

"We have a girl 14 and two boys aged 13 and 11, so finding a good place for them to grow up was an important consideration, but it wasn't the only one. We wanted a place where we could start over and get back on our feet. We picked the Gulf Coast because it has a stable economy, with plenty of high-paying jobs available within reasonable commuting distance, and the population is booming as people move down here from the north seeking work. We never had any experience with rental property before we moved here, so we didn't even think of that aspect. We just lucked out.

"We had tried other investments in the past. When we had the novelty business in Fort Worth we had quite a bit of money in stocks, but then we put up most of them as collateral for loans, and then we couldn't pay the loans back, so we lost them all. But even the stocks we were able to hang on to didn't do much for us. I mean, when you think about what inflation has done to the stock market . . . well, it was very disappointing.

"We also invested in a company which made steam carpet cleaners, and for a while Roger and his brother had a manufacturer's representative business, but none of them went anywhere. So all we had when we left Fort Worth was what we got out of our house when we sold that, and some money we got back on our taxes.

"We had built our house in 1968 for $36,000, and we sold it for $86,000 in 1977 when we moved here to Edna. Three years later I heard the buyers had sold it again for $165,000! It was enough to make me sick."

It was also enough to make Roger and Karen Hett truly motivated. It's not easy to start all over again when you're in your late thirties, have three kids in school, and are used to a comfortable, high income lifestyle. But Roger and Karen had no other choice, so they decided to make the best of it.

Karen was from the Gulf Coast originally, from a small town named El Campo, Texas, about 25 miles from Edna. Her parents still lived there, and they knew a lot of people in the area and had a lot of contacts, and her father knew of a convenience store for sale in Edna. It was a good business, but the owner was old and had recently retired. His son was running the store for him, but the son had his own business to look after in another town and was anxious to get back to that.

The store looked like a moneymaker, and Karen's father was able to help them arrange financing through local banks, so they took most of the money they got from the house in Fort Worth and relocated themselves.

The First Steps

Karen already had a vague idea by then (1977) that investing in real estate was a good idea in inflationary times, but she and Roger were too busy learning a new business and getting their lives readjusted to do anything along those lines.

"We did buy a house for ourselves as soon as we moved here," Karen says. "We had no choice because there was nothing to rent, and that got me thinking, but I didn't have the time to pursue it, and neither did Roger. We knew so little about real estate that we didn't even know that our house was on the 'wrong' side of town. We didn't even know there *was* a wrong side of town back then. We bought in a hurry, and we probably made a mistake, but back in Fort Worth we had a big, custom built house, and I had lots of furniture to fill it.

"Then we moved down here and most of the houses for sale were small ones, and the big houses were either all chopped up into rooms and apartments, or they were in terrible, run-down condition, and we needed something we could move into right away. So we bought the first liveable house we saw that was big enough for our furniture—and I still had to put a lot of it in storage and give some away.

"By 1979 our lives had settled down a little, and good friends of ours, Roland and Mayme Voise (Chapter 8), had started making good money with some rental properties they owned back in the Fort Worth area. They had been investing in real estate for about a year, and they were already starting to get some positive results, and talking to us about investing.

"There was a little house for sale across the road from our store, and Roger and I both agreed it was in a potentially valuable commercial location because it was right off the highway, so we bought it for $6,000, with a small down payment and the owner carrying a loan for the balance. That was in April, 1979. A short time later we bought the house next door for $10,000 the same way, and then we bought the vacant lot next door to our two houses. We now had three lots commercially zoned, and two run-down houses.

"About this time, I read an article in *Money Magazine* about Craig Hall, the author of *The Real Estate Turnaround*. He made a lot of money while he was still in college by renovating apartment buildings in Ann Arbor, Michigan, and the article told about how he did it. That caught my interest, and I tried to find the book, but I couldn't. While I was looking, though, I did come across an ad for *The Monopoly Game*, by Dave Glubetich.

"I was afraid it was going to be just another ripoff, but I decided to take a chance anyway, and I sent for the book. When it came, I was pleasantly surprised to find it had real substance. I read through it, and I learned a lot. I always figure that if I'm going to do something, I want to learn all I can about it. That's why I took a chance and sent for the book, even though I didn't expect to get too much from it. I figured that if there was one idea in there that I could use, it would be worth it, but instead, I got several good ideas.

"We bought a house in Victoria, a city of about 50,000 people which is 25 miles from here. It was a VA assumption for $36,500 with a $30,500 loan that we took over at a low interest rate with $6,000 down. This was money we had pulled out of our other properties in August, 1979.

"That was about the fair market price, but the financing was good, and the house was only a year and a half old, so we figured we wouldn't have too many maintenance problems. Our only reservation was that it's in a racially mixed area with a high proportion of rental housing, and the neighborhood could go downhill, but we figured we would only keep it for a couple of years anyway, and by then maybe the neighborhood would get better instead of worse, and we got solid tenants in there.

"We also bought a run-down fourplex here in Edna that is on a good commercial lot next to the local Pizza Hut and across from Dairy Queen. Now, if you've ever seen a restaurant row in a small town like this, then you know that once you get a couple of fast food places in one location, then someday you're going to have a whole row of them.

Adding Value for Higher Profits

"So we bought the fourplex for $25,000 with $6,000 down, and the owner carrying the loan. We renovated the apartments and switched from weekly rentals, which are fairly common for low income housing here in Edna—some people can't save up a whole month's rent, even if they make good money, because they spend it too fast—to monthly rentals to cut down on bookkeeping. Now, the renovations we did, better management, and the fact that there is a shortage of rental housing here in Edna, have allowed us to raise the rents to the point where we get a good income from the property.

"Next we bought a vacant lot in another, more residential part of town and moved the smaller of the two houses across the road from our store, to the lot. We now owned two vacant lots across from the store, so we went to the local bank for financing and built a laundromat.

"Some of the neighbors didn't like that idea at first. They said it was changing the character of the neighborhood, making it too commercially oriented instead of residential. But then they found out their houses were all on commercially zoned lots, so there wasn't much they could say.

"We also bought some land where we plan to build another convenience store. It was an old service station which had gone out of business after they routed the new freeway right around the town. It was sitting there vacant, and useless, with a rickety old building that used to be some king of saloon and needs to just be torn down now. The owner's carrying the loan at a low interest rate with a small down payment, and we're waiting for money to loosen up a little.

"Our store is paid down to about $80,000 or $90,000 on the loan, and it's worth about $300,000, and I would like to just sell it and put all that money into other properties, but Roger says 'No.' He doesn't want to kill the goose that's laying all the golden eggs. So we figure we will build a new store, hold it for two or three years, and build up its business and then sell it for a nice profit. But we would definitely have to get a manager to run it. As it is, Roger is on his feet from about 5:30

in the morning until 6:00 at night, and that's seven days a week—except Thursdays, when we close early so we can go into Houston and buy supplies.

A Growing Community Is the Most Profitable

"We also own a carwash now. This area has been good to us and it's great for investing. At first, I wanted to spread the word around, but now I'm starting to wonder if maybe I shouldn't just keep it to myself. I never have much trouble finding positive cash flow properties to buy, but prices are getting higher, and there is a lot of money around here.

"There are plenty of poor people, too. We have our share of them, but there are also lots of men making good money. There are not many jobs for women; unless their families really need the money, most women around here stay home with their children or do volunteer work, but there are plenty of good jobs for the men. A lot of them commute from here and work in the oil fields. It's hard, dirty work, but they make between $1,200 and $3,000 a month. That may not be much money in a big city, but in a small town like this it's a lot.

"There's also a nuclear plant which supplies a lot of jobs, and there's Dow Chemical, and then there are a lot of agricultural jobs too, so there's quite a demand for housing."

And Roger and Karen Hett are doing their best to buy and fix up their share of rental housing to help relieve the crunch and make some money at the same time.

"We bought two single family houses in Ganado, another small town near here, in August, 1979, because we got them at a very good price. The first one was a house with an apartment over the garage. It was in terribly run-down shape and was sitting there vacant. It needed a lot of work; more than we realized.

"We bought it for $18,000 cash. We went to our local bank and got a ninety-day loan, but then we had to put $12,000 of our own money into it. We thought we could refinance it and get all the money—the bank's $18,000 and our $12,000—back, but the appraisal came in at only $30,000, which is exactly what we have invested in the property, and the bank would only loan us 80 percent of that amount, or $24,000. So we have $6,000 cash tied up in the place, and so far we haven't built up any equity, although we do get a good cash flow from it.

"Then in November, 1979, we bought the run-down motel next to our fourplex, the one that's next to Pizza Hut and across from Dairy Queen, from two women investors who had started turning it into apartments and then decided to sell it instead. We bought it for $76,000 with $10,000 down, which came from our tax refund due to our previous business losses in Fort Worth, and the owners carrying the balance. We finished renovating it, and now have eleven apartments—

one- and two-room studios which rent for up to $75 a week to local people, and a big two bedroom apartment that used to be the restaurant, so it's become a real moneymaker.

"Plus, we now have six lots; 300 feet of frontage between the motel and the fourplex. Someday, when they build more fast food places along that strip we'll be in a good position to cash in. It will happen, too, because this is one of those small towns which was going downhill for 20 years or so, but is starting to come back. That's one reason why we located here.

"There's a dam being built near here, and it's a state recreation area with swimming, boating, picnicking, and so forth, and it's expected to draw a million visitors a year, and then this area will really take off."

After their ambitious start in the spring and summer of 1979, Roger and Karen took a break and began concentrating on their family business corporation. Roger was busy in the store seven days a week, and Karen, until just recently, did all the bookkeeping for the corporation which owns the convenience store (Bill's Drive In Grocery), the laundromat they built across the street, and a carwash they also bought, but Karen did find time to attend a seminar in October, 1979, at Rice University in Houston.

More Education Helps Investment Program

"I don't know if you know Rice, but that's our university for really smart people here in Texas. The seminar was given by a man named Barney Giessen. I saw an ad for it in the Houston paper, and decided that since we were getting involved in buying real estate, I ought to go and give it a try.

"It was really great. He gears the whole seminar strictly to conditions here in Texas, the Houston area mainly, but most of it applies to Texas in general. One thing he taught us, which I have never heard of anywhere else, is called the Roll Through. You go to a bank and get the money to pay all cash for a house on a ninety-day note; then you renovate it and go to another bank and get a new mortgage. That way you pay off the ninety-day note and the cost of the renovations, and ideally even put some cash in your pocket. That's what we had planned to do on the house with the garage apartment in Ganado, but we paid too much for the place and put too much into repairs.

"Another trick is to get the seller to carry the first mortgage for say ten years, and then ask him to also take a second mortgage for the down payment and have that note due and payable in sixty or ninety days. Then when you renovate the place, you refinance the second mortgage through a bank.

"In a small town like this, people tend to be conservative and suspicious. They like to do things the old way, where you put some money down. They want to know that you've got something in the property so you won't just walk away if something goes wrong. They don't go for these no-money-down deals like people will in the big cities, unless it's strictly short term. There's just not enough sellers who are really desperate. But on the other hand, there are plenty of good properties to buy with positive cash flow.

"I found Barney Giessen's seminar so helpful that I went back and took it again in March, 1980. We didn't buy anything for a few months there, but then we bought a house with a large lot for $7,500 and put another $6,500 into it, and now it appraises at $15,000, so we're about $1,000 ahead on that one.

"We also bought an older house here in Edna with 3 bedrooms and two baths. We have about $24,000 into it, and now it appraises at $30,000.

"After that, we didn't do much until January, 1981, when we bought a condominium in Galveston. Brand new, built by U.S. Homes and geared to investors: 10 percent down. That's a resort area here on the Gulf Coast. We wanted to spread out and have different types of property, so we listed it with a rental agency and figured we would have no trouble keeping it filled up, but it's been so rainy, no one's been going down to Galveston. It's just temporarily killed the tourist business there, so we haven't made out as well as we had hoped. Not yet, anyway.

"Then we bought a small two-bedroom house about sixty or seventy years old. We paid $26,000, with $6,000 down, 10 percent interest on the balance, and the owner carrying, with payments of $260 a month, and we rent it for $300, so we get a little bit out of that one each month.

"In February, 1981, we refinanced the fourplex and took the $15,000 cash we got out of that and bought five more houses.

"Then we heard about this man who decided he wanted to invest in rental property. He bought two houses, and then got sick of dealing with them. So we bought them both as a package deal. We put down $1,000 earnest money, and got a contract calling for a six-month escrow, with us to have immediate possession of both houses, at a total rent to the seller, of $400 a month. We turned around and sublet them for a total of $500, so we're a hundred dollars ahead.

"At the end of the six months we have to give him another $3,500 down; then we assume two bank loans, a first and a second, and he's carrying a third. We're picking up both houses, each with three bedrooms and one bath, for only $46,500.

"But about that time, we also decided we had made too many mistakes. We had been buying properties which needed more work than we realized, and by the time we got done renovating them, they were worth just what we had put into them. So, with the next house we bought, in the spring of 1981, I went in and made a list of all that needed to be done, and then priced it all before we committed ourselves.

"It's a three-bedroom, two-bath house we got for $30,000, and put another $3,000 into renovating, and now it's worth a little over $40,000.

"Right after that we bought another one, in April, 1981. It's one of the oldest houses in town, a Southern Colonial mansion about ninety or one hundred years old, but it's got green asbestos shingle siding, if you can believe that! So it's ugly as sin. It had been converted into a rooming house, and then about four or five years ago it was converted back into a single family home.

"There have been two owners since then, and the second couple bought it about two years ago for $55,000, and then they decided to get a divorce and put the house back on the market. It sat there for a year with no buyers, and then we got it for $40,000.

It Isn't Always Simple

"We have a couple living there now who have rented from us before, and they are going to stay there for a year while they renovated it for us. When they got done, they were supposed to have a choice. We would either pay them $5,000, or, one quarter of any profit we make on the house, or would sell them one of our other rental houses, whichever one they chose, for $6,000 less than it appraised for.

"We expected to spend about $10,000 on materials, and then when the house was done we expected to sell it for about $75,000. I know Dave Glubetich advises that you hold on for at least five years before you sell anything, but I figure as long as we can sell one property and then use that money to buy two more, we'll be coming out ahead. Right now it's too expensive to refinance with these high interest rates—that's what we did with the fourplex, but that was special—but we don't want to sell that one because of the location, so it's easier to sell and go for owner financing at a low interest rate on whatever we buy. But now problems have come up.

"The repairs have turned out to be more expensive than we antici-pated—again—and we've had to spend more money on materials. But worse than that, the tenants, the people who are renovating it, want to move out. They say it will be easier to finish the job if they're not living there, and that they can't afford to keep the place. They want to move back to the smaller place they were renting before.

"We are charging them the same rent, $290 a month, but they say they've been swamped by relatives moving down from up north and staying with them while they look for work, that they can't afford to maintain the swimming pool, that they can't stand living there and working on the house at the same time. So now we're giving notice to the people who moved into their old house, and this one will probably be vacant while they finish working on it. It's a big mess, and it was all my brilliant idea!"

Roger and Karen owned thirty-one units as of June, 1981, as well as their convenience store, laundromat and carwash. And they intend to keep expanding as Edna and the surrounding area expand. They have their name at the local Chamber of Commerce as landlords, and get most of their tenants that way.

"There's no trouble getting renters," says Karen. "Victoria's got about 50,000 people, but you look into the newspaper and there's never more than five houses and a few apartments for rent at any one time. Most of the time we know the people we're renting to, and we know their families, so that cuts down on problems, but we do make occasional mistakes.

"We once rented to a local girl from a good family, but she was kind of the black sheep. She just quit paying her rent, so we had to evict her. She kept saying she was moving out, but she didn't do it, so finally we just went in there, packed all her bags, and told her she had *been* moved out.

"Then we had a family in one of our houses that packed up one night and left all their possessions behind and about three or four hundred dollars owing in rent. They had a daughter who got in some kind of trouble up in Arkansas, so they just left and went up there to be with her. They eventually came back for their stuff and we got our rent, but it taught me a lesson.

"Now if people are not local or I don't have a good feeling about them, there is no way I'll rent to them. And everybody I do rent to, I check up on through the local credit bureau.

"You have to be organized to deal with management and maintenance problems. We would like to have regular maintenance people, but we can't find anyone who's reliable. We had one kid who could fix anything, but you had to stay on top of him constantly. You simply couldn't count on him to see a job through. Mostly we hire teenagers and ladies who want extra money to do the simple jobs, although my husband and I occasionally do some of the work ourselves, and we have a contractor we usually deal with for some of the heavier renovations. When it comes to heavy maintenance, like plumbing repairs, we deal with the regular plumbing company here in town instead of one of the cheapies. It costs more, but at least that way we know the job is done right the first time.

Small Towns Are Full of Opportunities

"There's a lot of money to be made in small towns. There's a company called River Oaks Investment Company—River Oaks is one of the nicest, most expensive parts of Houston, where they have their headquarters—and they have made a fortune in El Campo, Texas, my hometown. I've spoken to the man who is their exclusive agent in El Campo, and he said what they do is buy houses through him and let him manage them.

"They hold everything they buy for at least one year, and then they send a team down from Houston to evaluate the property and decide what to do to it. Then they renovate and sell.

"Their idea, according to this agent, is that there is no such thing as a bad neighborhood. They just look for properties which are sub-standard for the area. They don't do anything to them before they rent them, they just rent them out as is. Then, once they do renovate, they put the houses right on the market while everything is fresh. They won't rent them after that. They leave them vacant until they sell.

"Our approach is a little different. We renovate right away so we can get the rents up as high as possible. There's not too much creative financing you can do in a small town like this. Up until May, 1981, it was hard to even get any private parties who wanted to carry second mortgages, because there was a usury limit of 12 percent on private loans. Now, at least, that's been eliminated, because they changed the law. Everybody knows what you're up to sooner or later in a small town, and we think it's best to be honest with them and do things their way, so renovating our properties is the easiest way we've found to increase our equity quickly. There are some things we pass up, though, even if they are good deals.

"We had a chance to buy a four-bedroom house in a really substan-dard area, for instance, and we could have made a fortune renovating it and renting it out to illegal aliens from Mexico for exorbitant prices, but I just couldn't stomach that idea.

"But there are ways. Due-on-sale clauses are enforceable here in Texas, but a lot of the older loans never had those written into them, so we can just take them over at the old interest rate, and, of course, there are FHA and VA assumptions. So right now we've got a total rental income of $48,000 a year, and enough depreciation and write-offs to shelter that, and about half of the salary we pay Roger from the corporation.

"We use a standard Texas lease agreement, nothing fancy, but once a tenant's been in a house about six months and they express any interest in owning the place, we sometimes put them on a lease option. But we've had one experience recently which has made us stop and think twice about it.

"We had that house in Victoria, which we knew we didn't want to hold on to for too long, so we rented it to a nice older, working couple, and after they had been in there a year and expressed interest in buying the house, we gave them a one year lease option at $47,500. That was in August, 1980.

"Then we found a real estate agent who agreed to handle all the paperwork and help them get the loan for three percent of the sales price. We thought we were all set.

"The buyers wanted to get a new VA loan rather than assume the old one because they didn't have a lot of cash, and we didn't really want to carry a note. We wanted to get our cash out, so we could buy more property. The agent assured us that this would be no problem, but then the appraisal came in $3,000 low.

"It turned out that the only other houses with VA loans that had sold in that area in the previous six months had old loans which the buyers had assumed at a low interest rate. Therefore, the VA decided they were worth more, because of the financing, and would not accept them as direct comparables, i.e., if those houses had sold for $47,500 with the buyers assuming the old loans, then our house should sell for $44,500 because the buyer was getting a new, more expensive loan.

"Well, to make a long story short, we didn't want to lower the price to $44,500, and the buyers didn't want to come up with another $3,000 in cash, so they canceled the deal.

"Now, we had always figured that we could probably get more than $47,500 if we listed the house with a real estate agent and put it on the Multiple Listings, but we figured that by the time we paid a six percent commission instead of three percent, it would work out to be just about the same, and selling it to the tenants was easy and quick. We thought.

"But now, we had no choice, so we listed it on Multiple Listings and got it sold for $59,000, with us carrying a note for only $5,000. That kind of made us wonder about lease options and VA loans when we're selling property.

"We're coming out okay on the deal. The only thing that bothers me is that after we pay the commission, we may not have enough money to buy more than one new piece of property. Selling one property to buy one property is not my idea of progress, so I would like to buy *at least* two properties with that money. I know I'm certainly going to try!"

7

Broke and In Debt
John Broadfoot

"$250,000 Gift," reads the headline, Texan Receives One Quarter of a Million Dollar Windfall and When You Attend One of My (Mark O. Haroldsen) Financial Freedom Seminars® You'll Probably Write me a Letter Like This One . . . From John Broadfoot . . ."

Sound too good to be true . .?

"Everything in that ad is true," says John Broadfoot, of Amarillo, Texas. "I was worse than broke. I was in debt and I thought I would never get out of it. Then, in less than two years I acquired almost $400,000 of assets and ¼ million dollars net worth. I live in a 'nothing down' house and work out of my own 'nothing down' law office building. Last year my accountant advised me that I legally owed zero taxes. Mark O. Haroldsen changed my life around. When I saw what he was doing and getting away with, I decided I had to get into real estate and become successful so I could write a book of my own.

"I first heard of him when I was riding on an airplane and saw an ad for his book in a magazine I was reading. As soon as I read that ad, I just knew he was a crook. I was sure of it. He had to be, and I knew there was no way I was going to buy that book. After all, he wanted me to send money to a foreign country—Utah—and there was no way I was going to do that.

"I had been a lawyer for several years and built up a fairly successful practice, but this was kind of a low point in my life. I had originally graduated from Georgia Tech and intended to go to Dallas, Texas and become a tax lawyer. But my wife was from Amarillo, and somehow we wound up settling here.

"I worked for the D.A. for two years as an assistant prosecutor, and then spent 13 years in private practice, doing general civil and criminal law. Then I got divorced and remarried, and decided it was time for a change. A friend of mine had a very successful practice as a labor lawyer, and he told me that if I would go and work for the Labor Department for a year to get some experience, he would take me in as a partner. So my wife and I packed up and went to Fort Worth, where I went to work for the Labor Department for a year.

"The previous year had been a good one for me, and I had made about $70,000 in nine months. But now my wife was going to have a baby, and my pay at the Labor Department was so low that I wound up using $25,000 of my savings just to live on, and that meant I couldn't pay my taxes.

An IRS Lien

"At the end of the year we moved back to Amarillo. My friend had changed his mind about the partnership—when it came down to it he just couldn't stand to part with any money—and the IRS slapped a lien on my bank account and all my assets for $13,000.

"Well, I didn't know what I was going to do, but I figured I'd just have to borrow the money somehow, so I went to my banker, with whom I had dealt for many years, and I asked him for a $13,000 loan. I just knew he was going to turn me down, but amazingly, he gave it to me, instead.

"I got the IRS off my back, but then I thought I'd never get out from under that $13,000 debt. I figured I'd be paying it off for the rest of my life. Then a friend of mine told me how he had made about $200,000 in the commodities market in just a few months, and how that was the answer to all my problems. So I borrowed another $5,000 from the bank and promptly lost it. I thought *I* was in bad shape, but my friend lost the entire $200,000 he had made, plus another $200,000 on top of that, so there was no way I could blame him.

"I didn't know what else to do, so I began running four miles a day just to get myself in shape, and I decided I would have to practice law day and night until I got it all paid back. My wife couldn't do much, because she was home with the baby, so it was up to me.

"Then I saw another ad for Mark Haroldsen's book, and this time I sent away for it just to prove to myself he was a crook, but that didn't mean I was going to read the thing.

"I had it around for about a year before I read it, and even then, I didn't do anything about real estate. Then in April of 1979, I saw where

Mark Haroldsen was giving a seminar in Houston. Now that was clear across the state, but at least it was still in Texas, so I decided to go. After practicing law for 14 years and seeing most of my money disappear, I decided I had to do something about it. I was determined to see for myself if Mark O. Haroldsen was 'for real.'

The Turning Point

"Then I got to Houston and I went to the seminar, and there was no Mark Haroldsen. Just a bunch of guys I never heard of: Dave Cowan, J. C. Ebach, Bill Greene. Now I *knew* I'd been ripped off, but I was there already, so I decided I might as well stay.

"The first day, Dave Cowan taught us the nuts and bolts of buying income property. How to find properties, what to look for, and what to stay away from.

"Then Jake Ebach started off by telling us how he came out of a chicken house (he had been a chicken farmer) and how he borrowed millions of dollars on his way to success.

"It was amazing to me that here were men who had achieved phenomenal success and yet would sit down with you at lunch and discuss how you could do it, too.

"Even more amazing was the fact that some of the other people in attendance were already wealthy, with a net worth of as much as $1 million. When I told everyone that I could try a murder case more easily than write an escrow check, there was some laughter, but I was serious."

By this point, John Broadfoot was serious enough about investing in real estate that he had made it a point to get acquainted with a local Realtor back in Amarillo. As soon as he got home, he contacted this person and then began to go through the Multiple Listings, the local directory of houses for sale which were listed with any of the Realtors in the area.

"Within a week of returning from Houston I had looked through the local real estate listings several times, when I finally noticed a listing where the owner would carry the loan. The owner turned out to be the trust departent of a large commercial bank—the same one I had been doing business with for 14 years.

"It was a cute little house, a 2-bedroom brick bungalow. I immediately submitted an offer for $4,500 less than the asking price of $24,500. I also contacted the trust officer and told him I was interested in purchasing some property and had submitted an offer. The trust officer told me he never cut his prices, and that $24,500 was the minimum they would accept.

"I thanked the trust officer for his time, and went to my regular banker. I told him of my interest in the property, and requested a loan of $4,000 for the down payment. I was surprised, but he agreed to loan me the money if and when I bought the house.

"A couple of weeks went by, and then one day my phone rang. It was the bank trust officer, wanting to know if I was still interested in the house. I said I was if the terms were right. He said he had already talked to my regular banker, and they would loan me the down payment and then carry the rest at 9½ percent interest for 15 years, with no prepayment penalty. We agreed on a purchase price of $22,500, and they also loaned me the money for a new hot water heater and other minor repairs—105 percent financing at a time when money was tight in Texas due to a 10 percent usury law—and I closed the deal on May 25, 1979. I had my first property, and it didn't cost me one penny of my own money.

"After that, it just mushroomed. My banker friend who lent me all the money decided to move to a new house. The only trouble was, he couldn't sell his old one. He was sitting there, stuck with double payments, and he was desperate to get out.

"He knew I was anxious to buy more property, and so he called me and offered me the house for $67,500, but I wasn't sure I was interested. Finally, he agreed to sell it to me for $64,500, with no money down—it's a beautiful house, and I'm living in it now—and throw in a duplex I wanted, besides. That's how happy he was to get out from under those double payments. He's selling me the duplex for $22,000—I'm just taking possession of that one now (August 1981)—so that's $86,500 worth of property right there, that someone just dropped into my lap.

"Not all my deals have worked that easily, of course. Sometimes I even have to put down some money. For instance I have one seller who owns a $115,000 apartment house. The gross rents are about $1,600. The mortgages payments are a 9-year first for $50,000 with payments around $800 a month. This includes principal and interest. The second lien was a refinance of $45,000 for 4 years at high interest so the payments on that are $1,000. What? You mean the property produces $1,600, yet payments are $1,800? That's right. The owner is tired of the property and ready to give it away. I have asked an apartment manager friend and a doctor to join me in buying the apartment house for nothing except assuming the loans. We will share any small losses, but the four-year tax write-off will make us money. In four years the $45,000 refi will be all paid off, the remaining loan will be about $35,000 and the property, which has been appraised for $115,000, will be worth at least $125,000. The three partners will have acquired a $90,000 equity, or $30,000 each. Yet, none of us will pay anything down. This transaction is really being negotiated and anyone who looks can do the same.

Don't Wanters Are the Key

"I now own the building where I have my law office. I didn't put up any money, and I pay the same amount each month that I did when I was a renter. Why? Because the landlord didn't want it any more. This way, he gets the income every month and doesn't have to worry any more about maintenance problems. In 15 years, it will be mine, free and clear, so we're both happy about it.

"That's the way I do it, is to find people who don't want their properties any more or can't afford to hold on to them. Then I take their headaches off their hands. And besides building up my net worth and giving my family some security, it's helped me solve my tax problems, too.

"You know, it's funny. My accountant told me I didn't owe any taxes this year because I had so many write-offs from the real estate, and he used to be with the IRS Enforcement Division where they do all the audits. My next door neighbor, before I moved to my new home, is the head of the local Collections Division for the IRS. So, one day recently, as I was going into the County Courthouse, I met both of them on the front steps, and I told my neighbor that I wasn't paying any taxes this year, and if he didn't like it, he could sue his friend, the ex-IRS man, because he was the one who made out the return for me.

"Well, they both laughed, and then my neighbor said that not only didn't he mind that I wasn't paying any taxes, but he knew another IRS man who had some property he wanted to sell me, and then I would have even more write-offs. Isn't that something? Buying property from the IRS man so you don't have to pay any taxes!

"I blame it all on Mark Haroldsen, too. He's the one who got me started with all this. Now I've written my own book, called *Super Leverage Forms*—it's a bunch of forms to use for making different kinds of creative offers—and I'm trying to get Haroldsen to publish it for me, and if he won't do it, then I'll publish it myself.

"Mark O. Haroldsen had a big seminar in Lake Tahoe, Nevada, recently, and I went to that. I took some sample books with me, and I sold 20 of them for $20 each, just like that! Now I've got to refine it and get it all polished.

"I'm also going for my certification as a real estate specialist, as well as a general practicing attorney, and it's all because of Mark Haroldsen.

"And as for Jake Ebach... I would pay $500 just to sit down and have a glass of wine or two with that man. Aside from all he knows about real estate, it would be worth it just to hear his jokes and stories.

"I'm getting ready to sell one house soon for a $50,000 profit, and when I do that, I'm going to get all my debts paid off, and then in another few years, I'm going to be a millionaire. My net worth is already up around $250,000, which is a lot better than owing the IRS

$13,000 and having them attach everything I owned.

"I'm also planning to put an ad in the newspaper. For anyone who can't sell their house, I will lease it from them for five years or longer and take care of all the maintenance and the payments and everything in return for an option to buy it at today's price. As long as we have inflation, I can't lose. If inflation is running at only 8 percent—and we all know it's been a lot higher than that lately—the value of a house will double in 12 years. So, in only six years, you make $25,000 profit on a $50,000 house. Not bad, just for making the payments and doing a bit of maintenance."

"This story probably sounds like a fairy tale to you. It's not that I don't work daily to make it happen. This weekend I'm painting that new house so the tenant can move in Monday. The middle name of this game is "work," not "lazy." If you don't believe that I am a real person struggling to better my life and that of my family, call (806) 373–2886 and I'll be glad to visit with you."

8

Off to a Flying Start
Roland and Mayme Voise

Roland Voise of Fort Worth, Texas, is a Captain for American Airlines. He has a challenging and responsible position, and it pays well, but it offers no real security. If anything serious ever happens to affect his health, he could be out of work tomorrow. And even if he stays healthy, he must retire at age sixty. Besides, he was paying too much in taxes and losing too much to inflation as it ate away at his family's investments.

So in the summer of 1978, when many people were already saying that high prices and higher interest rates had caused the market to peak, he and his wife Mayme got into real estate.

"We had some stocks and some money in my husband's retirement fund," says Mayme Voise. "We also were in a cattle raising partnership with some friends, but we had no large investments and no really effective tax shelters until we became involved in real estate.

"We hadn't actually lost any money, but we were disappointed with our investments. You know what inflation has done to the stock market. So we were looking for something else. I think a lot of the pilots and flight engineers and all talked a lot about investments—and particularly about real estate—on long trips, so that got my husband interested. And also his parents were worried about us having so much money in stocks, and they encouraged us to buy property. They are very conservative people, not risk-takers, and they felt it was safer to have at least some of your money in something tangible where you had something more than just paper to show for it.

"But I guess the main thing that prompted us was taxes. My husband's retirement fund is set up so that you can't draw on it when you want to. You have to either leave all your money in there, or take it all out at once. Well, as I said, we got fed up with our investments, and my husband just decided the heck with it, and he took all our money out of the retirement fund.

"Now when we had put the money in there, we were in the 30 percent tax bracket, but when we decided to take it out, we had moved up to the 52 percent bracket, so we had to pay a lot of taxes on that money, and that got us thinking.

"My husband reads a lot, and he read a lot of books about real estate, so in August, 1978, we bought our first property, nine units on an acre and a half of land; it was six houses and three apartments."

"What my wife's not telling you," Roland says, "is that she thought I was crazy. She was dead set against buying the property because it was run-down and unattractive looking. I had to remind her that we weren't going to be living there, but she still wasn't thrilled about it. Of course, I wasn't too sure myself. I had never thought I had the personality or the skills to manage rental property. But we were disappointed by our other investments, and we were also concerned about our tax situation, so I decided it was at least worth a try.

"To me, the fact that the property was run-down was an opportunity. The owner wasn't getting much rent out of the place, and he wasn't really doing anything to keep the place up, so besides the fact that we were able to get the place at a cheap price, there was plenty of opportunity to increase the rents. He was only getting about $935 a month in total income; of course, he was living in one of the units. But now we've got it up to over $1800, so that place has turned out to be a little gold mine.

"The way my schedule is set up, I work three or four days and then I have three or four days off, so that gives me time to work on my properties, probably more than most people have. But then the schedule changes every month, so I never know more than a month in advance when I'll be working and when I'll be off. That makes it kind of rough sometimes in terms of keeping on top of maintenance problems, but I just decided I would have to work around that until we could get to the point where we could afford to hire maintenance people."

"I never had any experience doing any house repairs before, but I taught myself to do some of the simple things, and Mayme started doing the bookkeeping, so we both worked at it together.

"Mostly we have stuck to the middle and lower income range in looking for properties, for several reasons. First of all, lower priced housing is more affordable, so it was easier for us to get started that way and expand more quickly without having to put up a lot of money.

"Secondly, lower priced housing gives you a better return on your money. We can pick up run-down properties, fix them up a little, and get a positive cash flow, even if it's only a small one. With higher priced properties you can't do that. You're lucky enough if you can break even.

Bad Properties Equal Good Cash Flow

"For instance, a house we buy for say $15,000 can rent for $200 to $250 with a little fixing and cleaning, but a $50,000 house will only rent for $350 to $400. Besides, there's more buyer demand for the better properties. Everybody wants to buy something nice and clean in a good neighborhood, and so they pay more for it. Most of the other pilots I know are that way. They all think the only place to buy real estate is in good, middle class areas. To me, that's fine, if all you're interested in is the tax write-offs, but there's more to it than that.

"I think you get better appreciation by investing in marginal areas that are improving and by buying properties which can be improved. Like that first property we bought, where we've been able to double the rents in three years. We couldn't have done that if the property was in good shape and already getting good rents. As it was, the tenants were getting fed up because of the lack of maintenance, so they were happy to see us take over, and the owner was fed up with the place, so he was glad to be rid of it. He didn't want the responsibility.

"I remember when we first saw the place. A woman we knew had gone into real estate, and she knew we were interested in investing, so she called up and said there was a place for sale that wasn't a bad buy, but she was sure we wouldn't like it because it was such a mess. But I figured it couldn't hurt to at least look at it, and once I saw the place I decided right away that it had potential."

"In general, people in lower income housing have fewer expectations than people with more money," Mayme Voise adds, "so by buying cheaper properties we are also able to keep maintenance costs down. I don't mean that we don't try to keep the properties in good shape and fix things when they go wrong, because we do—in fact, we gladly buy the materials any time one of our tenants wants to paint or do something else to fix up the place themselves—but we do own a couple of duplexes which are newer and nicer and in a better area than most of our other properties, and there, the tenants are pickier and more demanding. In our cheaper properties most of our tenants are used to such bad service from the previous owners that they're grateful for anything we do.

"Of course, there is the other side of it, too. Not all of them keep up the places as well as I'd like them to, either, but I've learned to live with that. As long as they're not doing anything to destroy the place, I don't pay any attention to dirt or sloppiness. As long as they're not causing any damage, then the way they keep house is their business. If we find there are bugs after someone has moved out, we just call an exterminator and take it out of their deposit, which is a little bit more than half a month's rent, say $125 on a place that rents for $200.

Dealing with Tenants

"We always charge our tenants a deposit like that. We don't ask for the last month's rent in advance, but we do get a deposit and an additional deposit on top of that if they have pets. We get our tenants through ads in the newspaper and through rental agencies, and although we ask for references, we don't really check their credit too carefully because it is too time-consuming, so the deposits are our only real protection.

"In Texas, you have to wait until someone is thirty days behind in their rent, then you can get a three-day notice ordering them to pay up or leave. We've never actually had to take anyone to court yet. They usually just pay the rent they owe us, or they get out. But we have had people skip out with our furniture, drapes and things like that.

"That's why only our lower priced properties are furnished and our nicer units are rented unfurnished. People in the nicer units would expect nicer furnishings if we did rent those places furnished, and we would not be able to afford the loss if people walked off with things.

"You have to think of all this when you're in the rental business. You have to be a little hardened to other people's problems. You see a lot of hardships, but when you're into rental property to the point where we are (thirty-five units of our own and five more in partnership with another couple) you can't provide free rent. Period. You have to harden yourself.

"If someone doesn't have a month's rent and the money for a deposit, then they are just not the kind of people we want to rent to. Most of our tenants are on leases, except in the really bad areas where a lease would never be honored anyway, and we include a late penalty in there, too. We used to have all the rents due on the first, but we gave up on that because everybody gets paid at different times. So now we try to be flexible with our tenants, but once we do establish a schedule with them we expect them to get the rent in on time.

"We took a standard lease which we got from an office supply store and used that at first. Then we got a copy of another lease from a man from whom we bought some property. He had had his drawn up specially by a lawyer. We took both leases and combined them to create our own lease, which includes the late charge, the standard security deposit, and the extra pet deposit.

"Neither of us had any business experience before this. Roland's been a pilot, and I've been a housewife for the past twenty-five years, but we've had to learn, because since those first nine units, our rental business has just grown. Now it seems like I'm doing bookkeeping all the time. I never get away from it. There's always vacancies or something going wrong, and I'm always answering the telephone.

"I don't hesitate anymore to tell people not to call at 12:30 at night if it's not a true emergency, but with three children who drive and Roland away so much of the time, I'm always reluctant not to answer the phone. My husband would like to own fifty units some day, but I'm not sure I am quite that ambitious."

Setting Realistic Goals

"Originally, we didn't even want nine units," Roland says. "We were looking for a duplex, or something small like that. But they had such good potential... I was hoping to buy them in partnership with our oldest son, Kevin, who is a carpenter, but he wasn't interested. He works for us once in a while if he is between jobs, and we need some extra help, but it's hard being a father and a boss at the same time, and he prefers to remain basically independent.

"So we bought it on our own, and then shortly afterwards we picked up five more units from a friend of ours. He and his partner had lost their maintenance man and couldn't seem to find anyone else to replace him.

"They weren't doing anything to keep the places up, and they were all being condemned, and so most of the tenants weren't paying their rent. We took the five units off his hands and fixed them up and started collecting good rents.

"Not everyone is suited to owning rental property. Some people can't handle the problems involved, but I find it a challenge, and I know it will eventually make me a millionaire. I could have made a million dollars already if I just really worked at it, but it would mean giving certain things up, and I'm not prepared for that.

"I love to run, and so does my wife. I've competed in three marathons and I generally run about fifty miles a week. I also have a beautiful piano in my living room, and I love to play it. These things mean a lot to me, and I'm not going to give them up. But rents are constantly going up and so are prices, so I know I'll always make money in the long run. Plus, the depreciation really reduces my tax bill, so I'm much happier about real estate than I was about any of our other investments, and we've just kept going and growing.

"Our friend who is in real estate keeps telling us about deals, and we also hear about them through other sources—we don't work with her exclusively. We bought a house with an apartment over the garage, four duplexes, a few single family houses, and a fourplex. They are all within 25 miles of our home—around Fort Worth, in the city itself, and in Halton City and Arlington nearby—except for one place in Denton, Texas, about an hour and a half away, where our younger son, Phillip, goes to school. He's working for us this summer because we had a lot of hail damage this year, but he's not really interested in real estate. He's going to North Texas State University and wants to go into music.

"Our daughter helps her mother clean some of the places occasionally, but it's hard to say whether she'll really be interested in real estate or not. We're getting all of them involved to some degree, though. The only place we've sold so far was the house with the garage apartment, and we sold that to Kevin, our oldest son.

"We sold it to him at about the fair market price—well, maybe a little bit under—but we gave him the down payment as a gift to make it easy for him. We'll probably do the same thing with our other children as soon as they're old enough to move out, and that way it will help them to appreciate the value of property.

"Kevin already gets a good bit of rent from the apartment above the garage. It covers a nice part of his payments, and someday he'll be living in the house just about rent free, as the rent on the apartment keeps going up, while his payments stay about the same.

"And in our own situation, as soon as we get the notes paid off on our properties—which for some properties will be as soon as 1½ years, for others, as long as 7 years—we'll be millionaires. We will have more than a million dollars' worth of equity. I like that idea. It gives me a feeling of security."

"Roland is more ambitious than I am," Mayme Voise says. "I like to be comfortable and have all the bills paid, but I don't have any long range plans to get ahead like that and become a millionaire. Roland has goals for the next year, the next five years, the next ten years, etc. I don't, but my attitude towards real estate has changed. In the beginning we intended to make all we could in five years and then get out. Now we've both changed our minds and decided that it's not so hard to keep up with. In fact, if anything ever happened to Roland I would still keep all our properties except the ones in the really bad areas where I would be afraid to collect the rents by myself."

Knowledge Is Power

"My attitudes have changed, too," says Roland. "I used to take it too seriously. I was afraid to make low offers on properties because I always figured they would never be accepted. So I would pass on a lot of properties—not even bid on them because the price was too high and I was afraid the seller wouldn't come down. Now I bid on any property I look it.

"I carry a screwdriver and a flashlight with me so I can get an idea of the general condition of the place, whether there's any rot or termites or anything like that, and I put an offer in. If it's accepted, great. If not, what have I really lost? Once I spend time looking at a place I may as well put in a bid and see what happens.

"It's very important though, for me to get some idea of the problems a place may have. I've learned that much through experience. Sometimes a place will look great on the surface, nice and clean, but it will have all sorts of hidden problems. I bought two houses and a garage apartment once and they all looked nice and the numbers, the rents they could bring in versus the monthly payment, looked so good that I wound up paying too much for the property, because it turned out I had to put a lot of money into repairs.

"On the other hand, I've bid too low for other properties and lost out on them because I overestimated the amount of repairs needed. So now I check the plumbing, the wiring, the insulation, etc. Real estate is a hassle, but the money I can make is good enough to offset the hassle as far as I am concerned.

"Not all of it is a hassle, anyway. I like buying and selling, but I don't like dealing with the maintenance. In the beginning I did it all myself, then my wife started doing the bookkeeping, and I started getting part-time help with the maintenance and then full-time help."

"That has been one of our weak areas," says Mayme Voise, "because we are dependent on other people. We had one maintenance man who couldn't get anything done. He really took advantage of us and did as little as he thought he could get away with. Roland was so tired from trying to take care of everything with just part-time help that he didn't check his background and references adequately when he finally hired someone full time. He just was not keeping up with what had to be done, and that really cut into our profits, so eventually we had to get rid of him and look for someone else.

"We've never used a professional management company because first of all, it would be too expensive, and secondly, most of our properties are in relatively bad areas, so most management companies wouldn't be interested anyway. So instead, we put an ad in the newspaper to hire someone on a 30-day trial basis, with a possible 30-day extension."

"We finally got this couple who were working out well," Roland says, "and we even bought a house for them to live in, which we were going to rent to them. Then this summer (1981) they got divorced and we thought we were going to lose them, so we started looking around for someone else. But it looks like it's going to work out. They're not getting back together, but they're both going to keep working for us separately.

"You just have to roll with it. That's what scares a lot of people out of real estate, is that everything tends to happen at once. First a renter's baby will get sick and they can't pay the rent on time; then the dishwasher goes out and that's got to be fixed; and then that's when the city comes around and tells you you have to correct some kind of code violation and you get a bill for something you thought you had already paid, and that's when people give up.

"That's why I don't buy anything that doesn't have a positive cash flow, so I can hire someone to do the maintenance and stay on top of all the repairs and expenses without going broke. We have less income from our properties now than when we started because I don't do the maintenance myself any more. Once you own a few properties, you can sort of tailor the business to your own needs. If you want more income, you can sell a couple of places, either cashing out, or carrying the loan yourself; or you can refinance when you've built up some equity or make improvements that are designed to increase the rental and/or resale value.

"I intend to stay with houses and smaller income properties for about another three years, and then get into something like apartments with a resident manager. Right now, I like what I'm doing, because I have no real competition. Oh sure, there are other people doing the same thing, but most of them aren't doing it nearly as well.

"Most of my tenants are referrals from people already renting from us. In the last year, the only tenants who have moved out of any of our units have moved into other units we own. That's what we do with our good tenants. They start off in one place, and then if we get a vacancy in one of our other units that's a little bit bigger or nicer and they feel they can afford the extra rent, we let them move.

"We generally run about a 95 percent-plus occupancy rate, except on newer places like the one we've just bought. I don't really do that well at evaluating new tenants because I'm too trusting. I'm a positive person by nature. I think people are basically good, and I try not to let the occasional bad tenant throw me.

"What we normally do is to give people a six-month lease, and then if they turn out to be good tenants we renew it. We'll even keep the rent low if they keep the place up and do any work around there themselves, like gardening, stuff like that.

"Besides the units we own ourselves, we have gotten involved in a couple of partnerships, but I generally don't like them because I don't like to have my hands tied. For instance, I'm involved in one partnership where we own a place on a sale-leaseback where we bought the property from the guy who runs the business, and then we lease it back to him. Well, the guy is always late with his payments, and if it was my property alone, I would boot him out of there. But my wife and I only own 20 percent, and the other partners just let him slide, so there's really not much we can do.

"Besides that, we're involved with a partnership which owns raw land, and we recently started a partnership with another couple—friends of ours who want to cash in on our expertise and learn about investing—where we each put up equal amounts of money, but they will handle everything except the maintenance. They are responsible for renting the units, collecting the rents, bookkeeping, etc.

"This arrangement benefits them because they're new at investing and not sure what they're doing yet, and it benefits us, because my wife won't have any bookkeeping to do, and I won't be wasting my time running out to meet prospective tenants. I've found that in some of the areas where we buy property, people make appointments and then they don't even show up, but with this partnership I won't have to deal with that aspect of it. We already own 5 units together, and we've got 3 more in escrow (as of August, 1981).

"We've also gotten other friends of ours involved in real estate. Roger and Karen Hett (Chapter 6) used to live here in the Fort Worth area, and then they moved down to a small town along the Gulf and opened a convenience store. Well, there was an older property right across the road from their store, and Roger wanted to get it and put something else in there, and Karen said, 'Oh, but it's so run-down and ugly,' but we changed their way of thinking, and now they're buying up half the town and restoring it.

"Probably one of the hardest parts was getting our agent friend trained properly. Most real estate agents are only geared to selling residential houses to young owner-occupant couples. They don't have the faintest idea of what will be a good investment . . . what will make money. But we've been working with her long enough, so now she knows what to look for: ugly properties that don't really need expensive repairs, especially if they've got low interest assumable loans, or owner financing. The big builders and the people with money aren't interested in them, so that leaves the field wide open for people like us. I make good money as a pilot, but you never really get ahead working for someone else. You have got to have some business of your own, and real estate is mine. It's going to make us millionaires in another few years, and that's more than my job will ever do for me, no matter how much I enjoy flying."

9

$9 To $9,000,000 In 900 Days
Phil Drummond

"Nine dollars to nine million in nine hundred days." That's how Phil Drummond of Orlando, Florida, describes his experience with real estate investing.

"I owned my own house, but that was it," he says. "That was all the experience with real estate I had. I knew people who made a lot of money in real estate, but I always thought you had to have money to start. Then I found out I was wrong. I've been at it ever since. And all I've ever put into property is nine dollars of my own money on my first deal. I think it paid for some recording fees or something. Since then I haven't put a penny of my own into any of my deals. It all comes out of the properties I own already."

Nine million dollars in nine hundred days? It sounds almost too good to be true, and alas, it is. Phil is not *worth* $9 million (yet) and he doesn't even *own* $9 million worth of property, but only about $4 or $5 million at last count. However, he did manage to *control* $9 million worth of property during his first nine hundred days as an investor, and he made a profit on all of it.

What he couldn't buy, or didn't want to buy, he optioned, and then sold the option at a higher price. Or he would buy something, get the right to occupy and improve it prior to actually taking title, then fix it up and turn around and put it back on the market at a higher price. Where there is an honest dollar to be made in real estate, Phil Drummond has made it his business to find it.

He started by taking Nickerson and Lowry's seminar on how to buy and finance run down fixer properties and then went out to buy a fixer. He offered $16,000 for a three-bedroom, two-bath house, with central air conditioning, on a large corner lot. The seller said "No!" and refused to negotiate with him. Then a while later the seller called back, and Phil wound up buying the house for $17,000, a thousand dollars more than his original offer. There was a low-interest $12,000 first loan against the property which made it attractive, so Phil agreed to buy the house at the seller's price if the seller would take $1,000 down and carry a $4,000 note for 90 days.

The seller agreed, so Phil gave him $200 (borrowed) as a good faith deposit and promised to come up with the other $800 at the close of escrow. He spent the next few weeks hunting up money—not only the $800 he needed to close, but also the money he needed to clean up the place and do minor repairs—about $3,000 in all. He found passive investors who had money, but lacked the time or the interest to get actively involved in real estate investing, and he borrowed some from friends and relatives.

As soon as escrow closed and he took title to the house, Phil got hired workmen in there to paint it, put in new carpet, etc. He got an appraisal for $31,000, and a new second mortgage for $12,000. He paid off the $4,000 note held by the seller, paid off his creditors and investors, and walked away with almost $5,000 in cash as well as another $6,000 equity in the house.

After that he found another fixer, but this time the seller insisted getting $10,000 cash at the close of escrow. So, Phil got the right to fix up the property before the close. Once the property was improved, he found a buyer who was willing to pay him almost twice what he had agreed to pay the original seller. He got his money, paid the seller off, and put the rest right back into more property.

On another deal, he got the seller to carry back a $6,000 note, then a year later convinced her that she would rather have cash, and bought the note back for $4,000.

A Full-time Pro In Six Months

After six months he was doing so well and having so much fun, that he decided to get into real estate full time; not as an agent, but strictly as an investor. In the two and a half years since then, he has attended more than 25 different seminars and read over one hundred different books on investing, and bought and sold several million dollars' worth of property.

He is President of both the Central Florida Investment Group, made up of people who have taken the Nickerson-Lowry Seminar, and the local RAND (Robert Allen Nothing Down) group for graduates of

Robert Allen's seminar, and is in touch with investors and Realtors in other parts of Florida, as well.

Phil started with single family homes and still prefers them to other types of property, because single family homes are the most liquid. They are the easiest type of real estate to borrow against and to sell.

But Phil tries to avoid selling. He prefers to refinance or take out larger second mortgages, and so far, he has not sold any of the 80 or so properties he has actually owned. He figures that inflation isn't about to stop, so it makes sense that both prices and rents will keep going up. Therefore, he's determined to get all the property he can and hold on to it.

He's branching out now buying all sorts of property, wherever he finds a good deal. And he finds a lot of them. Just between January and May of 1981, he bought 28 single family houses, 8 duplexes, two four-plexes, one 20-unit building, one 30-unit building, 160 mini-ware-houses, and 20 full-sized warehouses. Phew!

Of course, these weren't all individual purchases; many of them were package deals. For instance, he recently bought seven houses and three duplexes in a run-down section of Jacksonville—all for $43,000! The deal did take $7,000 cash to the seller, but now that he has so many properties to borrow against, Phil can afford to put some cash into the deal when he has to. And in this case, the ten properties were all in good shape, with long-term tenants and management, so he didn't have to put any money into the property itself.

Besides, since all the money came out of other properties which he bought either with borrowed money or no money at all, rather than out of his pocket, Phil still feels as if he hasn't really put any of his own money into real estate. Instead, he just recycles it from one investment to the next as he pyramids his wealth.

"Not one of those properties that I bought between January and May involved a bank loan," he says proudly, "I just assumed existing loans or had the sellers carry the note. Some of them required a little cash, others didn't, but every one of them was at below-market interest rates. In fact, I've never paid more than 12 percent yet."

Occasionally, he will find a reasonable bank, willing to refinance one of their old loans below current interest rates, particularly once he has fixed up the property. This way, the bank gets to lend more money at a higher rate of interest than they were getting on the original loan, and Phil gets cash to live on, and to buy more property with, at a rate that is still favorable to him. When the bank refuses to cooperate, he just goes around them by keeping the original loan and getting a large second.

Florida law is still vague about Due-on-Sale clauses, which allow a lender to demand full payment of the loan balance whenever a property is sold or transferred. Although the courts haven't made a definitive decision yet, they seem to be leaning on the side of buyers and sellers. Therefore, Phil doesn't worry about asking the lender for permission when he wants to take over an existing loan. So far, he hasn't been challenged, and he feels that if and when he ever is challenged, the burden will be on the bank to take him to court and prove he has no right to do it. In the meantime, he is using their money on his terms.

The Other Half of the Job—Tenants

Of course, finding suitable properties and financing them is only half the job. After that, you have to get them rented. Phil is well aware of this, and of how it affects him as an investor.

"Shabby properties attract shabby people," he says bluntly, "so I never rent any house that I wouldn't live in myself under different conditions. But that doesn't mean fixing it up as if I *were* going to live in it. I've done that, and it was a mistake. Tenants don't appreciate it anyway. But everybody likes fresh paint and carpeting.

"First you have to know the market, both for sales and rentals. Then, when you find a property that's priced under the market, you have to find out why it's so cheap, what it will cost you to fix it up, and how much more rent you will get when you're done.

"It's a business, and you have to approach it that way. You don't want to make any improvements that aren't going to pay off, and not every property's the same. I try to put different amenities and different tenants into different properties. For instance, if I've got a house with a big yard, I'll let people with pets move in, but I'll charge them a larger deposit, and I'm sure not going to put brand new carpeting in there.

"On the other hand, if it's a small place, with little or no yard, then I'm going to look for people without pets or kids. It just depends on the circumstances. Here in Orlando, most of the houses are newer—about 20 years old—your typical two- or three-bedroom, but up in Jacksonville, where I also buy a lot, they have a lot of older, smaller places which have to be handled differently."

Phil finds his properties through the newspapers, word of mouth, the exchange groups he belongs to, and through real estate agents. He's found one good agent in Jacksonville who supplies him with just about all the properties he can handle up there. He would like to do the same thing in Orlando, but so far he hasn't found any one agent with whom he is completely comfortable, so he works with several agents who call him whenever they have a deal.

What Phil looks for, first of all, is a property that will at least break even. In the beginning, he stuck primarily to distress properties, since they were the easiest to get into with little or no money, but now that he has more cash and more experience, he no longer restricts himself to fixers.

"Lowry and Nickerson advise people to buy the worst, most run-down piece of property they can find, and Robert Allen advises people to stay away from fixers and buy good properties in good areas. I say they're *both* right. I've bought fixers and made money, and I've bought nice properties and made money. As long as it's a good deal, I'll go for it, but I try to stay away from real ghetto or slum properties."

Phil also stays away from fancy properties in expensive areas, aiming more for the middle ground. With ghetto property, he feels it's too much trouble to find decent tenants and collect the rent; with expensive property, it's almost impossible to break even (although it might appreciate faster), and again, the tenants wouldn't be the type he's looking for.

"I don't want to rent to doctors and lawyers and people like that," he says. "Lawyers will find a million reasons why they don't have to pay you the rent, and doctors, they don't know how to stop a leaky faucet or do anything for themselves. So I try to stick to decent but modest areas, where I can get working people as tenants, the kind who don't want to call you every time something goes wrong, because it's easier for them to just fix it themselves.

"I mean, I don't want the best house in the neighborhood when I'm done fixing it up, but I don't want the worst one, either. I want to know that it's going to blend in with the other houses and be fairly comparable, so I can get an idea of what it's going to be worth."

Phil uses many of the familiar devices for minimizing tenant problems: leases which specify that the tenant is responsible for all maintenance and repairs under $200; lease options, etc. But he doesn't believe in offering low rents as a way of attracting or holding renters. He feels that rents set toward the high end of the scale attract better, more responsible tenants; but once they move in, he doesn't raise the rents very much or very often, until they move out.

As he looks into the future, Phil Drummond sees only blue skies and green dollars ahead. Orlando is booming in spite of high interest rates, and he doesn't foresee any sudden changes. He doesn't believe all the stories of the coming real estate crash, although he has read all the popular doom-and-gloom bestsellers.

"Real estate is a good investment," he says. "It always has been and always will be. Just look at the insurance companies and really rich people like the Rockefellers. Where do you think most of their money is invested? And even if a crash does come, the banks aren't going to want property like mine, that's highly leveraged. They'll probably pay me to keep on managing them. The guy they'll foreclose on is the one who owes $10,000 on a $50,000 house. That way they can sell it at a discount and get it off their hands."

And so, after only three years as a full-time investor, Phil Drummond is having the time of his life, flying all over the country to go to tax-deductible seminars, meeting other investors, and getting new ideas. He has started teaching seminars of his own for both beginning and advanced investors, and now, in his spare time, he is putting out a bi-monthly newsletter called *Investment Footnotes*, for about 1,000 subscribers.

No, he's not doing too badly for an average guy who wanted to invest, but thought he didn't have enough money to ever get started.

STEP II

Paper Millionaires

10

An Unemployed Widow with Small Children Makes Good
Lucille and Bland Giddings

Although she is a relative newcomer to serious investing, Lucille Giddings is no stranger to real estate, or to creative financing.

"Heck," she says offhandedly, "nowadays all these books and seminars talk about wrap-arounds, owner carry-backs and all that stuff as if it's something new; I was doing it all twenty-five years ago, before I even knew what I was doing.

"I've always liked real estate and houses, ever since I can remember. When I was a little girl I used to make houses out of mud—not mud castles, but modern houses, with sunken living rooms. That was the big thing that was just coming out then; so all my houses had sunken living rooms, and I would furnish them like doll houses. I guess I decided then that I would own a house when I grew up. It was an idea I just always had."

But life doesn't always go the way we plan it . . . Lucille Giddings' life certainly didn't. It was a long time before she realized her childhood dream and bought her first house. There was a lot of living to be done first—a lot of hardship and enough romance to fill a book and have some left over.

She didn't marry and settle down right after high school, as many girls did in the thirties. Instead, she went on to Brigham Young University, where she majored in Home Economics and dated a handsome Chemistry major named Bland Giddings. But he was a senior, and the romance ended in 1939 when he decided to leave Utah and go back

East to attend graduate school at the University of Cincinnati.

"Girls didn't chase after men in any way, back then," Lucille says, "so once he left for graduate school, that was it. For me to follow him, or anything like that, just wouldn't have been the thing to do."

So Lucille forgot about Bland Giddings and went on with her life. She met someone else; but then he, too, was soon gone, off to fight in World War II.

"After the war he became a Land Management Specialist for the United States Foreign Service (he finished his B.A. in Biology on the G.I. Bill).

"We were married about a year and a half when he got leukemia. We had always intended to use his G.I. loan to buy a house. But then he was sick for the next two-and-a-half years, and he wanted to put off that loan so that I could get a house for myself and the two kids once he was gone; that way, we would at least have something.

"He thought I would be able to use his G.I. Bill when he was gone. So he died a happy man, because he thought his family would be taken care of. Unfortunately, he was wrong; I didn't get any of his benefits. But the idea of owning a house stuck with me, and I always knew that some day I would get one.

"My husband had always wanted me to go back to school and get my M.A. After he died I had to do something; so I began looking for someone who would give me some kind of fellowship.

"Well, Utah State Agricultural College at Logan offered me a teaching fellowship for $90 a month; so the three of us lived on that, plus some savings that I had. My B.A. had been in Home Economics, with a specialty in Clothing and Textiles. But you don't go beyond the B.A. in Home Economics; so I got my M.A. in Chemistry. Then I got a job back at my old school, Brigham Young University."

For a short while Lucille got to enjoy the relative affluence of being a full-time, full-fledged teacher again, after her struggle to get the Master's degree. Then she took some summer courses and her life was on the roller coaster tracks again.

"I told my department chairman how exciting it had been, taking those courses. She was a chemist too, a Ph.D., and she told me that I should go and get my Ph.D. I said I couldn't afford it, but she went ahead and made the decision for me, by firing me, sort of—she gave me an unpaid leave of absence and told me to go back to school and get my Ph.D.

"I went to Texas Women's University, in Denton, and they gave me a fellowship for $125 a month. Well, I don't usually tell people this, I'm not bragging or anything, but I finished in two summers and one winter. I wasn't about to waste any time... I had two children to support on that fellowship plus some small savings."

The next few years, Lucille and the children bounced around the country, from college to college, as she sought to advance herself in her profession.

"I don't know how much you know about college teaching," she says, "but if you stay in one place you never get anywhere. That's why I had to keep moving around like that. Every time I moved to a new school, I got a promotion and a pay raise. After a few years I had to move again, or stay frozen in place. That's just the way it is."

A House At Last

It was one of these moves that led Lucille to realize her lifelong goal and buy her first house. On a fall day in the late '50's she went into a school housing office, looking for a place to rent; instead, she heard of a man who wanted to sell a house for only $500 down. She contacted him right away and decided to buy the house. She knew it would go up in value sooner or later; so it would serve as a sort of retirement fund for her old age.

"If I had started working at an earlier age," Lucille says, "or if I were in a profession that gave me better retirement benefits, I might not have worked so hard at real estate—I don't know. But every four years or so I had to move to keep advancing in my profession, and each time I had to use up whatever retirement money I had accumulated to pay for the move. So my houses were my only pension.

"What happened is that each time I was ready to move I would call in real estate agents, who were so anxious to get the house sold and make their money that they would always tell me the house was not worth what I was asking. ('Oh, but the market has changed since you bought the house,' they would say. 'People just aren't buying right now.') They would tell me that everybody expected to take a loss when they sold their house, and that was the way it was.

"Somehow, wherever I went and whenever I wanted to sell, it was always the same story. The house was never worth what I thought it was worth, and I usually felt like I was being taken advantage of.

"Now, I had been reading the *Kiplinger Newsletter* all this time. I started in 1954, right after my first husband died. I was scared then and I needed information on how to get by. I discovered the *Kiplinger Newsletter* in the library one day, and it was like a lifeline for me to grab onto; it gave me hope.

"Well, Kiplinger always advised people to buy houses. 'Buy a house,' he said. 'Buy another house.' So I stuck to my price and decided to sell the houses myself. If I couldn't get the price I wanted, I would keep the property and rent it out.

"I usually had a lot of good friends and neighbors wherever I lived. So when I moved away they would watch the house for me, and then I would come back and visit every summer. The tenants just send the rent to a Post Office box; so it's really no trouble.

"On the ones I sold, I almost always carried the loans myself. No one ever advised me on that. I just figured it out for myself. If I had a 3½ percent loan, I wasn't about to give that up when I sold the place, especially when I could get the buyer to pay me 7 percent and I could pocket the difference.

"I never checked with the banks first to ask their permission. I never checked with anybody. I just did it. They never questioned it when I did my wrap-arounds. I don't think they even realized what was going on in those days. As long as they got their payments every month, they were happy. Banks have never done anything for me, except try to cheat me any way they could; so I never deal with them when I sell a house.

"Twice—in California in 1960 and then in Alaska in 1967—I've had bankers take me aside when I was buying a house and tell me, right to my face, that they couldn't give me the same loan that they would give a man, that I would have to take a shorter term and pay a higher rate of interest, because 'that's just the way it is.' "

But Lucille wasn't one to let things like that hold her back. She borrowed the money from her brother to buy her second house, and she kept the first one as a rental. After that, she regularly moved money from one house to another as she bought property in each new town she moved to. Most of the houses broke even or provided a small positive cash flow, but there were occasional problems. Once a tenant moved out in midyear and Lucille had to borrow from her credit union to make the payments until the summer, when she got back there and sold the house. Now that house gives her an income of $500 a month above what she pays the bank, since she carried all the financing herself.

Finally, she landed back at Brigham Young University once again, and she found a builder who was desperate. He had constructed a beautiful 5,000-square-foot showplace; then the market had gone bad and he couldn't sell it. He was willing to take almost no down payment and he would carry the loan. For $100 down, Lucille bought the house.

Old Friends and a New Life

"Bland's sister is about the same age as I am (Bland is older), and she and I had kept in touch over the years. Then she was also at Brigham Young again when I was back there in 1973. Her family still lived in the area, and we were friendly with each other. As I said, we had kept in touch over the years. She mentioned that Bland was coming home for Thanksgiving, for the first time in many years. I said that was nice. I had never asked about him. It was about thirty-five years since we had seen each other; so I didn't think too much about it.

"Then she mentioned that he had lost his wife to cancer a while before and that he had asked about me and was looking forward to seeing me when he came to visit. Well, as I say, I didn't take it all too seriously. I figured that when people come back home to visit after a long time, they always think they're going to see everybody and usually don't have the time. So I didn't even stay around. I went to spend Thanksgiving with my mother instead.

"Well, as soon as I got back the phone was ringing. It was Bland, and I found out that he had been calling the entire time I was gone.

"After that, we started seeing each other regularly and we found out we had a lot in common. For instance, I had gotten my Ph.D. in Textile Chemistry and he had a Ph.D. in Food Chemistry before getting his M.D. degree. So in some ways our backgrounds were fairly similar, even though we hadn't seen or heard from each other in all those years.

"I learned that he had taught at the University of Cincinnati after getting his Ph.D. there, while he worked his way through medical school, and that after that he had moved all around the country, just as I had, before settling in Mesa, Arizona, where he was working in nuclear medicine.

"We also had the feeling that we were related somehow. We have similar coloring and features; and when I mentioned that my mother's maiden name was Hadlock, it turned out that he also had Hadlocks on his mother's side of the family. It wasn't until recently, though, that he traced it back and found out that his maternal great, great grandmother was named Bessie Eliza Hadlock. Well, since my mother was named Bessie Hadlock and my aunt was named Eliza Hadlock, we're both fairly excited about this and are looking forward to going to England and tracing family histories back there.

"But that's getting off the track. We continued to see each other, and about four months later we got married. I sold my house in Orem, Utah, and moved to Mesa. This time I didn't have to buy a house, because my husband already had one. But I didn't want to just take that money and throw it into the communal pot, because I had learned from experience with my first husband. I knew we would only spend the money and never even know where it went in a couple of years. So I decided to buy another house in Mesa and rent it out.

The Doctor Needed Real Estate

"Now, my husband had no interest in real estate at that time. He was just not oriented that way. He's a doctor and his interests were science and medicine. Plus, I think he was a bit scared of real estate and business in general. What got him interested was the tax write-offs.

"He got hit by a large, unexpected tax bill right after we got married, and it really upset him. He had prepaid his estimated taxes on a quarterly basis, but he hadn't paid nearly enough. On April 14th the accountant showed up and told him he still owed the government a large sum. That just about wiped out his life's savings and left him pretty 'shook up.'

"Well, the next year we got about $9,000 worth of write-offs just from that one rental house of mine and, for the first time in his life, he got money back instead of owing the Government additional taxes. Suddenly, he was interested in real estate."

But that interest didn't go very far or very deep. The Giddings bought a couple more houses, and over the years they bought and sold a few properties, but it was strictly on a small scale. Both of them were too involved in Bland's nuclear medicine practice to worry about managing too many properties; so they kept it a part-time avocation.

Then some of the hospitals with which Bland was affiliated began to acquire their own nuclear medicine equipment and didn't need him any more. Suddenly, his income was cut in half. Financial insecurity was rearing its ugly head again.

That left more time for real estate . . . and more need for it, as well. It was obvious now that they couldn't count on Bland's medical practice to provide a comfortable retirement, any more than Lucille had been able to count on teaching. Once again, real estate investing looked like the only hope for a secure future; so they started investing more heavily.

"We were just in the process of buying eight units when I saw a notice about a free lecture by Robert Allen, author of the book *Nothing Down*. I attended and was so impressed that I immediately signed my husband and myself up for Mr. Allen's all-weekend seminar. Then I went home and told my husband about it and said that I was going, whether or not he was interested.

"Well, he wound up going, and it was quite an experience for both of us. For me it was not just a chance to learn new things, but to find out that I had been on the right track all those years when I didn't really know anything; that gave me new confidence. For my husband it opened up entire new worlds. That was late in 1979. Since then we completed the purchase of those eight units (which was a mistake; but that's another story), another building with seven units, five single homes (all here in Mesa) and a half interest in a trailer park in Flor-ida . . . We bought that for one and a half million last year and it was recently appraised for more than three million dollars!

More Profits with Less Cash

"The most important thing we learned at that seminar was financing techniques: how to use the banks instead of being used by them, how to to get sellers to carry back loans, and things like that. Actually, though, we haven't bought much property with nothing down. I've had more luck with the banks, letting them provide the down payments.

"We use the trick Bob Allen teaches in the seminar, where you open up accounts at three different banks and then borrow money against those accounts.

"By paying back the loans promptly, or even a little bit ahead of schedule, we were able to build up a good line of credit; and then we would keep going back and borrowing more. For instance, we would borrow $5,000; and when that was paid back we would wait a few weeks and then go back and borrow $10,000. We'd get that paid off and then, a couple of months later, go back and borrow $15,000. By dealing with three different banks we could always use the loans from one to pay back another one. Then, by the time the second loan is due, you take a new loan from the third bank and start the whole process all over again. It really works.

"We keep accounts at two smaller banks and one large one. We find we get better, more personalized service from the smaller banks, but they don't have enough money to make really large loans very easily; that's where the larger bank comes in. We try to stretch our credit as far as it will go, so that we'll always have money available when we need it. For instance, we were able to borrow the entire $250,000 for our half of the down payment on the trailer park, with just our signatures. We didn't even put up any of our property as collateral.

"That felt especially good to me after some of the troubles I had with banks in the old days. It's quite a change."

The Giddings also got ideas out of the seminar on how to find sellers who are ready to get rid of their properties and how to then negotiate a deal.

"It's probably one seller in twenty who's likely to give you a really good deal. To find them, you just have to call a lot of sellers and ask questions: Why are they selling? Why do they need the cash they want to take out of the deal—to invest in something else? to put in the bank? Then you try to show them that they don't really need all that cash, that they can get what they want without it.

"Not everybody needs cash. Some people are better off with a monthly income instead of one large chunk of cash. Other people really don't even need that. They can sometimes be talked into carrying part of the loan with no payments for, say, two to five years. Then you have one big balloon payment at the end, including principal and interest. But by that time you should be able to raise the rents enough to pay off a much higher loan; so you refinance.

"For example, you find a good house for $60,000 and it has a $30,000 loan at 9½ percent interest; your basic payment is going to be around $400 a month with taxes and insurance; the house will rent for about

$500, so you've got some kind of cushion. But you don't want to put up $30,000 cash; and, if the seller carries the other $30,000 but insists on monthly payments, you're going to have negative cash flow. However, in five years you should have the rent up to $800, or at least $750 a month; so you can refinance that $30,000 loan and not come out that badly. Plus, you're paying it back with cheaper dollars. Or, you sell the place for $100,000.

"What we usually do is to use our credit at the banks. Our $250,000 loan is for one year; when that comes due, we'll just borrow money from our other two banks and pay it back that way. Then, in another year or so, we'll go back to the first bank and keep the whole thing going around and around.

"*Kiplinger's Newsletter* always advised readers to buy real estate, but never went into detail about how to go out there and do it right. Bob Allen did. You just have to go out there and look through the newspapers and talk to people—other investors, anybody who might know of people who want to get rid of property. 'Don't Wanters' is what we call them. It's hard work, but it pays off."

Mr. and Mrs. Giddings also attend regular meetings of the local RAND (Robert Allen Nothing Down) group for the Phoenix-Mesa area. These meetings are usually attended by 50 to 75 graduates of the Robert Allen seminar, who come from a wide area, to exchange ideas with each other and to hear a range of speakers from mortgage and title companies, as well as attorneys and successful investors.

The Giddings find that the speakers help them explore new ways to profit from real estate. They also get to share ideas and information with the other members. A lot of trading and exchanging of properties goes on, and it's often a good place to find a deal.

Getting Tough with Tenants

The Robert Allen seminar also gave them a solid background in managing rental property and running it like a business. Then, on Robert Allen's recommendation, Lucille followed up by attending Jack Miller and John Shaub's seminar in Newport Beach, California, in the spring of 1981, on owning and managing rental property. Where she was lenient and easy-going before in dealing with tenants, she is now fair-minded and flexible but also tough and well-organized.

"You've got to make tenants feel like they're special," Mrs. Giddings says, "so we never let anyone see one of our places until we have it ready. Tenants have no imagination. You can't show them a place that's not ready yet and expect them to see the potential. It just doesn't work that way."

Mr. and Mrs. Giddings don't believe in showing a vacant unit until they are proud of it. That means fresh paint on the walls, clean—and if necessary, even new—carpets and drapes, and all the appliances spic and span. No matter how many call them saying they have found out about the vacancy and are ready to take it "as is," the Giddings stick to their guns and hold firm.

But don't get the idea that they go around making unnecessary repairs or improvements just for the heck of it. Owning rental property may be a matter of pride with them; but, first and foremost, it's a business. The Giddings are in the rental business to make money; they never spend money until they feel sure they will get it back and make a profit on it besides. If it's not going to pay off, they won't bother to do it.

"That's a lesson I learned a long time ago," Mrs. Giddings says. "I used to make improvements to places and put in the types of things I would like, and then I would find out that the tenants didn't even care. So now I'm much more cautious. But every good tenant likes a place that's nice and clean, with fresh drapes and carpeting. That just makes them feel as if they're being treated with respect and helps them to think of the place as their home."

And what type of tenant do they attract? What type do they look for? "The kind who strap on a tool belt when they go to work," Mrs. Giddings advises. "You know—blue collar workers, plumbers, carpenters, people who know how to change a light bulb."

The Giddings are busy people. They have no time to nursemaid their tenants and no interest in doing that; so they try to stay away from renting to people like themselves—busy professionals who are not inclined to fix things. Many of their tenants are young people on the way up, the type who can pay a good amount for rent and are steadily employed but who do not yet have the money for a house of their own.

They are the type of people who are too glad to take the standard deal the Giddings offer their tenants: a house at $20 or $30 below the market rents, in exchange for a lease that specifies that the tenant is responsible for any repairs under $200 and the first $200 of any major repairs which are the tenant's fault. This is one of the ideas Lucille picked up at the Miller-Schaub seminar.

Wealthier white-collar workers, the Giddings have found, are not usually enthusiastic about that type of arrangement. They prefer to pay the extra rent and "call the landlord" whenever anything goes wrong, no matter how trivial.

Ironically, they have found the same problem with low income people in cheap rentals.

"Some people have a lot of luck with junkers," Lucille says, "but we don't. We own one junker, but it's just been nothing but trouble. We find it's harder to get tenants, harder to keep them, and harder to get our rent. Plus, they seem to expect more from the landlord than people in better rentals do. They don't want to do anything for themselves.

It's almost as if they're doing you a favor by renting a place like that—in a not-so-great area—even though, of course, that's why they're paying so little rent."

All of Mr. and Mrs. Giddings' properties are now in good neighborhoods, where there are mostly single family houses and the majority are owner-occupied rather than rented. They have found that it pays to have, not only one of the cheapest houses in the area, but one of the few rentals around . . . "People are snobs. They like to associate with people who are better than they are: richer, smarter, better educated. This way, nobody has to know they're renters. Other people can think they own their own place, just like most of the neighbors."

Their tenants come from a rental agency the Giddings work with on a regular basis. The agency screens prospective tenants, takes care of the advertising, and even shows the property. It costs the Giddings nothing; the tenant pays the fee. "The agency sends them down to our office," Mrs. Giddings says, "and we collect a $20 deposit and let them have the key for an hour. When they return the key they get their money back. We used to go through the whole thing of advertising in the newspaper and meeting people at the house to show them the place, but this is so much easier."

Of course, no system is foolproof, and the Giddings just recently had a tenant take them for a month's rent before they could get him out. They collected the first and last months' rent and a half month's rent as a security deposit; but from the time his last month's rent was used up and they slapped him with an eviction notice, it took six weeks to get him out.

The Giddings figure that sort of thing is just part of the business; but they don't have problems like that very often and they do not willingly tolerate deadbeats. Every month Lucille sits down and sends a letter, with a return envelope, to each of their tenants, reminding them how much their rent is and when it is due. If one of them is late with the rent in spite of the letter, an eviction notice is served.

"If the rent is due Monday, November 1st, at 5 o'clock, and we don't get it by 6:00, I'll be at their doorstep with an eviction notice, all neatly typed out. I don't fool around. But, at the same time, you've got to be flexible with tenants. If the 1st of the month isn't good for them, that's okay. I'll work with them. I had one girl who used to pay on Thursdays. It didn't matter when the 1st was, or payday, or whatever, she'd always pay on Thursday, whether it was a couple of days before the 1st or a few days late. She got an eviction notice once, but after that we got it straightened out and we became good friends. She rented from us for more than three years.

"Another tenant always paid on the 20th of the month. I've had tenants who had to pay me in installments because they didn't have it all on the 1st. As long as they come to me and talk about it, I'll work with them. But once they set a contract with me as to when they're going to pay and how much they're going to pay, then I expect them to stick to it.

"The eviction notice is just to get them straightened out. As soon as they pay their rent, everything is fine between us and I tell them that. But I have a complicated set of penalties once I start the eviction, and it can cost them up to $100 in late fees."

Finding the Right Property

One thing the seminars did not change very much is their method for finding houses to buy. The Giddings drive around, and they look in the newspaper for houses that are for sale directly by the owner, with no real estate agent involved. All of their properties are in Mesa except for two of Mrs. Giddings' out-of-town rental houses that she used to live in, where she has friends and neighbors who take care of them; and the mobile home park in Florida, which is professionally managed. So they don't need, or use, real estate agents very often.

"I don't trust other people to run our real estate business for us. I like to be involved in the process of looking and deciding what properties are worth checking out, instead of letting an agent pre-screen them for me; and, up to a point, we even like to be involved in the maintenance work.

"I don't *really* like it," Lucille says. "I mean, I would enjoy going to Bermuda, for instance, a lot more than I enjoy working on a house, cleaning and painting it. But I don't mind it . . . let's put it that way . . . and I wouldn't want anybody else to do it all for me. I do want to be involved in the process. I'll hire other people to do some of it; like I've got a regular plumber with whom I work now, and a regular electrician, and a locksmith, and a carpenter, and an air conditioning man.

"I like people who will not only fix it right, but will let me help them so that I can learn something about it myself. Sure, it takes up a lot of time. But our kids are all grown up anyway, so my husband and I have the time to put in without hurting our family life."

But even with all their personal involvement, there have been occasional mistakes. For instance, they have discovered that apartment buildings require too much time and work—a lot more than single-family houses, because apartment dwellers seem to be more demanding and less resourceful, expecting the landlord to be right there at their beck and call.

"There's also a larger, more frequent turnover with apartments than there is with houses, and this is also a nuisance. We managed to unload—after eight months—our big mistake: an eight-unit building that was costing us $800 to $5,000 each month. And we are trying to unload our only other apartment building, a 7-plex, and our one "junker" house. At least for awhile, we plan to stick to single family houses in nice owner-occupied neighborhoods, and professionally managed investments like the mobile home park in Florida, so we don't overload ourselves with managing too many properties at once.

"I might buy another apartment building some day and give it another try, but I know I wouldn't want another one like my 8-plex. I bought that one only because I didn't know what I was doing. That was just before I took Bob Allen's seminar. Once I realized what a bad deal it was, I tried to get out of it.

"We had put up $1,000 earnest money, and I resigned to losing that amount. But I found out that the realtor had changed the contract to read that we would have to forfeit ten percent of the purchase price, or $21,000, if we didn't go through with the deal. They even had a meeting where they tried to convince us that this wouldn't be so bad, because it would give us a good tax write-off. But I wasn't going for that!

"I was tempted to take that realtor to court. But I had no way to prove that he had changed the contract and decided: why waste my time and energy that way when I could go on to something else instead?

"So I spent the next month and a half calling everyone I knew, trying to get up the money I needed to close that deal.

"They told me right out that they had another buyer, but they claimed he was willing to pay only $200,000 and, therefore, it would still cost us that $21,000 if we backed out. So I told them I had my own buyer who was willing to pay $201,000; finally, we compromised on $203,000. This meant we didn't have to lose the $21,000.

"We saved $7,000, but it was still a bad deal. We barely broke even when we finally sold the building, eight months later, for $220,000.

"It was a brand new building, and we learned from that experience that you have to wait until a building is at least three years old before it will pay for itself. New buildings have too many maintenance problems. You'd think it would be just the opposite, but we found that they're nothing but trouble. Lots of things break down, and it takes a while to 'get the bugs out' and to get the rents up high enough just to cover your normal expenses. For instance, the heaters were wired wrong—they had too much current and kept burning out all the fuses. Sure, if they had built it right, things like that wouldn't happen; but it takes awhile before you discover those things and then you, not the builder, are the one who gets stuck.

"Now we're a lot more careful when we buy, and we stick mainly to single family homes."

Enjoying Their Well-earned Success

Like all successful people, Bland and Lucille Giddings are too busy to let themselves be discouraged by their occasional mistakes. They simply deal with each situation as best they can and then move forward with renewed confidence. With over a million dollars' worth of equity and a fascinating and lucrative "hobby" to occupy their spare time, the future looks bright indeed.

"Yes, real estate investing has been good to us," Lucille says. "Christmas 1980, my husband and I had the first vacation we were able to take together when Bob Allen sent us to Nassau for a week as part of his 'Millionaires Club.' We had a great time. We were even part of a taped TV special.

"Before that, we had always taken separate vacations because, with my husband's practice, we felt that one of us had to be there all the time. But we realized that during Christmas week people don't want to see the doctor unless there's a real emergency. So we took a chance and slipped away. Now we hope to be able to do it again this year.

"No, our kids aren't impressed with what we're doing. Being paper millionaires doesn't mean a thing to them. All they care about is: shekels, money, what we can give them—which is usually not as much as they'd like. They can't understand why we're supposed to be so rich but never really have much money.

"My daughter, who is now 35, and her husband both work in the State House in Washington. They're finally starting to get a bit interested in real estate, after being disappointed by the stock market. My son is 31 and he is up in Alaska, where he finished his B.A. in Communications in June of 1980. I had given him some property, but he sold it to invest in other things. Now he's working for himself, building and selling log cabins; so he might get into investing some day. But my husband's children haven't shown any interest at all.

"Most people don't understand investing. They want instant rewards and misdirect their energy. You have to discipline yourself, especially while getting established. That means giving up a lot, but it's worth it.

"Everybody seems to think physicians are so well off and comfortable . . . They are—as long as they keep on working. Most physicians I have met would like to retire at 60 or 65; but they keep on working, not because they're so dedicated, but because they can't afford to retire without drastically cutting back on their lifestyle.

"My husband will be seventy in another five years, and that's when we plan to retire. At that time we'll either start selling off properties and carrying the loans ourselves in order to get income; or trade it all into income-producing (as opposed to 'break even') property and live off that. Then we'll be free to live comfortably and travel.

"Who knows? If my first husband hadn't died so young, or if I'd had jobs that gave me good retirement benefits, I might have been too lazy to do as much as I've done. But now, even if someone just dropped ten million dollars in my lap with no strings attached, I would still continue investing. What's important in life is to have a goal and to keep striving for it. Accomplishing that goal is far less important."

11

Ballplayer Hits a Homerun with Housing
Randy L. Green

Randy L. Green of Long Beach, California, believes in success. Why not? At the age of 28, he has already achieved the American Dream . . . twice. First, by becoming a professional baseball player, and then by becoming a millionaire, long before the age of thirty.

As a first baseman and outfielder for the Los Angeles Dodgers and then the Pittsburgh Pirates, Randy seemed to have it made. He was young, single, doing exactly what he loved doing, and while he was not exactly rich, he was making good money and his future was bright. What more could anyone want?

Not to pay all his income out in taxes, that was one thing Randy wanted. As a single man he was getting stung, but he didn't really know what to do about it. Then, almost by accident, he stumbled on the solution that wound up turning his life right around.

"I had always wanted to own my own home," he says. "It was a dream I'd had ever since I was a kid. When I was fourteen years old I told my mother that as soon as I was old enough I was going to move out of her house and buy a home of my own. Well, I didn't quite make it. I moved out on my own when I was 18, but it wasn't until 1975, when I was 22, that I finally got my first house."

Finding that first one was not easy. It took several months, and Randy figures he went through "about a hundred agents" before he found it. He knew exactly what he wanted—a three-bedroom, one and three-quarter bath house with a yard—and how much he was willing to pay: $30,000. But agents kept trying to sell him something more expensive than he thought he could afford. Now, he wishes he had listened to them.

"I was paying $150 a month in rent," he says, "and I decided that I would be willing to pay twice that much—$300—which meant I could buy a house priced at about $30,000. Agents were telling me I should be looking in the $45,000 range, but I didn't want to hear that. Finally this one agent found me a VA foreclosure that was just what I was looking for, so I bought it for $30,000, with $2,400 down, including closing costs, and four years later I sold it for $65,000. But the houses I could have bought for $45,000 were selling for $95,000 to $120,000, so I don't know whether to kick myself or pat myself on the back. But I wish I had listened to the agents instead of myself, since I really didn't even know what I was doing at that point."

Actually, to say that Randy did not really know what he was doing is an understatement. He was a twenty-two year old kid, fulfilling a lifetime dream of owning his own home, period. He had no idea of the investment potential of real estate; he just wanted a place to live and one where the monthly payments would not cut too deeply into his pocketbook. Beyond that, his only thought was that if anything ever did happen, and for any reason he decided to sell the house, a three-bedroom with one and a half or two baths would be the easiest to resell, because most buyers have at least four people in their family, counting children.

A Refund from IRS

It was not until the following year that he began to think about real estate as an investment. Since he was earning a better-than-average income as a professional ball player, the government took at least one-third of everything he made, and then he usually wound up still owing them money on April 15.

For 1975, the year he bought the house, he paid an additional $900 in taxes; but in 1976, a funny thing happened. He made about the same amount of money as he made in 1975 and had about the same amount of tax taken out of his paycheck, but this time, instead of owing the government money, he got $2100 back!

Something was going on and whatever it was, Randy decided he liked it. He realized that if just one house could save him $2100 on his tax bill, then by buying enough houses he could probably cut his tax bill down to nothing at all. That became his goal, and Randy soon set his mind to making it a reality.

Over the next two years he scrimped and saved and hustled and dealed and gradually he amassed a collection of houses—twenty-two in all—which did indeed cut his tax bill down to zero. Every dollar he kept out of Uncle Sam's hands went right back into property. He still had no real idea of what he was doing. Real estate was still a sideline to his baseball career, but he was feeling pretty pleased with himself.

Then came another major turning point in his life.

"One day I went to lunch with some people who were part of this organization I belonged to," he says, "and we were all sitting around bragging about our accomplishments. So I told them I didn't pay any taxes, and I did it all legally.

"Well, they knew I made good money as a baseball player, and naturally they were curious about how I did it, so I told them I owned a lot of real estate. Now four of the guys there happened to be real estate brokers, and they started asking me what my equity was and how much my properties were worth.

"I was embarrassed then, because I didn't even know what they were talking about. I said, 'Equity? What's that?' You see, I had just been buying real estate for the tax shelter it provided. I was not even aware of appreciation, equity buildup, or anything like that. I had just stumbled into it blindly. So, when these guys did some research and came back and told me I was worth about $750,000, it was quite a surprise."

Enough of a surprise so that Randy decided to take real estate a bit more seriously. By coincidence, his mother was studying for her real estate license at the time, so Randy agreed to go with her and help her study for the salesman's exam. They went to Accelerated Real Estate Schools, and after a day and a half of cramming, he decided to take the exam himself, just to see how he would do.

He got 93 answers right out of 150, and needed 105 to pass. Another day and a half of cramming, and he got 104 the second time around. Now he decided to get really serious, and he spent a full two weeks studying before he passed the test on his third try. Baseball was still his first love, as well as what he counted on to pay the bills. Real estate was just a hobby. But then he started having some problems with management, and the 1978 season had come and gone, but Randy still had no contract for 1979. Maybe it was time to think about alternatives...

Time For Decisions

In January, 1979, he began selling real estate as an agent. By March, he had sold $2 million and earned over $30,000 in commissions. When it came time to report to the Pittsburgh Pirates for spring training, he decided not to go. He still hadn't come to an agreement with the Pirates' management on a new contract, and he was making more money in real estate anyway.

By October of 1979, that decision was beginning to seem like a mistake. Randy was already getting bored with the traditional way of doing real estate by financing it through banks, mortgage companies, and savings and loans, using conventional, FHA, and VA financing. All the real decisions were made by the lenders and the title companies, and all Randy felt he was doing was running around town delivering various papers, like a courier. It was not very challenging.

On top of this, interest rates had started going through the roof, lenders were starting to refuse to honor previous interest rate and point commitments. They were holding up funding, waiting for the rates to jump. Randy decided to take a vacation.

When he came back, Randy celebrated the fact that he had reached his goal. He was only 26 years old, but already his net worth, the equity he had built up in his properties, had reached $1 million. At the same time, he decided he was disgusted with real estate sales, even though it paid so well, and he was going to quit. Then came the next big turning point in his life.

He went to a seminar given by a man named Al Brown, a very successful investor, real estate broker and lecturer, and Randy knew he had found the answer. The seminar was on creative financing: how to get around the banks, S & L's, and mortgage companies, get away from being just a paper shuffler or a messenger and learn how to put deals together. The participants were other real estate brokers and agents who felt the way Randy did and wanted to go beyond the boundaries of traditional real estate and find a better way.

In addition to his lectures and seminars, Al Brown had also organized a Creative Marketing Association which has now grown to cover seven counties in Southern California. By going to the weekly meetings, Randy gets ideas and makes contacts which enable him to become more innovative in dealing both for himself and for his clients. The members sit around and discuss marketing and financing strategies, problem properties they may be trying to unload, etc. Randy buys a good many properties from, or through, other people in the Association.

"I haven't used an institutional lender—except for hard money seconds (based solely on the value of the property and the accumulated equity, not the buyer's qualifications or credit rating) in well over a year. I can barely remember the last bank loan I got."

Randy uses owner carry-backs (where the seller agrees to carry a note for part of the purchase price rather than making the buyer get a new loan) and tries to determine the seller's needs (as opposed to what the seller may *want* and think he/she needs) and then tries to satisfy those needs with as little cash as possible—and *never* his own.

"All my life I grew up with the idea that if I won, somebody else had to lose. Baseball, school, everything I'd ever done was like that. Al Brown got me away from the idea of Win-Lose and taught me the idea of Win-Win, where everybody walks away happy. Now, that's the only kind of situation I will enter into."

Al Brown also gave Randy a book to read, *The Monopoly Game*, by Dave Glubetich, and that impressed Randy so deeply that he gives it to all his new clients and makes them read it and spend five hours discussing the ideas it contains before he will actually begin to work with them.

He Sets His Priorities

Randy does not work with just anyone. He is very selective about his clients. He does not work with home buyers. There are plenty of other brokers who can do that, so Randy works only with investors.

And, he is an investor himself. Commissions provide Randy with his living expenses, but his investments provide him with financial independence as well as a handy tax shelter. Since 1978, he has accumulated fifty more properties, most of them single family homes, for a total of seventy-two properties worth about $5 million. His net worth is about $1.5 million and growing all the time. That is what leaves him free to do what he wants with his life. But unfortunately, it does leave him with one small dilemma.

"It's a problem sometimes, trying to decide where to put my money, since real estate is the best investment I know and I never have to put in any of my own money when I buy. So I take a lot of trips and go to a lot of seminars and take frequent vacations."

Randy uses hard money seconds when he absolutely has to have some kind of down payment, or borrows the money privately. Whenever possible, he gets the seller to carry all or most of the note, with low interest and/or no payments until the note is due, but he will not put his own money into it. "You just have to ask the right questions," he says, "like 'Why are you selling?' and 'Why do you need the money?' " If it requires more cash than he can borrow, he will turn it over to one of his investors.

In spite of his stiff requirements—he also will not buy any property which will not at least break even—he has no trouble finding things to buy. He has picked up eight properties just in the last six months. He goes from county to county, to a different investment group every day, and between that and the newspapers and personal contacts, he finds all he can handle in the way of good deals.

One reason Randy has so little trouble finding properties is that he no longer haggles about price. "I don't worry about the prices any more," he says, "I learned that a long time ago. I once made an offer on a house that was selling for $31,000. I offered $30,000, and the seller said 'No.' I offered him $30,500, and I wouldn't go any higher. My ego got in the way; the seller's ego got involved; he wouldn't go any lower than $31,000, so I didn't buy the property. Today that house is worth

$95,000, so I lost over $60,000 by trying to save $500.

"So now I don't worry about the price if a property meets all of my qualifications. I'll pay full price, but I write it right into the contract that the seller's agent has to provide me with at least three comparable sales before the close of escrow to justify the price. If the comparable sales don't match and the house is overpriced, then the deal is off or we renegotiate the price. Once I do a deal with somebody and it works, then they bring me other deals.

"I don't mind paying full price as long as I'm not overpaying. Maybe I could get the property for $500 or $1000 less; inflation will eat that up anyway, and this way I accumulate more properties faster."

Management is not a problem. He uses rental agencies which charge only the tenant a fee and then turns the property over to a professional manager once it's rented. He has been managing his most recent acquisitions himself, since they are all in his own area, but expects to turn them over to a manager soon, because he's found he enjoys buying real estate much more than he enjoys managing it.

The one aspect of real estate Randy does not enjoy at all is selling. He does not believe in it. He sold only one of all the properties he has owned over the years, and he regrets that one.

"It was my own house, the one I lived in, the first one I ever bought," he says, "and the bank made me sell it when I bought this one. They said that was a condition for getting the loan. I didn't want to sell it. I never sell any of my property. Why should I? I don't believe anybody should ever sell property. It's just going to keep going up in value, and there's better ways to get money out of it—second mortgages, third mortgages. You won't get much more if you sell, anyway."

Money and Fun

But money is not everything. At least not as far as Randy is concerned. He is giving most of his away, to be put in trust for his 22 nieces and nephews, and starting over. It is not money he cares about, but inner satisfaction. He enjoys the challenges real estate investing provides.

That same spirit has caused him to leave the company he used to work for and start his own, because his associates were not receptive enough to his creative financing ideas.

"I want to save the world," he says. "I want to tell buyers, investors, about creative financing, but I can't reach enough people that way, so I realized I would have to train other agents. At first I went off on my own and I only took twelve clients with me, but in the next few months, from February to October, those twelve people brought me 288 more because of my success in finding them properties and financing them creatively. I couldn't handle that many people, so I've been hiring and training other agents."

Randy also makes believers of the sellers' agents he works with and expands his network of contacts that way. He is planning a nationwide realty company based on his investment ideas, i.e., buy, but don't sell, and a seminar as well. He has kept eight of his properties for himself, and is busily looking for new ones.

"I can easily have another seventy-two properties by this time next year," he says, "although, of course, it will take a while to build back up to the equity position I had. No, I don't buy real distress properties. The nicer and cleaner they are, the better I like it. I'm no handyman. My average house is a three-bedroom, one and three-quarter bath in a residential neighborhood. Nothing fancy, but nice. I just find people who can't handle the property, maybe they're getting divorced or something, so I take it off their hands. I'm a problem solver. I help people."

And he gets paid well for doing it. Randy sees life as a process of working towards ever-expanding goals, rather than sitting back with what he has. His long-range plan is to be the owner of the Pittsburgh Pirates, his old baseball team, within five years. What if the present owners don't want to sell? Randy will just make them an irresistible offer:

Something like $15 million down that will come from a hard money broker, and the owners to carry a straight note at 10 percent interest for another $15 million, all due in 20 years ... After all, you never know what people will accept until you ask.

12

Business Success Pyramids Wealth
Irwin Kief

"When I received *The Monopoly Game*, by Dave Glubetich," says Irwin Kief of Denver, Colorado, "I was disappointed at first. It seemed so short and so simple that I doubted its value. But then, once I read it thoroughly I realized how it tied together so much of what I knew about buying rental property. It gave me the confidence I needed to proceed at a rapid pace.

"I went back and reread *The Monopoly Game*, and it was great. Everything I needed to know was right there. It's funny, I had an M.B.A. from Harvard, a law degree and, later, a real estate license. I soon discovered I didn't really need any of them to make big money in real estate in a relatively short period of time."

Irwin Kief is not bragging. He doesn't need to. His accomplishments speak for themselves. He was already successful and financially secure before he began investing in real estate; he had a fine education, good credentials in his field, and an excellent job.

Irwin was well paid and he loved his work. He was not one of those frustrated, unhappy people who are looking to real estate investing to turn their lives around. But it did.

Today, 4½ years after he first started investing, Irwin Kief is still working for the same company he was then. Although he has no plans to quit, he now has a choice. He has control over his life. If he did leave his job tomorrow, his net worth would still increase by at least $200,000 this year, *after* he has paid all his bills and living expenses. In short, if

Irwin Kief ever does get tired of what he is doing, he can make a change without worrying about his bank account. Irwin Kief probably wouldn't have to work another day in his life if he didn't want to.

It is the appreciation on his real estate holdings—about 30 single family houses—which produced this windfall. Moreover, Irwin hasn't paid a dime in income taxes in several years.

"Before I got into real estate investing I saved a significant portion of my pay, but I still wasn't getting rich," he says. "First of all, too much of it was going for taxes. Even though I attempted to minimize my living expenses, my savings just weren't growing fast enough in conventional investments.

"Now, after four years of investing in real estate, my net worth exceeds a million dollars. I expect my net worth to increase by at least $200,000 this year, and I don't pay any income taxes at all. What amazes me is how easy it's been and what little difference it made that I had all those degrees!"

How did he start? Like many investors, Irwin's first purchase was his own home. As a young, single man with a good income, he needed some kind of tax write-off, and a home of his own seemed like a good investment. Through an ad in the newspaper he found one in an older residential area of Denver, about three miles from downtown. The agent turned out to be someone Irwin liked and trusted. After he saw how the home was appreciating and giving him tax write-offs at the same time, he kept working with this person, buying up as many homes as he could afford and could successfully manage.

"When I started out," he says, "I knew there were three things I was looking for. I work hard at my regular job, and at that time I was going to law school at night, so I obviously didn't have a lot of time to put into my properties. Requirement number one was that they all had to be reasonably close to where I live—within a mile or two of my house. Requirement number two was that they be in reasonably good condition. The third requirement was that all my properties had to at least pay for themselves. I wasn't rich when I started investing and I didn't want to end up with properties which would drag me down financially."

Personal Involvement Important

Irwin began pressing his agent to find him more properties, and one house led to another. Management was not nearly the problem he had originally expected. Since his houses were all in his own neighborhood, his tenants were his neighbors, too, and he developed personal relationships with most of them. He visited them each month to pick up the rent and to chat for a few minutes, just to keep it all on a more human, face-to-face basis.

Irwin's approach to sellers is to meet with them in person, talk to them and let them know he is not some unscrupulous hustler out to rip them off and run, but a serious, long-term investor who lives in the area and cares about what happens to his properties.

Like many successful investors, Irwin feels that tenant and seller alike respond better to personal contact. Although he originally used an agent (Irwin now has his own license), he never believed in letting the agent do all the negotiating. Sometimes he would call the seller; other times he would write a note trying to justify a low offer and to encourage the seller to meet with him to discuss the property.

"Usually I start off by pointing out to them what's wrong with the property and where I'm going to have to put some money into it. That way they are not too shocked when my offer is low. A lot of times I do it just to get a reaction out of them and to get them to meet me face-to-face. It's almost like a challenge to some of them to prove their house is worth more than I offered. Meanwhile, I've known that all along. I never start off by offering what I think a place is really worth, so ideally we 'compromise' on a price and everybody's happy.

"You'd be amazed at some of the responses I do get. I wrote a letter to one couple telling them everything that was wrong with their house and why I didn't think it was worth any more than I was offering. I included my phone number. Well, a few days later I received this phone call: 'Is this Irwin Kief? Look, you S.O.B. . . . do you want to buy our house or not? Who the hell do you think you are, writing a letter like that? What's wrong with our house?' Well, not only did I buy the house, but we became good friends. My wife and I get together with them about once a month. This example, of course, is an extreme case."

Irwin is quick to point out that most of the "problems" he calls to sellers' attention are minor ones. He avoids houses which have structural or other serious problems. The houses in his neighborhood are mostly about fifty years old, so there is always something which needs to be done. Irwin pounces on these deficiencies and calls them to the seller's attention.

He also tries to find out what the sellers want, what their motivations are for selling, and how he can help them. If an early escrow, or an agreement allowing the sellers to rent back for a short time will help him get a better price or terms, he is flexible. As long as a property meets the three requirements of location, condition, and ability to pay for itself, Irwin is interested and ready to deal—provided he can get it below market value, of course.

Irwin reads the local newspaper and checks with his agent frequently about any new listings (now that he has a license, he uses the Multiple Listings Book—the book which gives agents information on currently listed properties). Since he is only interested in the one area, he frequently drives around seeking "For Sale" signs. By limiting his area of interest, it is also relatively easy for him to keep track of what sells and for how much. This way he always has facts and figures to throw at unrealistic sellers.

Irwin also owns some rental homes jointly with his younger brother and sister who live in New Mexico. Irwin put up the down payment money, his brother and sister handle all the management, and they split the profits. The advantage for Irwin are that he gets to help his siblings and avoids managing the property at the same time. Irwin has made similar deals with a few friends in Denver.

As a way of spreading his own capital a little further and helping other friends invest in rental property, Irwin has also formed limited partnerships where he is the general, or controlling, partner, and his friends are limited partners. As limited partners, they share in the profits but have no real say in selecting or managing the properties. These limited partners put up their share of the down payment, closing costs, and any negative cash flow or maintenance expenses, plus Irwin charges the partnerships an hourly fee for management. In addition, Irwin will receive a percentage of the profits when the properties are sold.

Building a Pyramid

The first couple of houses were the hardest, Irwin remembers. "It took time to build up my confidence in handling sellers and tenants, in learning to negotiate and use creative financing. In the beginning, I put up more down payment money than I needed to." More recently, he has learned to buy more with less cash.

"I convince sellers they would be better off to sell now, carry a second mortgage, and receive a steady income, than to hold out to get all cash, which would then be deposited in an interest bearing account anyway. In the beginning I had some cash to put down. I was still hesitant about buying too much property too fast, so it really didn't seem to matter. But now I realize that the less I put down, the more properties I can buy, and that's the name of the game."

Once he caught on to this idea and really began to believe in it, Irwin began taking money out of his properties in order to buy new ones. He refinanced his home, took out second mortgages, and even sold a couple of properties, when it seemed advantageous to do that. Within two years he was well on his way to being independently wealthy. His properties were multiplying and appreciating, and his tax bills were going down while his net worth was going up. And in spite of his busy schedule, he was doing all his own management in his spare time.

Irwin would not trust anyone else to pick the tenants or collect the rents or do any of the other things connected with owning rental property. His wife helped some, but Irwin still did most of the work, because he says he is picky. If she did anything wrong or made any mistakes, it could affect their relationship, and besides, Irwin already owned most of his properties before they were married.

Not that Irwin himself has never made any mistakes. He admits to a couple of not-so-great purchases and some good ones he passed up at various times. But for the most part, he is pleased with his accomplishments. Buying and renting in only one area has made it easier for Irwin to know the properties, their value, any likely problems and repairs, and the types of tenants they attract.

This is important, and he feels it has really helped him to make money and avoid problems. Of course, like many successful investors, Irwin has found that prices in his area have gotten so high he can no longer find properties that will break even unless he puts up a large down payment or uses a graduated payment technique.

This has caused him to buy more cautiously. Fortunately, Irwin always could have afforded some negative cash flow. It's just taken time for him to build sufficient confidence to feel comfortable with it. As long as he has enough income to offset most of it and still allow him to live comfortably, he prefers investing locally rather than investing in some cheaper, but far-off and unfamiliar area where break-even situations may exist.

He could get better leverage by investing in a cheaper area; he could put up less down payment money and still break even on cash flow, but he feels the properties would be more difficult to manage. Everyone has their own way of getting rich, and Irwin Kief's way has worked just fine so far, so he sees no need to change it any more than necessary.

But times change, and so does real estate financing, so Irwin has been forced to make a few changes. For instance, he used to look for good FHA and VA assumptions, but they are getting harder to find because of increased competition for them. Rapid appreciation sometimes made secondary financing necessary to minimize the down payment.

For instance, a house with a $45,000 FHA mortgage at 9 percent interest was selling for $65,000. Although Irwin was sure it was worth at least $70,000, he put in an offer for $60,000 and finally got it for $62,000. He paid cash to the loan plus closing costs of $18,000. By assuming the FHA loan, he had payments of $367 per month, plus another $60 for taxes and insurance, for a total monthly cost of about $427. Conventional financing was available at the time for non-owner-occupants, but required 20 percent down plus 2½ points. Thus he could have reduced his down payment to about $14,000, but the interest rate would have been 12 percent. Principal and interest would have been $510; PITI would equal $570. Because the house would rent for only $475, Irwin chose to assume, even though it required more down.

A year later, however, the same house was worth about $80,000, and within two years, about $95,000. At $95,000, the $45,000 assumable loan was no longer very attractive, since it required $50,000 cash to assume it. But conventional loans were now going for about 13 percent. Thus, with 80 percent refinancing, the principal and interest payments alone would be $840. Taxes and insurance were now over $100 a month due to inflation. Thus, his total payment was $940 a month. Rents had not gone up nearly so much. Irwin had just increased the rent to $600 a month, leaving him with about $340 a month negative cash flow. Such refinancing would net Irwin about $30,000.

But if he could keep the $45,000 loan at 9 percent and then get a $30,000 second for 14 percent (payments of $373 amortized over 20 years), his total PITI payment would be only $840, or $100 less than if he utilized conventional refinancing. He would still net about $30,000, but at a much lower net cost.

He was caught in the classic bind many investors have had to face in recent years. Rents were not going up nearly as quickly as prices and interest rates, and consequently, it was getting harder to buy and to refinance property.

Changing Tactics to Suit the Times

What to do . . . like most smart investors, Irwin threw this problem right back at the sellers. He told them in effect that if they wanted to sell their property, they would have to help out with the financing. He began writing offers which called for the seller to carry large second mortgages at less than the going rate charged by mortgage companies—or in many cases, he asked the seller to carry the first. Sure, he got turned down most of the time, but occasionally he found sellers who wanted to sell their property more than they wanted to hold out for a lot of cash. Some sellers said "No" at first, and then reconsidered when they saw their properties were just sitting on the market.

"Again, being a resident of the area and being able to convince them I am a long-term investor and not a quick-buck speculator, really helps," Irwin says. "It's not true that sellers are motivated only by money and how much they can get for their property. Emotion plays a big part in it. Sure, the average seller wants the best possible price, but he also wants to feel comfortable about the person he is selling to— especially if he is being asked to carry back any part of the loan. That is the one area where my background does come in handy. My job involves negotiating with financial institutions, so I know how to deal with people and how to bargain. Aside from that, my B.A., the M.B.A., the law degree, even the real estate license, have made little difference. The license lets me keep part of the commission on properties I buy. The guy who used to be my agent is now my broker. I hang my license with him and get access to the Multiple Listings. Aside from that, the license hasn't done a thing for me. In fact, in some respects, it may have hurt, as the fact that I am a licensed salesman must be disclosed on all offers I make, and some people seem to get a little nervous over that."

Aside from *The Monopoly Game* and other investment books he has read, Irwin has found his best teacher to be good old-fashioned trial and error—learning from experience and his occasional mistakes.

Oh yes, Irwin has made some mistakes, but he feels he has managed to keep them to a minimum by being personally involved with his properties and his tenants. After all, he reasons, if they don't pay their rent on time they have to deal with him face-to-face. On the other hand, his tenants know that if something goes wrong, Irwin will get right on it without delay. In fact, he recently hired his own full-time handyman to help him stay on top of it all.

For the first three years he did much of the maintenance himself and relied on various free-lance handy people for anything he couldn't do. But now, with thirty houses, he needs and can afford someone full time. Hiring a full-time handyman has allowed Irwin to keep his properties in good shape, and practice preventive maintenance. It is not cheap, but Irwin believes in the long run it is cheaper and better than dealing with deteriorating properties and disgruntled tenants.

What are his plans now and for the future? Irwin isn't quite sure. He is very satisfied with what he has done so far, and expects to sit back and watch his equity and his net worth increase, for one thing. He is still buying property, but not as avidly—high prices, high interest rates, and lack of time to manage too many more properties have combined to slow Irwin down, but not stop him. He feels certain the growing housing crunch will drive up rents within the next couple of years and melt away negative cash flows.

"Denver is still growing," he says, "and a lot more people will be moving here in the next couple of years." He believes housing will become scarce as Denver becomes the energy center of the West due to its close proximity to shale oil and other deposits of natural resources, such as coal.

In the meantime, Irwin has written the first draft of a book about real estate investment with his brother in New Mexico. They are still editing it, and haven't decided yet whether they will submit it to established publishers or try to sell it on their own, and as yet they have no title for it.

They have also considered doing their own seminars, but Irwin is not so sure about that. "Seminars by Irwin Kief, real estate millionaire?" He sounds skeptical. "I am—I figure my net worth is about $1½ million now, and my properties are worth about $2½ million, so I'm a millionaire, but I'm not about to let my tenants know that. Or the people I buy from. I go to collect rents and to present offers in an old car. They don't have to know about the Mercedes sitting in my garage. But in six months or a year, I might change my mind. I do think I've got a lot to tell people."

Photo Album

Charles Carrithers
Newport News, Va.

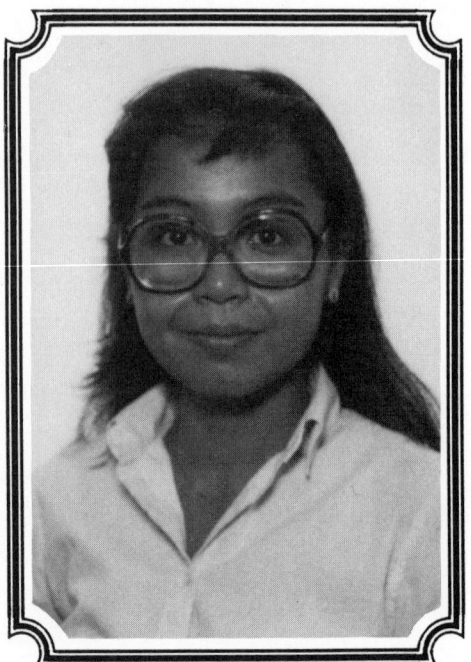

Rachel Cabarrubias
Long Beach, Ca.

Karen & Richard Hett
Edna, Tx.

Wayne, Kathy & Richard Phillips
Baltimore, Md.

Nick Koon
Columbus, Oh.

Charles Hughes
High Point, N.C.

Janet Little & Reverend Little
Houston, TX.

Lucille Giddings   Bland Giddings
Mesa, Az.

Jennifer Steves
Philadelphia, Pa.

Elbert Lee
Fresno, Ca.

Carl Crouch
Riverside, Ca.

John Broadfoot
Amarillo, Tx.

STEP III

Living Like Millionaires

13

A Poor Credit Risk
Carl Crouch

Carl Crouch of Riverside, California, is not one to sit back on his past success—not unless he can continue to make a profit that way. His motto seems to be: Neither a borrower nor a lender be—unless the interest rates are in your favor. He borrows when the rates are low, and then lends his money out to others at a profit when the interest rates go up again, just like the banks he never deals with.

Of course, it takes money to play this game, and lots of property to use as collateral for all those low-interest loans, but Carl has plenty of both—19 properties, and close to a million dollars' worth of equity in them at last count—so he feels he is in a good position to weather any economic upheavals we may face in the future.

Back in early 1977, Carl was just another struggling small businessman. After ten years of running his own motorcycle shop, he found that banks and other lending institutions still didn't consider him an acceptable credit risk. If he wanted to expand his business, or branch out into something new, he would have to raise the capital on his own, or through private lenders. So there he was, working too hard, paying too much in taxes, getting ahead too slowly, and not having much fun.

Then came the turning point, the event which helped Carl turn his life around and achieve almost overnight success.

Can a book really do that for somebody? Can you really learn to be wealthy and successful just by reading about how to do it? Carl did.

"Until 1977," he says, "I never thought about real estate. I didn't even own my own house. I had a nice apartment for only $125 a month, so I thought I would just be a renter forever. Then a Realtor I knew gave me a copy of *The Monopoly Game*, by Dave Glubetich. 'Carl,' the Realtor said to me, 'you're in business for yourself, so I know you must have a little money . . . why not start investing in real estate? Buy a house for your first investment, and if you decide you don't like it, in six months I'll buy it back from you at the same price you paid for it!' Well, with a deal like that, I figured, how could I lose? He was a nice, honest guy, and I trusted him to stick to his word about buying me out in six months, so I took the plunge. I read the book, and bought a house." Carl bought his first house, an FHA assumption, for $30,000, with $3,000 down.

After that, Carl never looked back. Within a year he had picked up seven more houses using the same technique—looking for good assumable loans—and he was on his way!

At first, he stuck with that same Realtor, and the deals just seemed to fall into his lap. The Realtor would call him about a house for sale, he would look at it and put in an offer to buy it. Through second mortgages—initially arranged through his Realtor, just like his purchases—he used one house as a stepping stone to the next. After the close of escrow, he got a second mortgage, or waited until he built up enough equity to refinance the first mortgage, and then he used most of the money to buy more property.

Confidence Grows with Experience

'Working in the shop full time and trying to buy everything I could get my hands on cheaply and manage it all at the same time was a bit much," Carl says, "especially since I was so new at it and had so much to learn. So I tried a couple of property management companies, but the trouble was, most of the good ones didn't even want to bother with somebody like me, because I was small time and there wasn't enough money in it to make it worth their while. But that's what everybody advised me to do, hire a management company, so I did. They didn't work out for me, so then I tried hiring individuals to manage some of my properties, but basically, my main interest was to learn how to do it myself. After ten years, I wasn't thrilled about working in the shop full time any more, so I decided my real ambition was to start spending more of my time on the real estate."

Then Carl began to branch out on his own. "As I learned more," he says, "and began to gain confidence, I started looking through the newspapers. I realized there were a lot of properties for sale directly by the owners, and I would never even hear about them through my agent. There were also people advertising who bought trust deeds and lent money, so I decided to expand my options and explore the possibilities."

Carl soon found he was making more deals—and often better deals—for himself, than he could by waiting around until his agent called him. He began to experiment more, finding some deals where he hardly had to put up any cash, others where cash was the magic word which could grab a property for a ludicrously low price because the owner was desperate. He found that meeting the seller face-to-face and negotiating with him or her directly without any agents involved could be a distinct advantage, as well as an excellent way to further his real estate education.

Of course, Carl was not willing to pay top dollar, or even true market value prices, for homes. But somehow, sellers seemed to feel better knowing that he planned to hold on to the property as a long-term rental. Also, meeting him made them feel more secure about carrying paper—first, second or third loans on the property—instead of getting all their money in cash.

As Carl got more and more involved in real estate, he had less and less time to spend at the cycle shop.

"I faced a choice at that point," Carl says, "I had to have help either running the shop or my properties; I couldn't do it all, so I decided it was cheaper, easier and better to hire more help for the shop and put more of my own time into the real estate. Now (mid-1978) is when the real work started. More people were catching on to real estate, and I had to hustle to pick up good deals and new financing. Besides, I wanted to get out of the shop more, anyway. Real estate was more exciting to me, as well as more profitable. The more I learned, the more fascinated I got.

"I got more into doing my own management, too. I found I never had trouble with the tenants I put in there myself—only the ones hired managers had occasionally picked for me—and fewer tenant problems left me more time to negotiate deals, so that's what I began doing." Banks were still reluctant to deal with him; but Carl was not about to let that stand in his way. FHA and VA loans are usually financed through mortgage companies and are automatically assumable with a minimal amount of paperwork. Carl concentrated on picking up properties that way, and got financing at a lower interest rate than the banks were charging, besides. He was coming out way ahead.

"The mortgage companies would try to discourage me," he says, "and tell me I should get a new loan through them instead of assuming the old loan. That way, I could have put less money down. Unlike the banks I tried, the mortgage companies were glad to lend me money, but that would have meant a higher interest rate and loan fees on top of that. So I said, 'No thanks,' and kept looking around for low interest loans I could take over. I haven't had to deal with institutional lenders in order to get a loan yet."

Private Investor the Best Money Source

Carl doesn't believe in dealing with institutional lenders for refinancing or tapping the equity in his properties, either. He just puts ads in the newspaper stating he will pay one percent over the going T-Bill rate for private loans secured by prime real estate. "All the little old ladies just come crawling out of the woodwork. One will recommend me to her friends, and soon I've got more money than I need, with no loan fees. I just pick them up at their houses, drive them by the property, show them the figures on equity, income and expenses, and guarantee them a fixed interest rate of return for at least two years. They practically beg me to take their money."

Although he doesn't mention it directly, it's obvious that Carl keeps a thorough, well-organized financial record for every property. This businesslike approach to his investments certainly aids the good impression he makes on his private lenders.

"Most of them are experienced investors. I can tell just by the questions they ask that they've done this before. They usually know just what they want. I show them some payment stubs—that show what the balance of the first loan is. Some of them will accept a verbal report from a title company—which you can usually get for free, especially if you use them regularly and give them a lot of business—but other times, I have to spend up to $150 for a written report showing that the property is free of liens, except for the first mortgage. Occasionally, I would go to a hard money lender, and they would get a title report at their expense, and I would ask for a copy. Then, if I got a private loan, instead of going through them, I would have it to show to the investor without having to pay for a new one. Once in a while, someone would ask to see the books, but not very often. Most of the time all I do is drive them by the property and show them how much equity I've got."

Of course, it also helps that all of Carl's properties are newer single family homes in comfortably middle class neighborhoods. This has been his rule of thumb from the beginning: find homes in good neighborhoods where you can get good tenants and good rents, with few maintenance problems.

Minimizing Tenant Problems

Carl tears out most shrubbery, since tenants usually won't maintain it anyway, and reduces the lot to a minimum-upkeep situation. He rents his houses with stoves, but no refrigerators, since stoves rarely break down unless they are abused, while refrigerators are breakdown-prone even with normal use and handling. "If the refrigerator comes with the house when I buy it," he says, "I take it out and get rid of it. In the beginning, I had a lot of problems that way. A house would come with an old refrigerator in it; I would rent it out, and six months later the thing would break down and the tenants would expect me to fix or replace it, just because it was there when they moved in. Now, I make the tenants supply their own refrigerator, and deal with any breakdowns themselves."

As for renting a place fully furnished, that's something Carl would never do again. "A few times I bought houses and paid the sellers a few hundred dollars extra for their furniture, figuring I would get more rent that way. It was nothing but trouble. Tenants would break the chairs and burn holes in the cushions, and soon the whole place was like a junk heap. People who have their own furniture seem to be more settled and responsible. They take better care of a house and cause fewer problems."

Problems are what every landlord strives to avoid, and for the most part, Carl has been successful at minimizing his through experience and common sense. "Whenever possible, I try to rent to working couples in their thirties or older, without children or pets, but my one strict rule is to never rent to anyone without a checking account. I go to their bank with them and make arrangements to have the rent money automatically sent to me each month in the form of a cashier's check. It costs the tenant about fifty cents a month, and it gives me peace of mind. If they don't go for it, or their bank won't cooperate, then I just tell them they can't have the place. It's as simple as that. By buying only nice, single family homes in middle class areas, I can get away with being strict. I never have trouble finding tenants."

The only properties Carl has sold so far are in neighborhoods which are starting to decline, or were too far away from where he lives. He is holding on to everything else, in spite of the current real estate slump. "I would get killed on taxes if I were to cash out now," he says, "and besides, I picked up a lot of my best deals from people who had held them from about 1974 or 1975 to 1977 and then got disgusted because they weren't appreciating. That was right on the tail end of the last big slump in property values, and shortly after that, prices started to go crazy. I wound up getting all of their profits, just because they got impatient and didn't hold on long enough. In fact, I got some of my best deals from Realtors who were going through hard times and were strapped for cash."

Finding Good Buys

Carl has also found other uses for Realtors. He buys property through agents whenever they bring him good deals, and he cooperates with agents whenever he sells something, although he does not list his properties with any one exclusive agent. "Some of them bring these clients from out of town," he says, "from areas where comparable houses are selling for a lot more money, I guess, because I always price my properties sky-high when I do sell; but some of these guys just snap them up like they are the world's greatest bargains, which is just fine with me. So sure, I always offer a commission when I do sell something. If agents can meet my price, why not?"

But, he admits, "I don't use agents that much when I buy property any more simply because most of them don't want to bother with the kinds of offers I like to make. I get a lot of properties directly from the seller. I always put the word out among the agents in my area when I'm looking to buy, but I also look through the papers on my own. If I find something in an area I like, I'll just call the owner and make him an offer without even seeing the property. Many times they tell me where to go when I offer them $50,000 for their house and they're asking $80,000, but I just leave my name and number, and sometimes they call me back a week, or even a month, later when they're starting to get desperate. Those are the ones I want. And the ones who don't call back? What have I lost but a phone call?"

Other times, when he sees a "For Sale" sign on an interesting-looking house, Carl will find out how much the owner owes on the mortgage, and then make an offer. "'Look,' I'll tell them, 'you owe fifty thousand and you want eighty-five. Well, I won't pay eighty-five, but I will give you ten thousand in cash and take over your mortgage. Think about it, and give me a call.' Some of them call me, and some don't."

What does Carl do with his money in between deals—especially all that borrowed money he is paying interest on? He loans it out again. "I don't borrow money right now," he says, "not with interest rates so high. I lend it out instead. I loan a lot of it to real estate agents on short term swing loans at up to 35 percent interest. Say they've got somebody who's buying a house but the buyer won't have any down payment money until their own house gets sold. I loan the agent the money, he loans it to the client. That holds two deals together—the house they are buying and the one they are selling—and the agent pays me back when the client's house sells. They don't mind paying me high interest if it helps them put two deals together, and the buyers don't mind as long as they get their house, so everybody's happy."

Carl also buys discounted notes and deeds of trust, a trick he learned from another book by Dave Glubetich, *How to Grow a Money-tree.* "I look through the papers under the 'Money Wanted' column. A lot of times someone will sell his house and carry back a second deed of trust for, say, $30,000 at 15 percent in order to help the buyer out and make the place sell faster. Then, six months or a year down the road, the seller decides he needs his cash out, so he decides to sell the note. I'll offer him $20,000 cash, or maybe even $15,000, and if he's desperate enough, he may take it. If not, I just leave my name and phone number, and call someone else who needs cash."

But property is still Carl's main game. He has branched out into limited partnerships—with himself as the general, or managing partner—to buy raw land in the Sacramento, California area, where a lot of residential construction has been going on in recent years. "Any land I buy in partnership I always buy outright, for cash," he says. "That way we get a better price, since the owner doesn't have to carry any paper (banks will not finance raw land, so it must be either a cash purchase, or else financed by the seller), and that way the only carrying charge or overhead is the property tax, so we can sit on it as long as necessary. With a partnership, I don't want someone complaining they can't handle the negative cash flow and have to cash out, so this way we avoid problems."

He has also bought himself a house to live in, the building his business is located in, and the one next door, as well. A contented renter no longer, Carl's motto is: "If I can't own it, I won't touch it."

Treat Investing Like a Business

Does he have any regrets about the way he's done things? Is there anything he would do differently? "Well, at first I passed up a lot of good houses because I wouldn't have wanted to live in them myself. Then someone told me that was no way to invest, and I realized they were right. I passed up a lot of good bargains. That was a mistake I don't make any more. It it's a good deal, I buy it, period, whether it suits my personal taste or not.

"This year I have also sold three houses, because I had too much equity in them, and because maintenance is a problem. These are houses I bought in 1977 and 1978, and they're about 20 years old, so things go wrong—roofs need replacing, pipes start to leak, etc.

"I got top prices for all three of them by giving the buyers great terms. I went to Beneficial Finance and got equity seconds at 18 percent interest, with only two points, for 75 percent to 80 percent of the value. That way, I got a nice chunk of cash—about $25,000—out of each one. They each had assumable first loans of about $30,000, payable at about $250 a month, and then the seconds added about $400 more to the payment. I took $3,000 down on each one, and then carried thirds for the balance of the purchase price—about $15,000—on straight notes, with no payments until the loans are due in three years.

"Now I don't have to worry about the possible maintenance problems, and I just put the cash into a money market fund until I decide what to do with it. As soon as I find a few good buys, I'll be ready to pounce on them. Now is a great time to have cash available, because there's so much on the market, so I'm just keeping my eyes open, waiting for the right ones. There are lots of opportunities available!

14

Salesman Profits by Buying
Nick Koon

Nick Koon is a Realtor who doesn't want to sell your house; he wants to buy it. But if you live in the Columbus, Ohio area and watch TV between nine in the morning and four in the afternoon, you probably know that already. Most likely you've seen his commercials on the local stations. If you haven't, you will, sooner or later.

TV commercials?

"Nick Koon, Realtor, will pay cash for your house!"

You can imagine the kind of shock waves that sent through the local real estate community! But then, Nick Koon is not your average real estate broker.

"I don't work for commissions," he says. "I don't sell houses. I work for a millionaire. My wife's a millionaire, not me," he jokes. "I just work for one. The nice part of it is, I get to sleep with her."

Of course, his wife was never anything near a millionaire until Nick started investing in real estate, but that's another story.

"All my life," Nick says, "everybody always told me that real estate was the way to make money, but I didn't really pay attention. Then, in college, I took an aptitude test and I just did not comprehend when it said I should be a real estate agent.

"I always thought real estate agents were all a bunch of well-dressed crooks—which, by the way, may not necessarily be untrue—and I didn't want any part of it.

"I didn't become interested in real estate until years later, when I sold my own home. I did it myself, with just an ad in the newspaper, and I was amazed at the number of calls I got—over ninety. I had been in sales, selling janitorial supplies, for several years, and I always had to chase buyers down and badger them to buy, and now here I had buyers calling me. I couldn't believe it, but I knew this was something good, so I started asking questions, trying to find out what it was really like to be a real estate agent. What you had to do, how much money you could make, etc.

"It was a real estate company that bought my house—they specialized in listing people's houses and guaranteeing to buy them at a certain mutually agreed-on price if they didn't sell. In my case, I never listed it, but they met my price, (minus the commission, of course, but I didn't mind paying that as long as I was getting what I wanted.) So I sold it to them.

"I went to the manager and told him I was thinking of getting my real estate license. He said he had no room for anybody else and couldn't hire me, but I went ahead and took the test anyway.

"When I passed it I went back to him and said, 'Look, it's not going to cost you anything to hire me. You don't have to pay me anything unless I produce, so I know you can squeeze me in somewhere.' And that's how I got started in the business. That was about 1971."

But after becoming an agent it still took Nick two years to work up the courage to buy his first rental property. He was just plain scared, but gradually it began to dawn on him that the smart money was not just in selling houses for other people, but in buying them for himself.

By this time, Nick had firmly established himself as a successful salesman, a million-dollar producer, but there was trouble within the company he worked for.

"There were two people behind the company. One was a millionaire who put up the money, and the other one was the broker-manager. For a while they got along fine, but then they started arguing a lot, and the broker decided to form a new company without financial backers. The company had gone from $2 million to $22 million in sales volume in two years, but now he was ready to chuck it all, to go out on his own. I told him he would fall flat on his face without more money to back him up, but he wouldn't listen, so I made two big moves within a short period of time. I started buying property on my own, and I moved to another company. I lasted there for six months, and then because of personality conflicts, I went off on my own and I've been on my own ever since.

"Nowadays I don't even sell houses anymore, except for occasionally selling one of my own. I've got ten people working under my broker's license, including three million-dollar producers, but my realty business just breaks even and pays for my overhead—the office, two leased cars, secretarial help, etc. It doesn't really provide me with any income. That comes from my properties; mostly from refinancing, not selling them, so it's tax free. It's up somewhere in six figures, but I live modestly, and my personal expenses are only about $1,000 a month, so I plow most of it right back into property. I own over one hundred houses, so I've come a long way from my first one eight years ago. I'll just keep buying until I figure I can't manage any more property."

Early Profits—and Losses

When he finally decided to buy that first investment house, Nick came back to his office all excited, but when he gave the details to two of the older, more experienced agents, they told him he was crazy. He had paid too much for the house, and would never get his money back. It would turn out to be nothing but trouble for him.

Nick was starting to feel down and gloomy, when a fourth person, also an old, experienced real estate veteran, came along and joined the conversation. He agreed with Nick that inflation was here to stay, and house prices would keep going up. That got Nick so excited that within two weeks he had bought a second house and then a third.

That second house really got him going. Within four weeks he had it cleaned up and resold for $6,000 profit. The other two were also profitable, but that one was the best of the three.

Then there was the other side of the picture, another house which also stands out in Nick's mind, and which he calls his Waterloo.

He gave the seller his down payment, took title to the house, and then found out he was in for all sorts of trouble. When he sold the house and got an FHA inspection, they wanted a new roof, new paint, a new furnace, water heater, electrical system, and plumbing. Also, it took the buyer six months for the deal to close because of some credit problem, and the loan points—which the seller pays—went from two when the escrow was opened, to ten by the time it closed. That meant ten percent of the sales price was chopped right off the top. Then the ceiling fell out of the living room, dining room and kitchen.

When he got done dealing with the Federal Housing Administration, Nick had to deal with the city. The house was in a mandatory inspection area, and everything had to meet city code approval before it could be resold as a habitable dwelling. Nick had bought it "as is," assuming there was nothing wrong, but he was not a contractor or an expert at housing inspections, so he found out the meaning of "assume." "It makes an ass out of you and me," he says ruefully.

The city made him put in new sidewalks and curbs, tear down a perfectly good three-car garage, put putty around all the windows, and install 220 volt wiring. They also refused to approve the water heater installations, so Nick had to tear that out and reinstall it to the city's specifications.

The only good thing about the house was that it did not have termites, but in spite of everything, Nick was rid of it in six months and
got all his money back. He got his original $100 down payment back,
plus about $5,000 in costs, i.e., repairs and loan fees, and even made
about $32 profit for his six months of work.

That might have been enough to stop some people, but not Nick
Koon.

Motivation + Faith + Knowledge = Success

"I figure this business is about 90 percent determination and 10
percent ability," he says, "and I figure I owe my success to several
things, starting with a mother who always told me there was no reason
I couldn't succeed, and I guess I was just dumb enough to believe her.

"I also listen to a lot of motivational tapes, by people like Zig
Ziegler, Og Mandino, Tom Hopkins, Norman Vincent Peale, Napolean
Hill, Clement Stone, etc., and I take real estate seminars and self-help
courses. The ones which have helped me the most are Robert Allen's
Nothing Down seminar, Paul Simons' Co-Investor seminar, the
Lowry-Nickerson seminar on distress properties, Jack Miller and John
Schaub's seminars, Clarence Jones from Cincinnati, Ohio, on main-
tenance, and Furman Tinon's investment seminar out of Newark, Ohio.

"And I'm also lucky to have a tight-fisted wife who only under-
stands 'Buy now. Never sell!' But nothing would have been possible
for me without God.

"I'm a Christian, and with God's help He has carried me through
many painful situations and general problems of running a real estate
business—i.e., dealing with tenants—and I've been able to get
through them through prayer. Like many times when I've been ready
to blow up at people—not that I never do, mind you—I've been able to
stop and go to God in prayer, and He gives me the peace and strength
to go on.

"'A hammer smashes glass, but a hammer also molds steel. When
the hammer—the problems of life—hits you in the side, you quickly
find out if you're made of glass or steel.' That's a quote from Norman
Vincent Peale. A tool of destruction can also be a tool of goodness."

Nick Koon long ago made his choice and decided he wanted to be
firm but fair, made of steel in a velvet glove, and that is what he likes to
do, "steal" houses from sellers whenever he can; that is, buy at the
right price. He only buys houses which are at least 20 percent below
market value, and he has developed an elaborate system for rooting
them out and then making sure they really are underpriced.

Nick has a complete file of all houses sold anywhere in his county
during the last six years. He has it broken down street by street from
figures compiled by the local Board of Realtors and a local newspaper,

The Court Reporter, which lists any sales in Franklin County. His secretary and his wife handle it all. His wife, who was an accountant, but now works only for Nick, keeps all records.

This way, whenever Nick goes to look at a house, he knows exactly what has sold in the area in recent years, what it sold for, and how long it was on the market. He then tries to use all the available information before making a decision. For instance, if ten houses have been for sale in a given neighborhood within the last few months and only two of them have sold, he figures something is wrong, and that is not where he wants to buy, because it is obviously not where people want to live.

Nick has also learned to avoid the city's targeted inspection areas and the inner city in general. He has houses scattered all over Franklin County, but they are almost all in suburban residential areas where he can attract respectable families as tenants.

Careful Tenant Selection

Although he is near Columbus, and Columbus is the home of Ohio State University, Nick tries to stay far away from the student rental market. He does not buy properties near the University, and he does not like to have students as tenants.

"Students cause too much trouble," he says. "I had a group of them once and they burned holes in the carpet and the kitchen linoleum and ruined the stove, all within four months. Another time I rented a house to four guys and the next thing I knew it had turned into a concubine situation; they had a bunch of girls move in there with them.

"Now this was a respectable family neighborhood, not near the University in a student area, so I was not about to tolerate that sort of thing. I still have one house that is rented to students, a four-bedroom place I rent to six guys, and the cops have been out there at least six times in the last 18 months. They're always making noise and disturbing the neighbors, and guys run around naked in the backyard and meanwhile, there's little girls, ten, eleven years old, living right next door. But they should all be out soon. I am aware that renting to students brings a better return, but I have elected not to deal with them. I don't think single family housing is the place for students, and I own only single family houses."

Most of Nick's tenants are far better behaved. He gets them through a rental agency which charges tenants $35 for a list of available rentals, with no fees charged to prospective landlords. Then, when he takes their applications, he submits them to a local private property owners' service called the Federal Adjustment Bureau.

This is a private, profit-making enterprise which charges landlords an initial membership fee of about $125 a year, plus an additional fee of

$6 for each tenant screened. They delve into a tenant's background, credit and work history to make sure he/she is really a good risk. For instance, they check the names and addresses of previous landlords against records of all property owners to make sure the tenant is not just giving a phony reference with a friend's or relative's phone number.

It is partly wise and thoughtful caution such as this which has made Nick Koon such a successful investor, and partly it is his willingness to just get out there and do it, while others are still debating. Or, as he puts it:

"There is no free lunch. That's the most important rule. If you want to *make* money, go work for the mint. In real estate you *earn* it, by accumulating knowledge and learning how to use it. When a man with money meets a man with experience, they exchange. One gets money and the other one gets experience.

"But I don't think that having a Ph.D., or giving seminars or whatever, is going to make you a success in real estate. You don't learn to ride a bicycle by reading a book; you do it."

Learn What Will Work

And Nick Koon does it. For instance, in September 1975 he got a call from a man who wanted to sell his house. The man wanted to sell the house, not list it. He needed a quick close of escrow because he was already behind in his payments and he did not know what to do, so he was not calling Nick Koon, Realtor, but Nick Koon, investor.

So Nick Koon, investor, went to look at the house and decided it was worth at least $24,000. The VA loan on the property was for only $10,000, with payments of $98 a month—far less than the house would rent for—so Nick asked the seller what he expected to net out of it.

When the man explained that he had lost his job, had already missed two payments and just wanted to get out before he was foreclosed on, Nick jokingly offered to give him $1.00 for his equity and take over the loan—including the two back payments. To his surprise, the seller jumped at the offer and they made a deal.

"I saw the house had all new cabinets and that sort of stuff," Nick says, "and the seller had obviously spent money fixing it up, so I expected there to be all kinds of liens against it by the people who had done the work. But when we got the title report it was clear, except for that $10,000 first. That was the first time I really felt I was stealing a house from somebody. But you know, that seller came up to me at the closing and he said, 'Mr. Koon, can I ask you something? I had three other agents come out to look at the house before you did, but none of them bought it, so how come you did?'

"Three other agents looked at that place, but they all wanted to list it; none of them wanted to buy it. In fact, one of them even gave the seller my name. He said, 'You ought to call Nick Koon; he buys houses for cash.' And so that's why he called me. That's how he got my name. Today, that house is worth at least $60,000. I wind up getting a lot of referrals that way, from other brokers."

And then, of course, there are his TV ads. He runs them on an irregular basis, he says, to avoid killing a good thing. But during downturns in the economy, such as we are now experiencing, he is on all the time between 9 a.m. and 4 p.m. weekdays to catch the unemployed person who is sitting home worrying about bills.

"I find that it works," Nick says simply. "Even if it only brings me one or two deals a year, it's worth it. I find people who are desperate to sell—or, I should say, I help them to find me—and then I buy their properties for less than market value and pick up instant equity. Then I hold the houses as rentals and pick up even more equity as they continue to appreciate."

Nick also finds that being a broker is helpful, because of his contacts in the local real estate world and the exposure it gives him, and he takes that part of his life just as seriously as his investing. In the past ten years, in addition to accumulating over $2,000,000 worth of his own property and building up a net worth of over $1,000,000, he has sold over $50,000,000 worth of houses to, and for, other people. Now he spends the main thrust of his time working his own investment inventory.

He also believes strongly in the value of education, in spite of his feeling that ultimately you have to learn about real estate by doing it, and he says:

"The real estate industry is working towards education that will kill the cancer that is afflicting us all—the ones who don't know what they're doing."

As for himself, he likes to take seminars offered in different parts of the country so he can learn new wrinkles, new ways of doing things, new problems, new opportunities. Right now, he is particularly enthusiastic about Paul Simons' TNT (Today, Not Tomorrow) Co-Investor concept, which he describes as working like this:

"You find a house worth, say, $40,000, with a $10,000 VA or FHA loan. The buyer offers to purchase it for $40,000 on the following terms: he will get the seller to obtain a second for 80 pecent to 90 percent of the value of the home, take his cash out of that, and carry the balance of the purchase price as a third mortgage on a straight note with no payments until it is all due, in say, five to seven years. That way, the buyer only has to make payments on the $10,000 first and the $20,000 second, so his costs are kept down.

"The payments, however, are still going to be more than the house will be likely to rent for, so the investor/buyer then finds an owner-occupant who is willing to move into the house, meet the entire payment (1st, 2nd, taxes and insurance), and be responsible for any repairs. In exchange, he will receive half the appreciation once they agree on an initial value for the property. They make an agreement to have the house appraised at the time the note to the seller comes due, and then the owner-occupant has the option to refinance or find some other way to buy the investor-partner out. Otherwise, they sell the house, pay off the original seller, and split the profits."

For instance, the investor buys that house for $40,000, then finds an owner-occupant and agrees to split any appreciation beyond $50,000. Five years later, they sell the house for $100,000 and after expenses of $10,000 are taken out, they split the difference between what is left ($90,000) and the $50,000 initial value they agreed upon—$20,000 each. But since the loans against the house total less than $40,000, the investor gets at least another $10,000 which she/he does not have to split with her/his partner.

Real Estate Is a Money Business

This concept appeals strongly to Nick, because he says he is not a high-leverage investor, and he does not like to have too much negative cash flow.

"The name of this business is O.P.M.—Other People's Money," he says, "but it can be deadly poison. You just have to know how much to take. I don't feel comfortable being too highly leveraged—and I don't need to do that any more—so why should I do it?

"I don't want to get caught if the market turns around. I've got too much to lose. I've already got enough positive cash flow to retire on if I wanted to, so I can afford to be a little conservative. That's why I try to buy houses in the $60,000 and under bracket so I can keep the payments down in relation to rents.

"But with this co-investor program, you've got nothing in the property, and no negative cash flow or management headaches, and a few years down the road you're going to get half the profits, so that's got to be worth something.

"It took me five years of buying and selling to realize that I'm not in the real estate business, I'm in the money business. I do not mind renting money at 18 percent interest, or even 22 percent, when I can turn around and make 50 or 100 percent on the money. Real estate is just the vehicle I use. That's why I look for houses that are in good condition, but where the seller is behind on a few payments, so I can make money with my mouth, not my back."

And, he might add, he is always happy to use his mouth to help others make money, too. He is a popular speaker at RAND groups and other investment meetings, talking about what it takes to be a successful single family home investor. He has also become somewhat of a minor expert on the tax advantages of real estate investing, having been audited four times in the last four years.

"When you have a six-figure income and you don't pay any taxes, you get audited," he says, "but they haven't gotten anything out of me because it's all legal."

His advice for aspiring investors?

"If someone is looking for a real estate attorney or a CPA to help them, they should ask one question: How much real estate does the attorney or accountant own? It's as simple as that. Real estate investing is a business, and you've got to work at it, just like any other business.

"Just because I'm a Christian, people sometimes misinterpret that to believe that I'm a soft touch, but it doesn't work that way. I once had trouble with a man with whom I was doing a shared equity deal. He was supposed to be making certain repairs and keeping the property up, and he was just not doing it. So I wrote him a note and told him that if he kept up his part of our agreement, he would someday get half the equity in the property, but that if he didn't, then I would just have to evict him and he would get nothing.

"He wrote me a note, saying something like, 'Mr. Koon, I thought you were a Christian, and so where is your Christian kindness?'

"Well, that made me so mad that after I wrote him another note I had to wait a little while and then let my secretary tone it down a bit. But basically, I said to him, 'Just because I am a Christian does not mean that God has given me the mission of raising you up in this world. So, you had better get up off your dead ass and raise yourself up.' And that's how I feel. I spoke at an investors' meeting in Dayton, and I gave them my definition of a good landlord, somebody who's qualified to survive and prosper in the rental business.

"I like to put back a little of what I've taken from real estate, by helping others. That's why I talk to investment groups, and that's why I agreed to be interviewed for this book. But my idea of being a good landlord is that you've got to be able to throw an 80-year-old woman out into the street on Christmas Eve if she doesn't pay her rent, while her husband is in the hospital, dying.

"I told that story in Dayton, and somebody at the back of the room yelled out, 'Yeah! And it's your mother, besides!'"

15

Interest Rates Don't Matter
Charles Hughes

What tricks or secrets do successful investors know which can be passed on to others who are just starting out? What separates the successful investors from the ones who tried, but couldn't make a go of it?

"Heck, there's no secret to it," says Charles Hughes of High Point, North Carolina. "If you're honest and you work hard, you'll make it. Real estate is about the only way that's left for the little person to get rich, and it's also the safest. If you find out all you can first, and then really work at it, there's almost no chance of failure.

"There's more opportunity now than ever before. There are more sophisticated buyers and sellers out there, and more ways to finance properties creatively. I bought 20 houses last year, and over one hundred and fifty of them just within the last two months. High interest rates don't matter. What counts is the return on your investment. If you're going to get a 50 percent return, or even 20 percent, on your money, then it's worth it to borrow that money at 16 percent or 18 percent, isn't it?

"I didn't know anything when I started. I just knew that I had a desire to own property ever since I could remember, and I didn't want to be a renter. My father owned his own home; in addition to his regular job, he worked after hours at a cotton mill, at $10 a month for 3 years, until he got $360 to buy a lot, and then it took him another four years to get the money to build a house. I wanted to do the same.

When you rent, you're just throwing away money that you'll never see again. It took me ten years to get the money for my first house, another two years to get my second one, and several years after that to really get rolling, but I started young, and just stuck with it.

"It all started with a paper route when I was 13 years old. Fifty-six papers to deliver along a fourteen-mile route, for $2.50 a week. I also worked in a grocery for three years, and then in a hosiery mill and a gas station. All through high school, I worked and put all my money into a savings account.

"I graduated in June, 1948, and went to work with my father at the Dallas Furniture Company store here in High Point, doing deliveries and repairs. Then after about a year, I moved up to the credit department.

"I went into the service, and continued to put my money in a bank account. When I came home to High Point, I had about $2,500 saved, and in 1953, I bought a piece of land, and with my father's help, I built my first house myself. I was single, so I didn't really need a house to live in, but by renting it out to someone else, I was able to increase my income and save more money. In two years, I had enough to buy a second rental house, but now my father started to caution me against getting in too deep.

"He was scared of owning too much property," Charles says, "and he held me back. I was kind of under his thumb at that time, and I was still scared, too, so I spent a lot of time checking out the market and trying to learn a bit more about investing before I really jumped into it. It wasn't until the early 60's that I really got started.

He Decided To Be Better Than Average

"I was married by then, and in 1959 I had replaced my father as manager of the Dallas Furniture Company store (where I still work—35 years now, and we've got three stores instead of just one; and now I also own part interest), so I had a little more confidence in my abilities, and I decided that I was not going to be ordinary. I knew I was going to have it better than the average man.

"I was ambitious, and hard work has never scared me, so I talked the Dallas family into opening a new store here in High Point. I also began buying more houses, finding people who didn't want to own rental property, or else didn't know how to manage it. The houses I was buying were all under $10,000 in price, and either they had assumable loans, or the sellers agreed to carry the financing. I would give them between $100 and $500 for their remaining equity in the houses, and take over payment of the loan. The houses all provided me with positive cash flow, and I would save that so I could buy more houses. Once people knew I was in the market for low-priced rental houses, I began hearing about them from brokers, friends and from the sellers themselves, people who were tired of owning property, and were looking for a way out.

"I was around 31 or 32 years old, and I began to set goals for myself. I decided that I wanted to own 35 properties by the time I was 35, fifty of them by the time I was 37, a hundred of them by the time I was 40, and two hundred by the time I was 45. I missed that mark. By the time my 45th birthday came, I only had one hundred and ninety five properties, so I was just short."

Today, Charles Hughes owns over three hundred properties with a combined value of more than $2.5 million—mostly single family houses—all within the city limits of High Point, a community of about 60,000 people. He figures his equity is over $2 million, and he has a substantial positive cash flow coming in above and beyond his mortgage payments of $9,000. How did he do it?

"Each house has its own story," he says, "and I learned something from each one. I never took any of those real estate seminars—I don't even think they had them when I started—I just learned by experience. There's a lot of people out there who really don't have the intellect or the desire to own income property. They don't know how, or don't want to deal with it, and there are always plenty of them around, so I would buy what they couldn't handle."

He has bought houses directly from the owners, through real estate brokers, and from banks and loan companies that have taken over properties they have been forced to foreclose on. Wherever there is a good deal to be had, Charles Hughes tries to be there to scoop it up.

He runs an ad in the newspaper offering to pay cash for properties. Generally, he pays between $100 and $500 to pick up the equities of sellers in trouble and assume the existing loan, but occasionally he will pay all cash for an exceptionally good deal. For example, he picked up one house for $9,000. The seller had to have cash, so Charles borrowed $6,000 from the bank and put up $3,000 of his own. It was worth it to him, even though he had to put up so much cash, because the house rents for $205 a month, and he figures it was worth at least $12,000 at the time he bought it.

The mortgage payments are only about $75 a month, so in less than three years he will have his investment back and start putting money in his pocket each month. One hundred dollars a month in positive cash flow may not seem like much, but it adds up over the years. One house he bought for $3,500 has already produced $13,000 in rents since 1970 and next year, when he sells it, Charles expects to walk away with another $15,000 in cash.

Getting the Figures Right

Charles will buy almost any small property anywhere in High Point, as long as the numbers are right. He has a series of formulas he has developed over the years to help him evaluate property and decide what it is worth to him. He says it all comes down to three old staples in real estate investing: location, location, location. The better the area, the smaller the rate of return you can expect on the rents. You will get more profit when you eventually sell the house, but you will get less monthly income in the meantime. In other words, a property in an area with good appreciation might be worth $15,000 and have an income potential of $200 a month, while another $200-per-month rental, in a slightly rougher neighborhood, might only be worth $12,000. The $12,000 house might give the owner about $100 a month in positive cash flow. In 3 years, it could be worth $15,000, so that is $3,000 profit, plus $3,600 in positive cash flow for a total of $6,600 over three years.

The $15,000 house requires more down payment money and produces a positive cash flow of perhaps $75 a month, but in three years it may sell for $20,000. That is a $5,000 profit, plus $2,700 in positive cash flow, for a total of $7,700 over three years. Clearly, the $15,000 house offers a better overall rate of return, and therefore is a better buy.

If, on the other hand, the $15,000 house offered no positive cash flow at all, or offered only $50 a month positive cash flow and a probable sales price of $19,000 in three years, then that would yield a total profit of only $5,000-$5,800 over three years, and clearly, the $12,000 house would be the better buy.

Other factors which Charles figures in when calculating his possible rate of return on a property are the amount of cash required and the amount of repairs or improvements needed and the potential for raising the rents.

"Price, interest rates, even location, none of that really matters as long as the rate of return is there. In some areas I figure on paying about 80 times the monthly rents—$16,000 for a place that rents for $200. That's about a 15 percent return. In other cases, I only want to pay about 60 times the rent—$12,000—so I can get a 20 percent return. It depends on the area, the property, and how much cash I have to put down."

For instance, Charles put down $3,000 cash for a $12,000 property he was able to get for $9,000. But when he bought a similar property, with the same rental income—$205 a month—for the full price of $12,000, he only put down $1,200, less than half as much as he put down on the $9,000 property. That way the rate of return on his investment still works out, in spite of the higher price.

Charles bought another building with four units for $32,000, with $2,000 down and the owner carrying the balance. He made some repairs as soon as he took over the property, and then raised the rents, which ranged from $85 a month to $110 a month, to $150 for each of the four units. With $600 a month coming in, he has a positive cash flow of around $300 a month, and he will get all of his original investment—

down payment and money for repairs—back within two years for a better than 50 percent per year return; and that is without even figuring in any appreciation.

How to Be Successful Starting with Nothing

This type of success has not come easily to Charles Hughes. Nobody handed him anything on a silver platter. He has worked for everything he's got, and he has enjoyed every minute of it. He estimates that real estate takes up about half of his ten-hour work day (the other half is taken up by the Dallas Furniture Co. where he now manages all three stores). At night he goes home and looks through the real estate ads, rental statutes, and anything else he considers relevant to his goal of learning all he can about the rental business.

Like many successful investors, he decided early on that he could not learn everything about all types of property, so he specialized—in his case mainly in distress single family homes and duplexes, those in need of repair, at the bottom end of the economic scale. In an area where he says the average house in a decent part of town is now about $50,000, and even good building lots can sell for $30,000 or $40,000, he has never paid more than $16,500 for a single family house.

"When I started out, I didn't have any money," he says, "and I was also scared, so I thought I'd better start small. I never bought any commercial property, because I felt there was too much risk for a small person starting out. There's a higher vacancy rate with that kind of property. And I stayed away from the more middle class areas, because I didn't like the numbers. You have to put up more down payment, and you don't get enough rent to make it worthwhile. Distress properties were the only ones I could afford, and since I didn't have to put too much in, I couldn't lose too much."

Although his properties and his tenants are both at the low end of the economic scale, he does not have too much trouble collecting his rents. With over three hundred properties of his own, and about a hundred and fifty others he manages for other people, he says he almost always has somebody in court, filing notices against tenants who are delinquent with their rent, but he has to go through with actual evictions only about three or four times a year.

He lays down a set of strict rules when he first rents to someone; no selling alcohol or drugs or sex, and nothing else that is illegal or will be likely to disturb the neighbors. Tenants get a 48-hour grace period when the rent is due, and after that they get an eviction notice.

For the first year, tenants are on a lease, which specifies that they cannot move out without Charles' approval, or they forfeit their deposit. After the first year they are on a week-to-week rental arrangement. This means that Charles can slap any deadbeats with a 2-day notice to vacate the premises instead of the three-day notice required with a month-to-month arrangement.

Management on a Schedule

Each week he goes through the files and sends letters to any tenants who are delinquent, and once in a while he visits each of his properties in person. He walks around the outside just to see how the tenants are keeping the place up, and to check if anything needs repair. If he feels it is necessary, he will then knock on the door and go inside.

Each spring he evaluates all of his properties, decides how much each one is worth, and then adjusts the rents so that he is getting a fair return on the value of the property (i.e., a property which is renting for $200 a month because it cost him $10,000 two years ago clearly needs an adjustment if the value is now $15,000, so he will probably raise the rent to about $225). The average rent increase is 10 percent to 15 percent, and he says that out of over 250 increase notices he sent out this year, only six tenants even commented about it.

Charles Hughes has developed a reputation as a good, fair landlord, and the Dallas Furniture Co. on North Centennial Avenue has become known as a place to go if you are looking for decent, inexpensive housing. Charles keeps his places in good repair and makes them as homey and liveable as possible. He has a full-time, four-man maintenance crew with all the necessary equipment, and he keeps them fairly busy.

He's on good terms with almost all his tenants; he has asked a couple to leave, over the years, because they did not get along, but not many. Most of them come right to the store each week to pay their rent, although some prefer to mail it in, and others pay for the whole month in advance.

He gets his tenants through word of mouth and newspaper ads. He does not really check applicants' references, but relies more on his own instincts in dealing with people. He simply asks them about their job history, recent housing, why they want to move, etc.; he doesn't take welfare tenants, because he feels they are too marginal and would more likely be unable to keep up with their rent than working people are.

For a long time he even refused to deal with "Section 8," the program where the government subsidizes the rent of low-income people by paying the landlord the difference between 25 percent of the tenant's income and the agreed-upon rent (i.e., a person with a $500 per month income and a $200 a month house, would pay only $125, and the government would pay the other $75 per month directly to the landlord). He does not believe in government programs like that, but when he saw that it was in operation all over town, he decided to give in. He now has about forty tenants on Section 8, including some who were already renting from him and then got into the program with his assistance.

With over 450 properties under his care, obviously Charles can no longer handle everything by himself. In addition to his maintenance crew, he also employs someone to do typing, filing, and record keeping. Every month he goes over the list of all the mortgages he owes and when the payments are due, and sends out the checks on the first or second of each month. Then he has the office employees send out notices to delinquent tenants. He's been at it so long that it's all a smooth-running operation by now, although he did sell off forty or fifty houses a couple of years ago because he felt he had too many, and is getting ready to sell some more in the near future.

The Safest Investment There Is

His biggest problem now is what to buy and how to buy it faster. He says he has owned many of his properties so long and paid down the mortgages so far, that he no longer has enough write-offs to offset his positive cash flow, and so he is getting walloped on taxes.

He used to refinance some of his properties—he's got one early one he's refinanced four times—and several he's refinanced twice—but now he feels the interest rates have made that impractical. It's cheaper to buy new properties.

"It's not good enough any more, buying one or two houses a week," he says, "so I'd like to start buying some units and apartment complexes for about $250,000. But I haven't put enough time in looking for them so far. I've put in some offers, but I haven't actually bought any yet." He has bought some industrial land, though, and intends to develop it himself.

His father never felt it was a good idea to keep too much money tied up in real estate, but Charles Hughes feels just fine about it. A real estate crash? He isn't worried. People will always need a place to live, and sooner or later prices will go up again. He believes real estate is not only an enjoyable challenge and a way to get rich, but also the safest investment there is.

"I don't remember where I got these figures, so maybe you shouldn't quote me," he says, "but somewhere I read that there's more money invested in real estate than all other business and industry combined. I really wish more people were interested in it. I've helped some friends get started, but I say the more people in it, the better. I'm not worried about the competition. If more people were interested, then people would have better places to live.

"In the future, it's only going to get better. There's a lot more opportunities now than when I started. You just have to get out there and do it.

"The government has scared off a lot of the timid investors with all its regulations and redevelopment programs that tear down private housing and build public housing projects instead, so that means there's less competition and more properties available, because those people are anxious to get rid of them.

That doesn't scare me off, because I've studied the laws that affect my business. I've read the laws concerning rental property here in North Carolina. I've gone to the library at Wake Forest University in Winston-Salem, which is right near here, and studied landlord-tenant acts and North Carolina Supreme Court decisions. Real estate is simple if you know the rules to go by. I've designed my own lease that Legal Aid has tried to break on three different occasions, but they have never been able to do it.

"My wife helps me on occasion, but for the most part she just tells me to go ahead and buy whatever I want to, and she signs her name without even seeing the place. I am giving each of my four children four units of their own as a way of getting them involved, and I think my two boys are interested and will eventually come into the business with me. I imagine the girls will probably come into it also, if they settle in this area. But they're all in school now, so none of them helps out too much.

"I have occasionally thought of selling most of my houses and just collecting an income from carrying the loans. I have a friend who's doing that, and he's doing pretty well. He used to laugh at me and tell me I wouldn't get anything but headaches owning property. Then, about ten years ago, he saw I was starting to accumulate something after all, and he came to me and said he wanted to buy some property too, but he had only $700. So I started trying to help him.

"He found a dirty run-down house belonging to a dentist who was asking $3,500, with $1,500 down. My friend wanted to buy it, but he didn't have enough money, and he didn't know what to do. So I told him there was no way that dentist was going to get $1,500 cash with the house in the condition it was in, and no way he was going to bother cleaning and fixing it himself, so it was a perfect situation. My friend wound up getting the house for $3,000, with $300 down, by assuming the $1,700 first mortgage, and having the seller carry back a second for the remaining $1,000, because the dentist just wanted to be rid of it. My friend got in there, cleaned out the trash, repaired the windows, plumbing and wiring, painted the place, and raised the rent from $35 a month to $97.50.

"Ten years later he sold the house for $27,000. He got $2,000 cash, and he's got a note for $25,000 at 12 percent interest, bringing him

$257.16 a month for the next thirty years, with no maintenance headaches. With all the properties he picked up in the past ten years, I figure he's going to have a total income of about $8,000 or $9,000 a month by selling them all on the same terms.

"It's a tempting situation, but I'm still buying houses faster than I'm selling them. I recently bought a couple of houses in a light industrial area, and in a few years, when the depreciation runs out, I'll tear them down and build a small industrial building. Between my own and the ones I manage for the Dallas family, it doesn't give me much time to myself, but I'd probably get bored anyway if I didn't have something to do."

16

The College of Hard Knocks and Big Bucks
Bill Felix

"I get by with a little help from my friends." These famous words from the old Beatles song could well be the theme song of self-made millionaire Bill Felix. A millionaire friend first inspired him to become rich, and then other friends helped him to achieve that goal.

Not that he didn't work for it and put in a lot of effort of his own, because he did. For close to three years, he knocked himself out, buying properties, fixing them up all by himself, with only his wife to help him. And all the while he was working full time, eight hours a day, seven days a week, to earn money to support his family and to realize his dream of becoming a full-fledged millionaire by investing in real estate.

"I had only five hundred dollars when I started in 1967," he says, "and I thought the only way a poor person could make it was to work yourself sick."

His first purchase was a single family home that everybody advised him against. He paid $6,000 for it, and today he admits it was probably worth no more than $4,000, but Bill had more enthusiasm than knowledge. He didn't really know how to invest—he just knew he wanted to do it, so he jumped in with both feet—and went right through the floor...

The house had a broken furnace, the water heater broke and flooded the whole place, and the place wasn't even hooked up to the city sewer system, so he had to take care of that, too. It took Bill several months to fix the property up and sell it, and when he did, he made a profit of all of ten percent. This might have been enough to scare off a lot of people, but not Bill Felix. He just got excited over his success and decided to do it again.

He bought a duplex for $19,000, lived in one half and rented out the other half. Like all his early purchases, this one needed a lot of work, which Bill did in his "spare" time, i.e., from 6 p.m. to 1 a.m. (he worked at his regular job from 8 a.m. to 5 p.m.).

He bought a third property by taking the last $500 out of his savings account and borrowing another $700 from his father. This one also netted him a ten percent profit on his investment, after about six months' work, and he was on his way, one property after another, in a string of never-ending fixer projects . . . or so it began to seem.

More than two years went by and Bill made money during those years, but not much. He was a lot better off than he had been. He had a net worth of over $40,000, but he was still an awfully long way from being financially independent.

Bill's problem was money. He had a lot more than when he started, but he still didn't have enough to enable him to move ahead as quickly as he wanted to. But what he did have now was experience. He knew how to buy property, how to sell it, and how to manage it, so he went to a friend and made a proposal.

Partnerships Were His Best Tool

Bill's friend was to come up with a certain amount of cash, which Bill would then invest in real estate. Bill would sign a note for half the amount of money his friend put up, plus seven percent interest, to be paid yearly. In return, Bill got half interest in the property and a contract to fix the property up and manage it for seven percent of the gross rents.

The partnership would not include the wives, so each partner would have an insurance policy on the other partner. That way, if either of them died, the other one would automatically have enough money to buy out the widow for cash.

The partnership would have no set time limit—it could go on forever if they both agreed—but neither partner would be locked in. With proper notice, either one of them could buy the other one out, or offer to let his partner buy *him* out.

Every year the partners would reappraise the property themselves and put their own value on it. This did not necessarily mean the true value of the property on the open market, but simply what each of them would be willing to pay the other one for his equity. That way, if one partner did want out, they would both know approximately how much money he would get for his share at any given time.

His friend agreed, and Bill was off on the next phase of his investment program. This one worked better than the first phase, so much so that Bill was soon able to enter into a second partnership and the third phase of his program.

Now, Bill had some cash, but still not enough to get him where he really wanted to go, so he went to another friend—the self-made millionaire who had first inspired his ambition to improve his life—with a new proposal. This time, Bill would put up half the cash for the partnership, and his friend would put up the other half. Once again, Bill would do all the purchasing and managing and the partnership would pay him for it. In this way, he was able to accumulate more cash than he could investing on his own, and he could get into more and larger properties, and build his equity faster.

This worked so well for Bill that eventually he was able to buy out both of his partners and enter into a third partnership where he and his partner again put up equal amounts of cash; but this time, his partner was responsible for the management. Bill had come a long way in a few short years. Such a long way, in fact, that by 1978, he was able to quit his regular job and live entirely off the income from his investments. He also formed a limited partnership that specialized in paying cash for tax sale properties which were selling at prices well below market value.

By 1979, Bill Felix owned 25 units outright: 13 single family homes, and the rest mostly duplexes and triplexes. Plus, he owned another 98 units in partnership. He had reached his goal of financial independence and achieved a net worth of over $1,000,000. He also had a $100,000 line of credit at one bank, and $50,000 at another, so that today he can snap up good deals that come along, even if he has to put down a large down payment or pay all cash. Not bad for a poor boy who started with only $500.

But, of course, it's not all a bed of roses, either.

Student Tenants Are Different

"Most of my tenants are students," Bill says, "so it's like a whole different business. Renting to students is not like renting to normal people. First of all, my units all become vacant at once, and then, during rental season, I will get maybe 125 phone calls a day. And students have no conception of time. They'll call at midnight, wanting to know about an apartment for rent."

Then there's the fact that Bill and his partner have to go around and check every apartment at Christmas time, to make sure the tenants didn't shut off the furnace to save money while they are away on vacation. Midwestern winters are cold, and a furnace that's completely off can mean the water pipes will freeze and crack, causing extensive damage and costly repairs. And, of course, there is always the patching and plastering to be done.

Each summer when the students move out, Bill makes the rounds to inspect all the holes in the walls and ceiling, the torn, stained and burned carpeting, and to make a general assessment of the damage. Before the apartments can be rented out again, they have to be returned to something at least approaching their original condition. This is an annual rite, since the new tenants rarely keep up the place any better than the old ones did.

And students are young and emotional, and tend to see their landlords as heartless money-gougers. This can lead to numerous headaches for the college town landlord, and Bill has probably lived through most of them by now.

"They wrote about me in the school newspaper once," he says. "They ran a picture of my house, and next to it a picture of one of my rental units. It was supposed to show how I rip off the students. Felix, the greedy slumlord. That's the main reason I don't want my name used." (Bill Felix is a pseudonym.)

But the problems have not stopped Bill, and neither have the bad economic conditions in his area.

"There's too much competition now. Too many people wanting to invest near the college," he says. "Prices have gotten too high, and with the high interest rates it's hard to find anything that makes sense to buy. None of them give enough income any more. Bank interest rates are 16½ percent (as of May, 1981) and you can't assume old loans because the banks either raise the interest rate or foreclose and insist you pay the whole thing off.

"Even older people don't want to carry mortgages at less than that. They all look at the money market rate and want to get high interest, too."

But Bill isn't out of business yet. It may not be profitable any longer to buy old properties near the campus and rent them out, but it is profitable to build new apartments, so that's what Bill is doing.

The apartments have four bedrooms, a living room, and a kitchen, all crammed into 850 square feet. They cost Bill $31,000 a unit to build ($10,000 a unit for the land and $21,000 a unit, or $24.70 a square foot, for the building) and rent for $600 a month. Even at 16½ percent interest, that makes more than good sense, especially since the college is growing, and demand for housing is going up all the time.

Now that he has made it in the rental business, Bill has learned a few tricks of the trade, and has accumulated enough cash to make life a little easier for himself. For instance, he no longer does his own repairs, but deals with a free-lance maintenance contractor who specializes in dealing with rental properties.

Although most of his tenants leave during the summer, Bill leases his places on a twelve-month basis, so he doesn't have to worry about summer vacancies. In spite of the article in the campus newspaper, he has a reputation among his tenants as a pretty decent landlord, and he has no trouble getting renters.

He is down to about 100 units, all told, and he fills them by putting up notices around town, running an ad in the paper, and by word of mouth.

Since he gets so many calls all at once, he has also hired a temporary answering service that he uses at rental time. And since students tend to damage whatever places they live in, he charges first and last months' rent, plus a security deposit.

Now that he has made it and has it made, Bill is able to indulge himself in out-of-town, negative-cash-flow properties with built-in management, so he owns three condominiums in Florida. He bought them partly for the appreciation potential, and partly because they give him a good excuse for tax-deductible vacations away from the Midwestern cold. After all, he's earned it.

17

The Bankrupt's Road to Riches
Elbert Lee

"You don't have to be Jewish to get rich," read the ad in Bill "Tycoon" Greene's *Real Estate Newsletter.* "I was poor and black and I became a millionaire by investing in real estate. Now you can find out how I did it by reading my book."

Intrigued by this, I contacted the author.

"That's right," says Elbert Lee of Fresno, California. "I was born poor and black, but by the time I got into real estate I was worse off than that; I was in a negative position. I had tried to go into business for myself, doing landscaping, but thanks to some employees who didn't follow through on what they were supposed to be doing, I went bankrupt.

"I'd been trying to put myself through school with the landscaping business, but now I was not only poor, I was broke and had no credit rating left. This was in July, 1975.

"I went to work as an insurance claims adjuster, which I had done before, and tried to get myself back on my feet. The company I was working for kept harassing me because I was black, trying to claim I was incompetent. Finally, in 1976, they fired me. However, I wasn't about to let this keep me down.

"I saw an ad for Clement E. Stone's insurance sales training program, and I signed up for that. I left after four days, because I knew it wasn't what I wanted, but the motivational training was really helpful to me. I'm a strong believer in motivation and positive mental attitude as keys to success. If you believe in yourself, I feel you can achieve anything you set out to do.

"About this time, Home Savings started a training program for appraisers, so I enrolled in that. I'd already dealt a lot with real estate as a claims adjuster handling claims involving real property, so I knew something about it, and I had also read a lot of books about real estate and real estate investing, so I was convinced it was a good field to get into. This was in 1976.

"Around this same time I also took Mark O. Haroldsen's (*Wake Up the Financial Genius Inside You*) seminar on real estate investing and took a gamble and bought my first investment property. I had been around real estate long enough, both as a claims adjuster and an appraiser, to know that a lot of people were making big money as investors, and Mark Haroldsen's seminar convinced me I could do it, too, so I decided it was time to start.

Investing With No Credit

"I found a house where I was able to assume the seller's FHA (Federal Housing Administration, a division of the Department of Housing and Urban Development) loan at a low interest rate. FHA loans are automatically assumable. The buyer doesn't have to qualify, pass a credit check, or even submit an application. You just pay a small assumption fee, and that's it. No one can turn you down or stop you from taking over the loan as long as you pay the assumption fee and can make the monthly payments.

"This meant that my bankruptcy and my nonexistent credit rating didn't matter. The only problem was that the seller wanted $38,000 for the house, and the loan was for only $28,000. The seller wanted the $10,000 difference in cash, and I didn't have it.

"I knew the seller wanted to get rid of the house quickly, so I persuaded him that his asking price and terms weren't realistic, given the price of other homes in the area, and I convinced him to accept $33,000 with only $5,000 down.

"I borrowed the $5,000 on a short term basis from someone I knew, and then as soon as the deal closed escrow, I went to a hard money mortgage broker. That's the kind who charges a slightly higher rate of interest and a higher-than-normal loan fee, but loans money on the basis of the property's value, not the borrower's credit rating. I got a second mortgage for $4,000, so then I only had $1,000 tied up in the property.

"I was out looking at houses every day appraising them. I knew what was on the market and where the good buys were, so it wasn't long before I was able to pick up a second house, this time for $19,500, with $1,500 down. I immediately put a second mortgage on that one, too, got more back than I had put into it, and paid back the $5,000 I had started with.

"Bankruptcy had forced me to be creative; since I couldn't get new loans through banks, I took advantage of that fact and explored some of the available alternatives. I had a lot of experience dealing with property, and I owned two houses now, but I still had no money. So I found a partner who did, and bought my third house with him.

"The price was $47,000, with a $43,000 assumable loan, so my partner put up $5,000 cash, while I put up my time, talent and experience.

"This worked out well for both of us, and we bought a second house together. The seller wanted $38,000 for this one, and there was a $30,000 assumable loan. I talked him down to $33,000, and my partner put up $3,000 cash for the down payment.

"While this was going on, I quit my job with Home Savings after being with them for about six months, and decided to go off on my own. I spent the next six months pounding the pavements, hitting all the lenders in the Fresno area who were too small to have their own staff appraisers, trying to find work on a freelance basis, building up contacts, before I finally got established. This taught me a lot about determination, and it also gave me a chance to increase my knowledge of the area and the local moneylenders. This was extremely valuable to me in pursuing my investment goals.

"I found a fifth house I wanted to buy, this time all by myself. The seller wanted $33,000, but the property was free and clear. There was no loan to assume. I had to get a new loan instead, so I went to a hard money mortgage broker again and got a $20,000 first mortgage against the house so the seller would get a substantial cash down payment out of the deal. Then I got the seller to carry back a second mortgage for $15,000. That way I got $2,000 cash for buying the property, and the seller got $18,000 in cash for selling it to me, plus a monthly income from the second mortgage he was carrying, so everyone was happy.

Never Give Up

"It was Mark Haroldsen and Bill Greene—especially Bill Greene—who helped me by showing me *how*. My wife helped me *do it*. We work together as a team, and I couldn't have done it without her.

"I found houses through real estate agents, newspapers, leads from people I knew, any way I could. By 1978 I was going so strong that I bought $1.7 million worth of property within 8 months.

"I'm a very positive person. I just stuck with it and refused to get discouraged. The one snag I hit was management. Neither my wife nor I like managing property, and we had no luck with professional management companies because there don't seem to be any good ones, at least not here in the Fresno area. But we didn't let that stop us, either.

"I bought mainly single family houses in working class areas. They are easy to rent and easy to sell or refinance when we need cash. I read a lot of books about how to manage property; I have over $20,000 worth of investment and motivational books at home. And I *worked* at it along with my wife.

"I wouldn't buy anything without a positive cash flow, so I was able to absorb the losses when I had vacancies. I refinanced some properties, sold others, and put all the money back into more property. The values kept going up and up until I became a millionaire. Then I wrote a book, called *How To Make Money 24 Hours A Day*, and published it myself.

"The book has done quite well, and now I devote most of my time to writing, lecturing and giving seminars, and am not buying real estate as aggressively. We still have about $1 million worth of equity, but we have also sold a lot of our properties and put the money into gold and other commodities which don't require any management so that I can put my energies into other things.

"I'm working on a new book on positive mental attitude, called *Strive to Arrive*, and I'm also doing a lot of lecturing and personal appearances. My wife edits my books for me and schedules my appearances, so neither one of us has that much time right now to spend looking for, or managing, property, and we don't need to any more.

"Now that we have some money there are all sorts of opportunities open to us. But when we were starting out, real estate was about the only one. It's still the easiest way I know for a poor person to get ahead in the world. You just have to be creative, honest and hardworking.

"You have to have faith in yourself and just get out there and *do it*. If I could do it after going bankrupt, then anybody else can too, if they really *want* to. That's the message I'm trying to get across in my lectures and in my new book: never give up."

18

Buying Low in a Sellers's Market
Simon Lantzer

Passing up good buys because they don't suit his own taste has never been a problem for Simon Lantzer of Oakland, California. He owns more than twenty rental properties, and he has never yet bought one he would want to live in. His houses are in a poor area of the inner city. "When I first started," he says with a laugh, "I was afraid to get out of the car. Now I know almost everybody on every block where I own a house, and I never worry about walking around there."

Simon saw the potential in real estate when he sold his own first home—a small, three-bedroom his family had outgrown—for far more than he thought it was worth. He got $65,000 for the house he had bought for $28,500 only four years earlier. That struck Simon as a neat little profit; and it allowed his family to move to a larger, $95,000 house on a secluded one-acre site with plenty of money for the down payment. Not bad for someone who had always lived in rented apartments.

In more than one way it was the move to this new, more expensive house which propelled Simon into the world of real estate investments. Even with the equity from his previous home as a down payment, the mortgage on his new home was higher than his old one. He needed some extra income to help with his bills, so he decided to buy a cheap house or two, the kind that would rent for more than the mortgage payments would cost him.

His interest in real estate had been awakened, and Simon went to his first investment seminar, given by a local attorney and real estate broker named John Beck. After that, Simon knew real estate was the way for him to go, because he could get not only income, but tax benefits as well. He decided he would have to buy in the less desirable parts of town because the good areas were so overpriced that investors had to subsidize any rentals they bought. In order to avoid negative cash flow, Simon would have had to put up a substantial amount of cash down payment—as much as 40 to 50 percent of the purchase price—and he did not want that type of investment. He wanted to leverage his money, putting down as little as possible.

By the mid-1970's you couldn't get a house in a nice, middle class neighborhood unless you could put down a substantial down payment, usually at least 20 percent. Then you had to submit credit applications, tax returns, and pay bank loan fees. There were very few assumable loans available, and not many owners who were willing to compromise on the price and terms—or even take back a second mortgage. They didn't have to accommodate the buyer in any way, since good properties were being snapped up almost as soon as they hit the market—many with multiple offers for more than the asking price. It was a seller's market all the way, and a buyer had to have plenty of money just to play the game.

On the other hand, Simon knew he did not want to invest in any really bad areas where he was likely to have trouble with vandalism and tenants who didn't pay their rent, so he decided to find a real estate agent to help him. He called several whose names he found in the want ads, and finally talked to one who seemed to understand what he wanted to do and was willing to work with Simon to find the kind of property he was looking for.

Making the Right Buys

"If I'd had enough money to buy decent properties in decent areas," Simon recalls, "I probably never would have bothered with real estate in the first place. I'm an electrical engineer by training, and I had my own electronics business, but things were slow, and it wasn't bringing in enough money. At that point I was mostly interested in expanding my income, not sheltering it, so I only wanted properties with positive cash flow."

So while Simon had no interest in being a slumlord, his houses were usually the neighborhood eyesores. Simon would buy them cheaply, fix them up, and then rent them out. Not only was he making money, but he was performing a public service, restoring properties. Before he rehabilitated them, some of his houses were barely liveable.

"I paid ten to fifteen thousand dollars for most of them, usually with anywhere from five hundred to a few thousand down. But sometimes if I got something really cheap, I would even pay cash, and then get a loan after I fixed it up. I bought my first investment house in August, 1977. It was an FHA assumption, where I bought the house for $12,800 and assumed a $9,800 loan with $3,000 down. I got it painted, and then, six months later, I got a second mortgage for $4,500. I walked away with $1,500 cash, and still had positive cash flow."

Simon picked up a lot of these FHA and VA assumptions, but instead of sitting there with a low mortgage at a low interest rate, he usually continued to fix the places up and then refinance them. For instance, a run-down house with three bedrooms was going for $20,000 at that time (1977). Simon would offer the owner $15,000: $3,000 cash, and Simon assumed a $12,000 loan at 8 percent interest, with payments of $105 a month, including taxes and insurance. Simon had a full-time handyman working for him, so he could put the house in good shape for another $2,000 or so and then rent it out for $350 a month. As soon as the house was rented, he would go to a bank and get a loan for $20,000. Even at the new interest rate of 9¼ percent, his payments were still less than $200 a month, so he had $150 a month income and his down payment back, too.

Once the $12,000 FHA loan was paid off, Simon still had $8,000 cash. Take out five thousand for his down payment and his investment in improving the property, another thousand for closing costs, and he still had $2,000 more than he put into the property, and he was ready to buy another one. All this took three to six months.

Of course, not every property yielded instant cash returns, but they each provided positive cash flow of at least $100 a month, and began to appreciate steadily once they were put into liveable condition. At first the cash flow was modest, but as Simon kept buying properties, the amount kept growing, until he now has an income of about $40,000 a year from his properties alone, all of it tax free.

Keeping It Simple

"Almost all my properties are rented under Section 8 (the federal subsidized rent program for low income families)," Simon relates, "because that way, I'm guaranteed that I'll get my rent. The tenants pay part of it themselves—up to 25 percent of their income—and the city pays the rest, or even all of it in some cases. Someone from the city comes in and inspects the place before the tenant moves in, and takes an inventory. Then, if anything is stolen or broken when the tenants move out, the city has to pay for it. Another advantage is the rent. Section 8 isn't profitable for a landlord with a nice rental house in a good middle class area, because he can get more rent on the open market, but in the neighborhoods where I bought, Section 8 was paying better than anybody. Section 8 pays the same amount for a 2-bedroom house in a ghetto area as it will for a luxury home in a rich neighborhood. The rent is based on the property, not the area.

"I just give tenants twelve stamped envelopes—one for each month—with the address of my Post Office Box, so they can send me their portion of the rent. I usually get it right on time with no trouble. I've found that if you give people a decent place to live and you help them keep the place up by fixing anything that goes wrong, they appreciate it. A lot of them are so used to bad landlords that they thank me any time I do anything to improve the place."

Simon tries to make his houses attractive without spending a great deal of money. He finds that painting, putting in new carpeting and other cosmetic touches like that bring back more than they cost, but he rarely puts in new kitchens or gets involved with other types of expensive renovations. Clean, but simple, has been the winning formula for him.

"Once I saw how easy it was," Simon now says, "once I realized I was not going to get mugged or robbed just because I was a white person in a black neighborhood, I just kept going. It was fun, and it was so easy it practically fell into my lap. I didn't even know what I was doing. I bought one house for $5,500, spent a couple of thousand fixing it up, and then got a loan against it for $20,000.

"I had a handyman who used to do odd jobs in my business, so once I got my first couple of houses I let him fix them up for me, and he even became one of my tenants. He came to me one day and said he had found a house for sale that he wanted to live in. He said if I would buy it, he would fix it up and pay me $250 a month rent, which I could take out of the money I paid him to work for me.

"So I bought the place for $20,000, and gave him a couple of hundred dollars more for materials. I probably could have gotten more rent from somebody else, but this made it convenient for both of us, and I was still coming out ahead. The rent he paid covered the payments, I didn't have to pay him for fixing the place, and I always knew where to get in touch with him."

A Good Word for a Good Agent

Simon's real estate agent knows the area and keeps him aware of any good buys as soon as they hit the market. Simon has never really worked with anyone else—except when he buys property elsewhere—and has never felt a need to do so. He feels that by sticking with the same agent over the years he gets better service, such as being the first one to be called when a hot deal becomes available, instead of being on the bottom of several agents' client lists, the last one to be called after everyone else has turned a property down. He also considers his agent a friend, someone he can trust to deal fairly and honestly with him and give him sound advice, rather than hustling him into buying questionable properties just to generate commissions.

Of course, he does not rely solely on his agent's judgment. Once Simon had his first three rentals and realized he had indeed caught on to something good, he began trying to learn as much about real estate as he could. He read books on real estate investment and attended seminars by local realtors Ralph Hines and Dave Chodack, as well as others by well-known investment experts such as Bill "Tycoon" Greene and Albert Lowry and William Nickerson, in order to pick up any tips he could use. After that, he began to feel more confident, and his investment program expanded even faster.

"My agent's been good to me," he says. "He's shown me many good deals, and I've bought most of them and have made a lot of money, so I trust his judgment. But I had to trust my own judgment, too, in order to feel comfortable, and that meant learning all I could about real estate investing. Everybody you talk to in this business has helpful ideas, and I try to learn as much as I can from all of them. No one person has thought of everything there is to know, but I think Bill Greene helped me the most. He gave me his phone number, and I used to call him when I had problems. For instance, I found a duplex I wanted to buy, but it had a termite report calling for eight thousand dollars' worth of work. That seemed like a lot to me, so I went through the house with the termite man. I put on a pair of coveralls and took a flashlight and asked him to show me where the $8,000 worth of work was. He pointed out some termite tubes and showed me where the termites were eating into the wood underneath the house, but it still didn't look like $8,000 of work. 'Well,' he said to me, 'you come and talk to us after the close of escrow and we can knock that price down a little. The termites are not that big a problem. They won't eat the whole house away, or anything. They'll just eat the juiciest parts and then they'll leave.

"That's what he said to me. But this was when I was just getting started—I owned three or four rental houses, I can't remember which—and so I still wasn't sure what to do. I called Bill Greene and told him the situation, and he told me it was a perfect situation and I shouldn't worry about it, but just go ahead and buy the property 'as is.' He told me to ask the seller for a credit back for the termite work rather than taking it off the sales price, because that way I could get a bigger loan and put up a smaller down payment. I followed his advice, and when the escrow closed I got three thousand dollars back in cash.

"All my loans were through Home Savings, and they never required a termite report anyway, so that made it easy. I would have my handyman do what was important, and just ignore the rest. Termite companies put a lot of unnecessary things on their reports, and they charge a minimum of $35 an hour, so I saved a lot of money by going around them."

Using equity in one house to pay for the down payment and repairs on the next, Simon kept adding to his string of properties. His agent would find them, his handyman would fix them, and then Simon would rent them out at a profit. It became a comfortable, prosperous pattern for all three of them.

Good Judgment and Experience Pay Off

"I had two rules," Simon states. "I would stay away from anything in an extremely poor area. I was always looking for the worst house in the neighborhood, not the best, because it's a lot easier to improve your own property and bring it up to the quality of the other houses than to bring the whole neighborhood up to match. And I would stay away from places which needed really extensive repairs. Plumbing, painting, simple carpentry work, my handyman could do, and wiring I could do myself. But I wouldn't get involved with a house which needed a whole new foundation or anything which meant bringing in a contractor and a whole construction crew, because that usually meant too much money out of my pocket and having the place empty for too long, with no rent. A couple of times I got involved in minor remodeling, but only if my handyman could do it and it was going to bring in a lot more rent when I was done."

The other thing he learned by experience was to stick with single family houses and duplexes. He tried a couple of larger properties, but didn't like them. He found the larger the building, the harder it was to find only the type of good tenants he wanted, and the harder it was to keep up. He also found that larger buildings, at least in the areas where he bought property, did not appreciate as quickly as duplexes and single family homes, and were not as easy to borrow against.

As for fancy extras such as decks or hot tubs, fireplaces and stained glass windows, he never got into that, since common sense told him his tenants could only afford to pay so much, no matter how nicely he fixed the place up. Therefore, he left the frills to those who could afford to buy in wealthier neighborhoods. He wanted to make his properties attractive, but he didn't want to waste money on over-improving them.

"Even before I took any courses or read any books," Simon points out, "I had the sense to realize that my tenants' taste was not always going to match my own, so I try to fix up a house when I buy it, make it clean and attractive, but I leave the decorating to the tenants."

After his original handyman left the area, Simon tried a succession of low-priced "Mr. Fix-its," but came away dissatisfied. Now he has a man he pays ten dollars an hour on a full-time basis, and feels it is worth the additional cost to have someone who is always there on time, does his work conscientiously, knows what he is doing, and is not about to pick up and disappear on a sudden whim. Simon has too many properties now, and too many other things on his mind, to be worrying about whether his properties are being well maintained. If ten dollars an hour is what it costs to achieve this peace of mind, Simon considers it well worth it.

The one aspect of buying and owning property which Simon has never delegated to anyone else is the actual management. He does that himself. He picks all his own tenants, and goes around personally to collect the rent on the rare occasions when it is late, or when tenants have a complaint the handyman can't take care of. It isn't that he objects to spending the money for a manager, but he has heard only complaints from others who use them, and he has reduced his management problems to a minimum anyway. Therefore, it is easier for him, and better for landlord-tenant relations, to take care of them himself. He feels that when you know your tenants and they know you, it is far more human than being an absentee landlord no one ever sees, represented by a manager with no personal interest in the property.

After five years, though, Simon is looking around for other areas to invest in. "The houses I used to buy for $10,000 or $15,000 now sell for $50,000 and $60,000, and won't even pay for themselves at today's rates—and the shortage of investment money has changed the whole game. I used to deal with one large savings and loan. I knew the people there, and at one time I had many different loans with them, all supposedly owner-occupied so I could borrow up to 90 percent of the value. Now you can't do that anymore."

And Simon Lantzer is not really hungry enough any more to look for new areas where he could still get positive cash flow. He has a good income, and his existing houses have already made him a wealthy man, so he is content to hold on to what he has for now and buy only what looks good to him.

High interest and tight money haven't knocked Simon out of the game, they have just caused him to change his emphasis. The income from his houses not only enabled him to expand his original electronics business, but to start two others as well, so he is now in the comfortable position of needing some negative cash flow as a tax write-off.

"My wife wanted a place in the country where the kids could have horses," he says, "maybe ten acres or so, but I guess I got a little bit carried away. It costs me close to three thousand a month."

What Simon bought was a total of 240 acres, about two hours north of San Francisco. The land is divided into six 40-acre parcels, and Simon started off by buying one parcel. Then, when he found he could get options on the other parcels at a little over $1,000 an acre, for $100 apiece, he decided to take a chance. The options were for six months, and by the time they came due, a similar parcel sold for $80,000—$2,000 an acre.

Needless to say, Simon exercised his rights to buy all six parcels he had tied up, with the owner carrying at a good interest rate, and Simon putting up a modest down payment. He already has one on the market for $86,000—enough to cover the down payment on all six—and is holding on to the other five. He plans to build some houses and sell them at a profit, too.

Simon's original plan was to build up his holdings to twenty-five houses, and then hold them for at least five years without selling anything. Circumstances have caused him to stop at twenty-one temporarily, but as soon as he decides when the next big price jumps are likely to be, he'll be buying more. His houses have already doubled, or more, in value—all in four years as of August, 1981, and he knows they will go up in price again as soon as interest rates come down, so he's comfortably waiting, taking opportunities as he finds them.

19

Millions from Rentals and Wrap-Arounds
Charles Carrithers

Almost everyone in Newport News, Virginia, knows Charles Carrithers. And those who don't know him, probably know of him. After all, he is one of the town's more prominent and successful citizens. He has his own real estate brokerage company, his own property management company, and over 400 rental properties, mostly single family homes, worth an average of $30,000 to $35,000 each.

He is not one of those big spenders, but he lives well, and sees no reason to hide it. Middle class homes in the area average $55,000 or so in price. The Carrithers place is a big five-bedroom house on a large plot of land overlooking the James River, and it is valued at around $250,000. For the past 20 years, Charles Carrithers has been a one-man growth industry, making money almost faster than he can spend it.

But those who have been around long enough remember a different Charles Carrithers...

"I started around 1957 or '58," he says. "I was selling insurance, and not doing all that well. Then one day, a client called me up and told me he had this rental house he was sick of dealing with. He'd had the thing for awhile, and he was just tired of it. He didn't like being a landlord. And he told me I could have the house if I wanted it, if I'd give him five hundred dollars and assume his 4.5 percent VA loan.

"Well, he told me what the payments were, and I did some checking. I found out I could rent the house out for about $25 more than it would cost me each month, and that sounded good to me. I mean, I was only making $75 a week, so $25 was a lot of money. I figured if I could get about five rental houses like that, I would be okay."

So now Charles Carrithers was in the rental business. He was a landlord. But he could not afford to keep his $500 tied up, so he had to sell the house. He sold it for $2,000 more than he had paid for it, with $500 down and a wrap-around loan at 6 percent. The underlying loan was a VA assumption which he had taken over at 4½ percent when he bought the house, so he now had a small income each month—the difference between the 6 percent interest he was taking in, and the 4½ percent he was paying out.

Turning Hard Times To Good Times

Times were hard in those days. There was a lot of unemployment, and a lot of houses for sale, but no buyers. Charles Carrithers began buying. People tried to talk him out of it, friends and relatives told him he was crazy, but he kept buying houses and either renting them out, or cleaning them up a little and then selling with low down payments and wrap-around loans. For $500 down and six percent interest with no loan fees, people would buy, even in hard times, and there were always people who needed a place to rent, so Charles Carrithers prospered.

"Interest on new loans was about seven percent by then," he says, "so I was picking up VA and FHA assumptions at four or four and a half percent. Then when I offered them to other people on a wrap-around loan at six percent, it was still a good deal for the buyers.

"There were a lot of people who lost their jobs, and also, we have a lot of military people who get transferred and have to sell, so I would pick up houses cheaply and then put ads in the paper right away. I used to run two ads: one to rent a house, and one to sell it. If I had $500 or so tied up in a house, I couldn't afford to let it sit there vacant, so whoever came along first, buyer or renter, that's who got it. Either way, I got some income out of it each month, and that was what I was after."

And on it went. From the late '50's through the early '60's Charles sold insurance for a living and dabbled in real estate on the side. He took the stoves and refrigerators out of the houses he bought and sold them to second hand appliance dealers before renting or reselling the houses. That way he got a couple of hundred dollars back almost immediately, since the houses and the appliances were generally fairly new and in good condition. It all went back into property.

"Most people don't make it," he says, "because they don't have the self-discipline. Something comes along that they want, like a car or a boat, and they start spending their money instead of pyramiding it. I'm not one of those big spenders."

By 1965, he was making more money in real estate than he was in insurance, and enjoying real estate more, too. By 1967, he quit the insurance business entirely, went into real estate full time, and became a broker. Now, he feels that may have been his one mistake.

"Being a broker restricts me," he says. "I don't know that it was such a good idea getting a license. I guess at the time, I thought it would help me make more money and that's why I did it, but now, I don't know.

"I run ads in the newspaper all the time as a broker and an investor, and when somebody calls me up and they want to sell a house, I say to them, 'Okay now, am I coming out there as a buyer or as a broker? I've got to know which hat I'll be wearing so I'll know how to behave. I mean, if I'm a buyer, then I'm looking out for my interests and you would be looking out for yours, but if I'm a broker, then I'm looking out for your interests, and that's a different story.'

"Sometimes I think I would make more money without the license. This way, I think some people are afraid to deal with me because they think I know so much more than they do. If I had it to do again, I don't know if I would get the license or not."

Management

The one area where it definitely has helped Charles to have a real estate license is in managing his properties. He has a management company which takes care of all his properties, as well as managing others for clients. This affords him the luxury of full-time maintenance crews, with all the necessary equipment.

It is a business, and that is the way he runs it. He no longer believes in getting friendly with tenants, because he's been burned too many times and had too many bad experiences, but he does treat his renters fairly and professionally. As long as they pay their rent on time and maintain the house in reasonably good condition, he has a contract with them and he strives to hold up his end. If something goes wrong, he takes care of it.

"I know a lot of people use those leases where the tenant is responsible for any small repairs, but I don't believe in that. I figure I'm in the rental business, so it's up to me to take care of it. Oh, sure, sometimes I use discounted leases, lease options, net leases, etc. But generally I take care of any problems."

He also cleans up a house each time a tenant moves out, to get it fresh and ready for the new tenant. He feels he gets his houses rented faster that way, gets more rent, and also gets a better class of tenants.

Charles Carrithers, landlord, keeps ads running in the newspaper, along with Charles Carrithers, real estate broker, and Charles Carrithers, investor. He gets his tenants that way, and also through walk-ins and call-ins. Prospective tenants have to pass a credit and reference check to weed out the bad ones, and then they are signed to a strong lease. Everyone has to put up a good security deposit. If they have pets, the deposit is doubled. Having a separate company to handle all this helps keep it an arm's length, businesslike transaction.

"I don't want to be friendly with my tenants," Charles Carrithers says. "The first time they come to me and they say, 'Can I ask you a favor?' I say, 'Sure. As long as you don't want my money, my time, or my wife.' Now that doesn't leave much else, does it? So what else could they want? It lets them know right away where we stand. As long as they pay their rent on time and keep the place up, I'll leave them alone. I expect them to do the same for me."

Built In Tenants

Charles Carrithers believes in being businesslike, but he is no hard-hearted profiteer. When someone stops meeting the payments on a loan he is holding, he does not foreclose on them immediately and throw them out the way many lenders do. In fact, he tries very hard not to foreclose at all. If somebody absolutely can't make their payments or catch up with what they owe, Charles will take title to the property and hold it, rather than formally foreclosing and hurting the other person's credit rating. Then he will usually allow them to continue living in the house as renters. He's gotten many houses this way, with built-in tenants to sweeten the deal.

Nowadays, Charles can also afford to pay cash for houses he can get for well below market value. He buys foreclosures and distress properties, where the owners have to sell in a hurry. Some he rents out; others he resells at a higher price in order to get his cash out.

He is now a multimillionaire, and his net worth will be growing by a million a year soon. His biggest problem is where to put it all. "It's gotten to the point where I can't even spend the interest," he says, "on the loans I'm carrying. I've got so many of them, there's some I'm trying to terminate. Some of the old wrap-around loans I made fifteen, twenty years ago, aren't even paying enough to justify the bookkeeping. It's just not worth it, keeping track of them."

What Charles Carrithers does keep track of is the latest developments and trends in real estate. He goes to seminars and exchange groups locally and around the country to learn more. Twenty years of experience in buying and renting houses has taught him most of what he knows, and he finds that most seminar leaders don't have too much to teach him; but usually he does get one or two new ideas, a new twist on an old technique, or whatever, and that makes it worthwhile. In real estate, one small idea can easily be worth $500 or $1,000, and you can use it again and again.

Besides that, seminars and conventions are great places to meet friends and make contacts, and Charles Carrithers enjoys them. He enjoys almost everything to do with real estate investing. It gives him the freedom to do what he wants to do, when he wants to do it, and he enjoys traveling, but not enough to buy many out-of-town properties—except for an occasional partnership.

"I know people and I have contacts all over the country," he says, "and I own property from New York to Florida. But I like to stick mainly to my own backyard. There's fewer problems that way. You buy property out of town and you can never find good management. Besides, I don't like to fool around with what I don't know. That's why I don't buy commercial property or get involved in big deals. I don't know commercial property, and I'm a little afraid of it. And in big deals I wouldn't have the same control I have with single family houses.

"Individual homes are also the most liquid, and I know I can always rent them or sell them to somebody as long as I carry the loan. A lot of people are afraid to do that, but not me. If I get the house back because somebody doesn't meet their payments, that's just fine. After all, I'm in the rental business, so I don't mind. I'll either rent it back to the former buyer or rent it to somebody else."

Charles Carrithers doesn't think there are any special secrets to what he's done, besides working hard and pyramiding his earnings. He says that when he started he had no real idea of what he was doing. He wasn't working with an agent, just looking through the papers on his own, and all he knew was that he wanted positive cash flow and to try to get back his original investment within eighteen months.

He has, of course, learned quite a bit since then, but he says the main thing is that you can buy property and make money at *any* time. Conditions will vary from time to time and place to place, but there are always opportunities in any kind of market if you are creative and use your imagination.

People need a place to live, and sooner or later, one way or another, property will increase in value. Times such as those we're going through now don't scare Charles Carrithers. He looks confidently toward the future, wheeling and dealing, looking for new opportunities. His big worry is not losing what he has because of a sudden crash, but planning his estate so that it doesn't all go to the lawyers and the tax collector.

"If I don't find someone to help me figure out my estate," he says, "I figure the vultures will wind up getting about $5 million. Yes sir, I sure think real estate is great. It has been good to me."

20

Success and The Single Woman
Jennifer Steves

"Tell me the truth," said one of the successful investors I interviewed (Nick Koon, of Columbus, Ohio, Chapter 14). "Didn't you find there is one thing all the people you've talked to have in common? Wouldn't you say they are all single-minded? That they set their minds on one thing and then work at it to the exclusion of almost everything else? That they set their goals and then just work like crazy to get there?"

This question was on my mind as I interviewed Jennifer Steves of Philadelphia, Pennsylvania. By anyone's standards, she is successful. She heads four separate corporations dealing in real estate investments, and owns thirty properties in a rapidly gentrifying area near downtown Philadelphia, and adjacent to the University of Pennsylvania, as well as buildable land in Hawaii and British Columbia, Canada. She receives hundreds of letters each month from people who have seen her on Phil Donahue (or one of the other dozen or so TV talk shows on which she has been featured), in *Money Magazine*, or on the front page of *The Wall Street Journal*, and a publisher has asked her to write a book.

Yet she hardly comes across as single minded, or obsessively devoted to making money. A bright, personable blonde in her mid-30's, she is attractive and feminine; not exactly the hard-bitten millionaire business woman.

"Some people who don't know me very well think all I do is play. They never see me working, so they think I just travel a lot," she says.

"But if they saw me when I *am* working, they would realize it's not that way. When I work, I do it very intensively, and I get a lot done. Most of my travelling is for business.

"And I have good people working with me and for me, so they can usually carry on by themselves when I'm not around.

"I love what I'm doing, so for me, there's no distinct line between business and pleasure. I own land in Hawaii and Canada, and I go there to vacation, but then I am constantly looking around and finding good buys. I meet people, and they decide to invest money with me; I was even in Egypt recently, working on a film about women in business. There are so many opportunities opening up for me that my only long term goals right now are to go on enjoying my life and letting other women know it can be done. I want all people to know that, but especially women, because they need it more; they often lack confidence, and so they never realize their potential. I don't know what my exact income is, but it provides a very interesting life-style. It's great."

From Humble Beginnings

But Jennifer Steves' life was not always like that. Although her mother happens also to be a self-made real estate millionaire in Houston, Texas, Jennifer's family was far from wealthy when she was growing up. Her father was an Episcopal priest, and her mother a housewife and church organist, and Jennifer and her two brothers learned to work for whatever they wanted; nothing was handed to them unless they earned it first.

When she was 21, Jennifer got married, but that was hardly the beginning of the life she enjoys now. After the wedding, she and her husband moved from Houston to Philadelphia, and for the next five years they got by on her salary as a social worker, while he pursued his Ph.D. at the Wharton School of Business at the University of Pennsylvania.

During this time period, she had little time, energy or direction to think about creating an independent business empire of her own; it was not until her divorce, in 1973, that Jennifer even got involved with her first real estate venture.

"I was on my own, and I felt a need to be independent," she says, "so I took the little bit of money I had, about four thousand dollars, and bought a house. It was a run-down old Victorian, and I fixed it up myself to save money. I did almost everything except the electrical work, because that was the only way I could afford to do it. I even knocked out walls myself and personally did most of the heavy remodeling.

"The house was in the University City area, right near the University of Pennsylvania and downtown Philadelphia, and a lot of the people I knew around there were doing the same thing, because that was the only way most of us could afford houses. So I had people I could call on for advice, but I still had to learn most of it as I worked, which was after my regular job hours and on weekends.

"I also knew it was possible to make money in real estate, since by that point, my mother was already fairly successful, and I did think of that, too, even though I really bought the house to live in.

"I wanted to be independent, to be able to support myself without being dependent on a man. It's not that I'm against men, because I'm not. I love men, but I just don't see any need to be financially dependent on them. If I'm dependent on a man emotionally, that's one thing, but it has nothing to do with my business.

"That's what makes real estate so great. It's probably the least discriminatory field for women, because you make all the decisions on design, construction, purchasing, etc. I've never really felt discriminated against because I'm a woman. I just go to the bank, show them my plans, and I've always been judged on that and on my track record, the projects I've already done.

"There was one time I was turned down for a loan, and that was probably because I was a woman. In any case, I didn't feel I had gotten a fair hearing from the man who handled my application, so I went to the higher-ups at the bank and told them I felt I hadn't been judged fairly on my past performance, and I indicated I would complain to the Equal Opportunity Commission.

"I got the loan.

"Aside from that one time, I've never really had a problem obtaining financing. When I was finished with my first house, it was worth about $70,000. I got a new mortgage loan against it for $35,000 and bought five more houses in the same neighborhood, but I didn't quit my job. Real estate was still a part-time venture for me at that time; but from then on, I've never had less than six houses I was working on at once.

Expanding the Business

"Of course, I couldn't do it all by myself anymore, so I started hiring friends to help me. I had lived in that neighborhood for a long time, so I knew a lot of people with different skills. I frequently hire friends. Even today, most of the people who work for me are friends, people I care about, people who care about me.

"It works out very nicely. We all enjoy working together, and the work gets done the way I want it done.

"Sometimes, when I was starting, I put too much work into a place and too much money. I bring things up to resale quality, with everything gleaming, and then rent them out. Maybe I should wait and not put so much money or work into them until I am ready to sell them in a few years. But on the other hand, I get better rents this way, and a better class of tenants."

Her tenants are mainly students or young professionals: college professors, lawyers, anyone who wants to be close to the university and/or downtown, and who is willing and able to pay $450 to $800 or more per month for a house or apartment. Often, they are single, and several of them will split the rent. They expect the best, and they're paying for it, so Jennifer goes out of her way to accommodate them.

"I look for buildings with character," she says, "stained glass windows, old wood, exposed brick, things that can make a place special. Also, I stay on top of maintenance problems and try to fix things as soon as they go wrong. Some of my tenants are kind of picky—they expect everything to be perfect—but they have a right to be that way, because they're paying high rents, and they keep the property in good condition. That way, the neighborhood improves, and my property appreciates faster, and I've rarely had to advertise for tenants. They usually seek me out.

"Some buildings only need painting and plastering and cleaning up. With other buildings, I have to tear out walls and change the number of units, and do whatever I think will increase the resale value.

"Once I decided I was interested in real estate, I took a course at Temple University's Real Estate Institute from Jay Lamont, who inspired me to go on in investment real estate. I didn't take the course to get my license as an agent but just to find out what I was doing.

"I don't believe in highly leveraging my properties at today's interest rates. I know I could build up more equity that way, and do it faster, but I like to keep at least 50 percent equity in anything that I hold on to as a rental. That way I can get through some hard times without getting caught in a cash squeeze.

"Instead, I try to use what I learned by buying cheaply, and doing a good job of restoring and renovating. Most of the houses I've bought in recent years have been vacant shells, and I've had to replace everything—plumbing, wiring, roofs, furnaces, the works—in order to make them liveable, so I'm helping to provide housing and improve the area.

"I've rarely been criticized for my rents by any of my tenants or anyone else in the neighborhood. In spite of all the negative talk about gentrification—middle class professionals (the "gentry") moving into poor minority neighborhoods and displacing the residents by driving up prices and rents—I feel I'm doing something positive for the city.

"These changing neighborhoods can't stand still. Older buildings need maintenance, and that costs money and drives up rents. If they don't get maintenance, the older buildings fall apart, and the neighborhood falls apart with them. People like me are helping to keep the neighborhood alive, and we're keeping people and tax money in the city and helping to bring some money into the neighborhood. Without the middle class, the city willl die, and now that neighborhoods like University City are being renovated, young professionals and working people are starting to move back from the suburbs, not necessarily displacing the existing residents, but taking over properties which were lying vacant and abandoned.

Caring About People

"I was a social worker for ten years, and I haven't lost that attitude. I care about people, and I care what happens to the neighborhood. I'm not one of those people who are just out to make a fast buck and run. In some ways, I still think like a social worker. Of course, that has caused occasional problems for me, especially when I was first starting out, but I've just had to learn how to deal with it.

"For instance, the first tenants I ever had went four months without paying rent and I had let them move in without paying any deposit money. Then I had one woman living in one of my apartments for a whole year without paying rent. She had children, and so I felt sorry for her and I didn't know what to do.

"Finally, my mother came to visit me, and I was upset, so I told her about it. My mother just looked at me and said, 'You're just going to have to talk to her and explain to her that she has to leave.' So my mother talked to the woman for me, and sure enough, she moved out.

"Then another time a savvy squatter moved into an abandoned building that I had bought, and he changed all the locks so we couldn't get in to renovate. I knew it could be a long, drawn-out, painful process to get him out legally, so instead I just offered him $300 cash if he would leave, and he got out. After that, I learned to have somebody stay in vacant buildings while I worked on them so squatters couldn't take root in the first place.

"I had to learn all these things the hard way, because I had absolutely no background in business when I started. Before I became a social worker, I was always involved with the arts and humanities— my B.A. was in English Literature—so I had to teach myself as I went along.

"I bought my first rental house in 1974; by 1975 I owned three houses, and by 1977 I owned thirty. I was also working full time as a social worker. Once I got into buying houses for investment, I started using other people to do most of the labor, but right up until 1979, I was still doing the taxes, bookkeeping, etc. Finally, it all got too big for me to handle. I've renovated about 60 houses since 1975. I've sold half of them to raise capital, and have held on to the rest as rental properties. It was a lot of work, and it finally caught up with me.

"In 1978, I just collapsed from exhaustion, and the doctor told me I couldn't keep it up. He ordered me to quit either real estate or social work, so that's when I had to make a choice.

"I thought about it, and I realized I simply couldn't see myself chasing after street gangs when I was fifty years old. By that point, my real estate deals were already bringing in more money than my salary from social work. But I also knew I couldn't go on doing everything myself, so that's when I began hiring other people to take care of some of the details and paper work.

Employer-Employee Relations

"How did my business grow so big, so fast? Well, for one thing, I wasn't spending any money on myself; it was all going back into my properties. Also, there was just a tremendous demand for good, nicely renovated houses in the downtown Philadelphia area. The main downtown area was already far too expensive for investing by the time I got involved in real estate, and the University City area, where I have done most of my renovations, is just west of there. People have been moving back to Philadelphia from the suburbs, and they all want a nice place to live.

"I knew the area well, and found properties on my own through word of mouth and through agents; any way I could find a good buy. My workmen were people I knew, or people who had been recommended, and there, too, it was a matter of trial and error, seeing which people worked out and which ones didn't.

"I've only had one bad experience. I've never had to fire anyone, but I did use one contractor who just didn't work out, and then when I didn't use him any more after that one project, my buildings started getting sabotaged and things were stolen. It was kind of scary.

"But I couldn't prove anything, so I just waited it out, and eventually things stopped happening just as suddenly as they started. Beyond that, most of it has gone smoothly. I mean, there are always problems, but half the time I don't even know about them. The people who work for me handle them well and only call me if there's a major decision to make.

"I treat my workers well. I don't necessarily pay them a lot more than anyone else would, but I give them interesting work to do and good working conditions. I don't have the time to do it any more, but I used to show up at the rehab job on Friday afternoon and bring a case of beer for everybody, and things like that. Just because it's business, is no reason why we can't all have a good time together.

"I have anywhere from 10 to 50 people working for me at any one time on various projects I have going, plus office help, lawyers and accountants, etc. I've got my own designer, and people who supervise the projects, as well as actual workmen. Most of the time they can run things themselves without even checking with me.

"Without the people I have around me, I wouldn't be able to do all the projects I do at once, and my business wouldn't be as big as it is. They're all just great, and I try to give them as much responsibility as they can handle so they can grow, too. For instance, my personal assistant, Mary Byrnes, has authorization to hire one or two people to work under her any time she thinks she needs them. So far she hasn't done it, but she can do it any time; she doesn't even have to check with me first.

"An interesting thing happened to me a couple of weeks ago. I have a couple of women who come in and clean my house on Saturdays. Most of the time I haven't been around when they've come, and I was feeling guilty, because I hadn't had a chance to get to know them. So, one Saturday, I deliberately stayed around, and then I drove them home when they were finished.

"I knew they were refugees from Vietnam, and they were obviously educated; I figured they were middle class. But then when I started talking with them, I found out they had been extremely wealthy in Vietnam before the Communists took over. They had owned and run a *chain* of expensive hotels!

"It was odd. Here I had grown up relatively poor, and now I was living very well, and these women, who had had much, much more money than I do, were scrubbing my floors. It didn't make sense. I mean, here they have all this experience running a large enterprise, so why should they be wasting that? Why should I waste it? So I'm thinking of creating a new company, a cleaning service for my buildings, and I'll let them run it. They can hire other people to do the actual cleaning, and they can be the managers.

"My people take pride in their work, and so do I, and it pays off. Until recently, when I've started getting into big, multi-million dollar projects, I never even thought primarily of how much money I would make. I thought about what I could do with a house, how nice I could make it, what kind of challenge it would be.

If It Feels Good, Do It

"If a project seemed to have potential and it interested me, I did it, and I guess people like what I've done, because I've never had to seek out investors. *They* always contact *me*, because they're familiar with other buildings I've done, or they've heard about me from other people.

"Some of the houses I've sold in the last couple of years have been to out-of-town investors, people from outside the Philadelphia area, who just want to own something I've been involved with.

"I buy properties that are on the edge of fashionable neighborhoods which are spreading, and then I modernize the heating, because most of these places were built back in the days when fuel was cheap and furnaces did not have to be energy efficient, as long as they kept the house warm. I'll turn several small, dingy rooms into one or two large, airy rooms more suited to the types of renters and buyers I want to attract.

"For instance, I recently took a Victorian home with several small, ugly apartments, and turned it into an elegant, three bedroom, three bath home with a huge atrium with a skylight, and one apartment in the back which rents for $500 a month and helps to offset the monthly payments.

"As time goes on, the rent on that apartment will keep going up, and eventually the owner will be living there almost for free. Naturally, that sort of setup appeals to home buyers, because it gives them the best of all worlds, a home with old-fashioned charm, modern conveniences and extra income to help make it affordable.

"In addition to modernizing my houses and making them energy efficient, I deliberately try to give them charm. After all, if modern efficiency and convenience were all people wanted, they wouldn't need me. They could just go out and buy new houses. But the fine older homes have a certain quality to them which newer homes just can't match. This is what renters and buyers are looking for, what they're willing to pay for, and so this is what I try to bring out and/or to preserve.

"In the beginning, I bought older homes because they were inexpensive and that was all I could afford. Of course, I was attracted to them because of their style, too, and because I knew the neighborhood and saw the potential, but the main factor was the cost. That was also why I started off doing everything myself: because I couldn't afford to hire other people. But as I got better at it, more experienced, and started selling a few of the houses I had renovated, it got easier, and cost became less of a factor. As I got more money to spend, I spent more of it on my renovations—not only hiring other people to help me with the work, but doing more extensive renovation work and constantly trying to improve the quality. John Pierre Lafont has designed and been the contractor on most of my homes.

"Quite often I spend more on the renovations than I do to purchase the property initially. After all, most of these places have been allowed to deteriorate over the years while the neighborhood was going downhill, and no one thought it was worth it to put any money into them. That's why I'm able to pick them up cheaply. But the people I'm renting and selling to don't think of it as a declining neighborhood; they want homes they can take pride in, and it's that kind of positive attitude which is helping to turn things around and increase the value of my investments.

"What makes real estate such a good investment is that all houses are going to keep going up in value. They have to, because all the components—the labor, the materials, the land itself—are all constantly going up in price. And I invest in neighborhoods which are constantly improving and attracting more and more middle and upper middle class young professionals, so prices go up even faster. The $75,000 building I've finished renovating is going to do a lot more to improve the neighborhood—and will appreciate a lot faster—than the run-down building I bought for $25,000.

Life At the Top

"I don't have to work with any investors I don't like. I can be choosy about whose money I invest, and that means a lot to me. But it took a lot of hard work to get to this point.

"That's why there are certain things I still handle myself, or in conjunction with hired experts, rather than just turning everything over to other people. I work with my designer, John Lafont, but I'm the one who has the ultimate responsibility for the way the project will look when it's completed. And even though I buy most of my properties through brokers, I like to deal with the sellers directly when I present an offer so I can explore all aspects of creative financing and terms. Most of the brokers insist on being there, but I'm the one who does the negotiating. I think that maintaining this type of personal involvement in the business, staying on top of certain key areas such as financing and design, is not only good for me, personally, by keeping me challenged, but it's also good for business.

"The investors I work with have a lot of money, usually a lot more than I do, so they can afford to be choosy, too. If I was just cranking out houses as fast as I could without worrying about doing a nice job, I might make money, but I wouldn't be offered some of the really interesting projects I'm starting to get involved with, and that means a lot to me. Money isn't everything. If I wasn't interested in what I'm doing, challenged by it, I would have gotten out of real estate by now. In fact, I almost did get out last year (1980) when it all got to be too much for me.

"When I quit social work in 1978, everything I made went right back into my business. I wasn't really spending anything on myself, and I wasn't really having any fun.

"In 1979, I started hiring other people to take care of the taxes and bookkeeping and some of the other details I had been handling by myself, but that still wasn't enough. I found I was still driving myself too hard, and it got to the point where I was even having nightmares about tenants, and things like that—and my tenants don't even give me much trouble!

"I just decided I had to get away and start making some changes in my life. Sure, I was successful, but if I wasn't happy, then it just wasn't worth it to me to continue.

"So I decided to take my first real vacation in years, and I went to visit my brother, who lives in Maui, Hawaii. As soon as I got there, I fell in love with it, and I wound up buying a condominium there, as well as some residential building lots I'm holding on to for investment and planning to develop some day. I even wound up starting a new company: the Western Islands Development Corporation, headquartered in Maui, to buy property there and in British Columbia, Canada, which is a booming area because of all the oil they have up there.

Urban Renewal

"When I got back from Maui, I decided to stick with real estate, but I also decided to reorganize my business so it wouldn't dominate my entire life, and to start spending some of my money and enjoying myself. I got some good tax and real estate lawyers and accountants, and set up one corporation for my rental business, to manage my own properties and those I handle for out of town investors, and another corporation that is allowed to be a dealer in properties: buying them, renovating them, and then putting them right back on the market and selling them for an immediate profit. That way, I keep the different aspects of my business separate.

"The funny thing is, not only am I more relaxed now, but I'm making more money, and my business is expanding faster than ever. Before, I was working primarily on my own, just doing houses, but now I meet investors through referrals from attorneys and accountants, and by using their money, I'm able to get into bigger, more interesting projects than I could on my own.

"I'm still doing houses, both for myself and for investors, but now I'm also getting into restoring historical buildings which I couldn't afford to do on my own, or which might not be that profitable. Some of the people I'm working with now have enough money that their main concern is the special tax write-offs they can get by investing in historical restoration projects.

"I love doing those kinds of projects. It's something new and challenging for me, but I couldn't afford to do them without having investors to back me up. I don't have enough capital, and I don't need the tax write-offs, because I have enough already. So now, the bigger my business gets, the more I enjoy it, because I'm constantly getting into new things.

"I'm negotiating now to buy some industrial loft property in Philadelphia at $6 a square foot and turn it into residential and commercial condominiums which will eventually sell for $100 a square foot. Why hasn't someone else grabbed it up if there's so much money to be made? Well, first of all, it just became available, and secondly, why didn't other people grab up all the houses in University City when I was picking them up in the 'teens, putting a few thousand into renovations, and renting them for $500 a month? Who knows?

"I'm also negotiating on several other deals, including one which would involve buying an office building for $6.5 million and then spending another $6.5 million on renovations. And in my spare time, I've started doing occasional lectures and seminars.

"At first, I wasn't sure if I would like doing that, but now I've decided I do enjoy it, and I think I'm going to start doing them on a regular basis. I've been on TV and done several interviews besides this one. At first, I wasn't sure if the publicity was a good idea, but now I've decided it gives me credibility and helps attract investors.

"I'm also working on a book about renovating properties, and I'm considering doing another book about my life and all the experiences I've gone through. I want to show people it *can* be done, and I particularly want to show women they can do it without giving up anything, without losing their femininity or becoming hard.

"I haven't let myself become hard, and I don't see why I should. Most of the people I deal with have a high degree of integrity. They may be tough negotiators looking to get the best deal they can, and obviously they are in business to make money, but they are fair and honest. Most entrepreneurs are pretty interesting people. They're out to make money creatively, not by cheating anyone, and that's my attitude.

"I don't have any long-term goals beyond going on with my life, enjoying it and continuing to grow. I have my short-term goals all laid out—the various projects I want to take on, but in the future, who knows?

"The person you should really speak to, though, is my mother. She was a housewife all her life—my father is an Episcopal priest—and then someone left her an old broken-down house—a woman she had been good to and taken care of—and then when I got married—I was the youngest of three children, and the last to leave home—she fixed it up, made some money, and then went on to make a million dollars in real estate. And she was fifty-five before she ever got started. She's a lot more interesting than I am."

21

Pets and Children Welcome
Janet Little

"If I ever write a book," says Janet Little of Houston, Texas (Jennifer Steves' mother), "I'll probably call it 'Pets and Children Welcome.' When I started in the rental business, I was so naive that I put an ad like that in the newspaper, and I couldn't understand why I was swamped with calls. I continued to use that ad for several years . . . I never had a vacancy problem.

"When I looked at property, I asked myself if it would be a good home for families and children, not how much money I could make on it. I wanted to provide good housing for people who needed it.

"Real estate was something that had always been in the back of my mind, but my family came first. I don't know if things like that are hereditary and can be passed down from generation to generation, but my father and grandfather were both builders, stonemasons, and my father was a designer as well. He never went to architectural school or anything like that, but he could design anything, and I've had an interest in real estate ever since I can remember.

"Then about the time my daughter Jennifer was married—she was my youngest, and the last one to move out—someone died and left me an old run-down house. My husband was the Rector of St. Andrew's Episcopal Church here in Houston Heights, and although the woman who died wasn't a member of the parish, I had helped to take care of her while she was ill, and so she left me her house. I got it fixed up, rented it out, and started getting a nice bit of income each month.

"That got me started, and then I bought five units which were run-down, for $8,500. Now this was in the same area, known here in Houston as the Heights, because it looks down on the rest of the city, the downtown area and all. It's a curious thing. It's part of the city of Houston, but it's got definite boundaries, because when 'the Heights' was incorporated into the city back in 1918, it was under the condition that it would be legally and forever dry. There are a lot of Baptists here, and they insisted on that before they would join the city of Houston. So now the Heights is forever legally dry.

"Anyway, one night I was looking out over the rest of the city, and I thought to myself that if that view was in New York or somewhere like that, it would be worth a fortune. Now, this is a beautiful neighborhood, with many fine old Victorian homes, but at that time, prices were pretty low; a lot of the people in the neighborhood were poor, and a lot of the old houses were run-down. But I looked at that view, and I knew that someday property here in the Heights was going to be worth a lot of money.

"Wages were low then, also. I knew skilled carpenters and people like that here in the Heights who worked for as little as $2 an hour, so that made it easy for me to get started. I did all the contracting and managing myself. I hired the workmen, I supervised the jobs, I kept the books and everything. I didn't do much of the actual labor myself, but I did everything else.

Earn While You Learn

"Before that, I never had any real business experience. I was a wife, mother, piano teacher and church organist, but I had to learn about being a landlord and a businesswoman as I went along, and I worked hard at it for eight years, from 1967 to 1975, buying properties and fixing them up.

"I have never had any special problems being a woman. I'm lucky, I guess. I found a good banker who believed in me, and I also managed to get some good deals and pick up some properties with old loans, at low interest rates, which I was able to assume. For instance, I got 19 units and a pool, with a loan at 6 percent, from an owner who had to get rid of them.

"But, of course, I've had my headaches, too, and my share of interesting incidents. Once I went to collect the rent from a young couple in one of my apartments, and I knew right away the boy was high on something because he was acting strangely. I wanted to get out of there, so I just told him I would come back when his girlfriend got home from work, and I would collect it from her. Then, just as I was turning to go, he came at me and began chasing me.

"I got out of there okay, but later I found out he had been sniffing glue, and that's what had made him act that way.

"I also was threatened once, when I had to ask someone to leave. It was a nice building here in a good part of the Heights, and all of my tenants were solid working people. Well, I had an apartment for rent, and this beautiful girl came along and she had no husband, but she had four children, so I felt sorry for her and let her have the apartment. And then, pretty soon, I'm getting calls from the other tenants threatening to leave unless I get her out.

"It seems she had men coming in a steady stream at all hours of the day and night. She was a call girl. When she was moving in, I had noticed a man in a Cadillac dropping her off. I didn't think anything of it at the time, but apparently that was her procurer. When I told her she would have to get out, he started screaming at me, wanting to know why I took her deposit if I wasn't going to let her keep the apartment, and then he threatened me.

"Nothing ever came of it, though. They just left coffee grounds in the bathtub, and put ketchup all over the mattress when she moved out. But she did get out. I've never had to call the sheriff on anybody yet.

Home Is Where the Investments Are

"Anyway, I kept on buying run-down property here in the Heights, in spite of the occasional problems. I bought one house for $4,000. The city made me spend $600 to get it rewired; then, before I could even rent it out, the city bought it from me and tore it down to build a community center. I bought some units for $25,000, with $1,000 down. I also bought some land back in Virginia; that's where we are originally from. The property is near my sisters, between Monterey and McDowell. I got the land for $54 an acre, with a big old house, and we use it as a summer place. That one is the best buy I ever made. It's worth a lot more than I paid for it, and it's the first house we restored.

"But for the most part, I've stuck to investing here in Houston Heights. I'd find places just by knowing the area, as well as through agents, but most of them didn't want to bother with me too much, because they knew I was choosy and would only buy really good deals.

"Most of my properties were in poor areas, and many of my tenants were from Mexico and didn't even speak English. I used to visit with them, and my husband baptized some of their children, even though they were mostly Catholics.

"My husband, Father Haskin Little, was the Rector of St. Andrew's for 25 years, so he was too busy with his church and community work to do much with the real estate we owned, although he has been involved with real estate in his own way.

"He is the Chairman of an inter-church group, a nonprofit corporation which has built two high-rise apartment projects for senior citizens. Four churches are involved: our Episcopal church, the Heights Christian Church, the Presbyterian church, and the Roman Catholic church. We built 223 apartments for people 62 and over, or who are handicapped in some way. The government subsidized 20 percent of the units, but the building is owned by the nonprofit corporation and the rest of the units all break even. It cost $3 million for that project, and then five years later, when we built another 151 apartments, it cost $5 million to do it. That is why real estate is such an easy investment. Prices just keep going up and up and up, because land, labor, materials, everything else keeps going up.

"Here in the Heights, a lot of other people started getting the same idea I had, buying up old run-down properties and renovating them, and now (1981), this has become a fashionable neighborhood. There are young professionals moving in, and some of the houses are selling for $150,000 and more. I was lucky. I got in right at the start of it all, and so my properties just kept going up in value along with all the rest.

"I had one man who was after me for years to sell him one building I owned, and I kept telling him I wasn't ready to sell it, but he wouldn't give up. Finally, he got me by offering me a good profit on the building and then agreeing to let me collect all the rents for the first year after he bought it.

"Why did he want that building so badly? Probably because it was a moneymaker rather than a troublemaker. All my properties were in good shape once I finished fixing them up, so there was no deferred maintenance, and I would get mostly good tenants in there who knew that and appreciated it.

Fair But Firm

"I never saw real estate as just a way to make money. It was a way to help the community, to improve it and to give poor people a decent place to live. In that sense, it was an extension of my work for the church, just like my husband's projects for the senior citizens, only I was able to make a profit on my work, besides.

"I suppose some people have tried to take advantage of me because of my husband's position in the community—everyone here in the Heights knows Father Little—and so they thought I might be a soft touch. But for the most part, I think if you treat people fairly, then that is the way they will respond.

"And besides that, I now have a full-time manager for my properties. I'm down to only two now, a 19-unit luxury building with a pool, and an eight-unit building. My husband retired a few years ago—I think he just decided that 25 years at the same church was enough, and it was time to give someone else a chance—so we travel a lot. When he retired, they made him Rector Emeritus, and now we have a life estate in the Rectory, so our expenses are very low and we can afford to get away a lot.

"My husband considers it part of his mission to take people who are afraid to travel on their own, so we have taken tour groups all over the world. And then we also go to visit our three children and our families, so I couldn't keep up with the properties any more without a manager, and I'm lucky—I've got a very good one.

"She was a sergeant in the Air Force, where she was in charge of policing drugs and camp followers, so she doesn't stand for any nonsense. It's like the story about the Quaker who's trying to milk his cow, and the cow keeps kicking over the bucket and refusing to be milked. This goes on for awhile, and then finally he says to the cow: 'As thou knowest, I am a man of peace who does not believe in violence, so I cannot beat thee and I cannot kick thee. But keep acting up like this, and I shall sell thee to a Baptist, who will beat thee and kick the hell out of thee!' She's my Baptist.

"But don't get me wrong. All my tenants love her. She's firm, but she's fair, and she keeps a tight rein on the properties for me. Now that I've moved up to a higher class of property, I don't let the tenants have pets anymore. It's too much trouble, and I'm not quite as naive as I was when I first started. But some of them try to get around it. Just recently, one woman with 'no pets' written into her lease, tried to hide her mother cat and kittens in the oven when my manager came to collect the rent. She gave the woman a few days to find homes for them, or, one for herself!

"Owning rental property is rarely dull, although I've gotten a lot more professional about it. Now I belong to the Houston Apartment Association, the Texas Apartment Association, and the National Apartment Association, and they have all sorts of educational programs, and I also read some books on real estate investment. I had a real estate license from 1975 to 1980, but then I gave it up. I never used it very much, anyway.

"Except for my daughter Jennifer, who has done quite well on her own, my children don't seem to have much interest in real estate, but they've done very well in their own fields. Christopher is a lawyer. He was counsel and a vice president for the *Washington Post*, and now he is publisher of *The Herald*, at Everett, Washington, which is owned by the *Post*. Michael is an English professor who lives on Maui, Hawaii, so I think I did a pretty good job raising them. My two grandchildren, Timothy and Meg Little, age 14 and 11, are pretty terrific, too.

"For me, real estate is exciting and challenging, but my family has always come first. But that's just one more good aspect of investing in real estate. Not only was I able to start later in life, after my children were grown, and without having much money to invest, but I have always been able to fit it to my own schedule and my husband's schedule. It's flexible. You've got to put in a lot of time, at least in the beginning, but you can set your own hours and decide what days or weeks you want to take off.

"I just love houses. I always have, ever since I was a little girl; especially the big old stone houses they have back East. The kind my father and my grandfather used to build. I also love people. I love working with people, trying to help them. Fixing up old houses and apartments, building new housing for senior citizens and the disabled, creating nice places for people to live, just came naturally to me, but it's definitely not my only interest in life. I like to keep active in a variety of ways.

"I was Ladies' Golf Champion when we lived in Lampassa, Texas for four years, and I swim a lot. I have constantly read all my life, and I also paint in oils. My husband and I like to play Bridge, and have played in the Nationals, and in my spare time—mostly in the middle of the night—I write poetry. I want to call my serious book, *Time Us Too Shall Cover*.

"I am also the free decorator for the high-rise apartments we built for people who are 62 and over, or handicapped, and for our conference center and for Camp Allen, built by our church on 750 acres near Houston. My husband says when you work for free, you can get plenty of work, but I enjoy it.

"I believe that if you care, you can make a building beautiful—decorations, furniture, etc.—with the same amount of money it would take to make it look ordinary. I buy good reproductions of oriental rugs, Chinese lamps, good art for the walls. The beautiful atmosphere makes the people who live there happy, and we almost never 'lose' anyone to nursing homes. A man in a wheelchair in Heights House, our last project, saw me hanging pictures, and said, 'It's looking more like the Biltmore every day.' (What a sad thing to have the Biltmore destroyed!)

"I do it all as inexpensively as I can, to make the money we have available go as far as possible. Recently, I saved a lot of money on a free decorating job by buying beautiful handwoven woolen hangings in a little village in Spain, called Mijos, instead of buying oil paintings or other art for the walls. I saved about $1800, and I got satisfaction from it, too, so everybody benefitted.

"It was the same with buying rental property. Investing in real estate gave me a chance to combine two of the things I enjoyed, so I did it and I prospered, and so did the community. And my daughter Jennifer is the same way. She was a social worker for many years, and she was involved with the theater and the arts in general, and now she is restoring old buildings, and she's become independently wealthy and has helped bring back her community, too. Maybe it does run in our family."

22

Share the Wealth
Paul Simon

"All you have to do is to figure out how things really are, and not how people say they are," says Paul Simon, of Modesto, California. "And with real estate, people care about two things: how much down, and how much a month. You work that out, and the rest is easy."

In slightly more than four years, Paul has used that philosophy to become a top real estate salesman, the founder of a successful flat fee brokerage company, and the owner of several million dollars' worth of property, most of which he never even has to see, let alone manage. He is also one of the hottest new speakers on the real estate seminar circuit, and the author of one popular book, *An Offer You Can't Refuse*, a compilation of sample real estate contracts he has used successfully, and a new book to be put out by Impact Publishing Company, called *A License to Steal*, all about the various ways you can buy real estate without money.

He lives in a beautiful $150,000 house rent free, and even makes $25 a month positive cash flow on the deal. He spends most of his time travelling around the country first class, lounging in the sun at quality hotels, giving one or two seminars a week and three or four previews, buying up property all across the country, and spreading the word through his "Get Wealthy Clubs" for graduates of his seminars. All this from a man who went bankrupt in 1973 and was laying carpets for a living at the beginning of 1977 . . . less than five years ago.

Starting at the Bottom

"Yes, I've been bankrupt," Paul Simon admits. "It started back in November, 1971, when I quit my job as a carpet salesman for Montgomery Ward and my wife Glenda and I started the Anchor Chemical Company, manufacturing commercial and industrial chemicals. We took over an existing company and started with only $700 in cash, and by January 1, 1972, three months later, I had set up a complete network of distributors and we had $30,000 in the bank.

"In August, 1972, we sold out to a company called Bio Ecology for $50,000 cash and 667,000 shares of their stock, which was supposedly worth $20 a share, but within seven months, they had gone bankrupt.

"Our arrangement was that we were supposed to keep selling them supplies, and we were supposed to get a royalty payment equal to five percent of their gross sales. But after a couple of months, they stopped paying us the royalty, so we stopped sending them supplies. Eventually, they were forced into bankruptcy, and we lost about $300,000 worth of equipment they had inherited when they took over the business. Plus, we incurred liabilities of $880,000 as John Doe defendants, because of our relationship with them and all the stock we held, so that drove *us* into bankruptcy, too.

"I went back to Ward's for about a year, then in 1974, I went off on my own again and opened a carpet business with two partners. In those days, we used to just throw away the remnants, the pieces that were left over after we carpeted a room, and leave them in the trash out back. Well, one day I noticed that people were always going through that trash barrel, and some of them acted like it contained pure gold. So then I decided that maybe instead of throwing the stuff away, we could try selling it. Nobody was doing that back then, and everybody thought I was crazy, but I convinced my partners to give it a try, and we opened Big Foot Remnants.

"We made a fortune with that idea. We would get the remnants free from some of the big carpet places; they were glad to be rid of them. Then people were paying us good money. But my partners and I had some disagreements, and I decided to open a carpet shop on my own, and that's how I eventually got into real estate.

"I couldn't get anyone to help me in the carpeting business," he says, "because I worked them too hard. My son didn't want to work with me, and I couldn't find anyone else, either. A friend of mine, who was a remodeling contractor, was having the same problem. He couldn't get anybody reliable to work with him, either, so we made a deal. I would help him, and he would help me.

"Well, it didn't take long to realize that we were making a lot more on the remodeling than the carpet laying, so I just gave the carpet business away to another friend of mine. I told him all I wanted was the accounts receivable and the money for all the stock as that got sold, and I threw myself into the remodeling business full time.

"We were remodeling kitchens, and there is a lot of lag time on each job. For instance, you put in a set of cabinets, and then you have to wait for the stain to dry before you can do anything else, and that's a day or two of doing nothing. So I decided that we ought to find a house of our own that we could work on when we had extra time like that, and then sell it for a profit.

"The idea was to get someone else to put up the cash, and then we would do all of the work and split the profits, once the place was sold. We put an ad in the paper, and sure enough, we had no trouble finding people who had money to invest. So we bought one house, fixed it up, and made money, then we bought two more.

"Since it looked like we were going to be doing this on a regular basis, I decided I should get a real estate license, so we could save the commission whenever we bought or sold something. So I began studying for the test.

"Around this same time, the friend I'd given my floor covering shop to, ran into problems. He just wasn't making a go of it, and so he spent the accounts receivable, sold the remaining stock, and walked away from it. So I had to go back and deal with that business again.

"Meanwhile, my partner was sitting around doing nothing, just waiting for me to get my real estate license, and I decided there was no point to that. I didn't want to hold him back, and I didn't want him holding me back, so I told him I thought it was best if we each went our separate ways.

"I sold the floor covering shop in April, 1977, got my real estate license, and on April 15, my first day on the job, I sold my first house. My broker told me it was beginner's luck, but I knew better than that. Wherever I've worked, I've always been the number one salesman, and I didn't see why real estate should be any different. I had learned the secret of making sales on my first job, and it had stuck with me ever since.

Knowledge Is Power

"I was 18 years old, and right off the farm when I walked into a Chrysler dealership in Porterville, California, and told the owner, a man named Blane Syttes, that I wanted a job detailing cars. You know, cleaning them up inside and out and making them sparkle.

"He told me they really didn't need anyone to do that, and I said, 'Fine.' I loved to do it so much that I would do it for free if he'd just let me hang around. So I worked the first two days, and I did such a good job that he called me over and said he was going to start paying me after all, including the two days I'd already worked.

"He knew I really wanted to become a salesman, and so he gave me the Chrysler manual and told me to study it and learn all I could about the cars if I was going to try and sell them. Now, I'm sure he probably told all the other salesmen the same thing, but most of them probably didn't pay much attention. But I thought he was such a neat guy, that I took him seriously. I went home and studied that manual until I knew it backwards and forwards, and knew everything about those cars. Within three months of getting hired, I was a salesman, and within six weeks after that, I was outselling everybody in the place and I became sales manager.

"I knew so much about the cars that the guys in the service department used to ask me questions about adjusting certain parts, things like that. I was making $2,500 a month, and that was more money than I'd ever dreamed of.

"When I got into selling carpeting, I worked for Sears, and I developed a system of prospecting customers which they still use today. At Montgomery Ward, I was number eight salesperson in the entire country.

"I had my volume up several hundred percent, while all the carpet departments in all the other stores were way down in the volume of business they were doing. They gave me seven stores all through central California, and I got the volume up in all of them. I took my people to carpet mills so they could see how carpeting was made. I took them to visit distributors, so they would understand why it took so long to get to the stores. I figured the more they knew about carpeting, the easier it would be for them to sell it.

"When I got into selling real estate, I just applied that same principle. I figured that the financing was all people really cared about, and if I learned all there was to know about financing, then nobody would ever be able to outsell me.

"Of course, I didn't know how to write up a contract. Passing the test for my real estate license hadn't taught me a thing about that, so I went to my broker for help, but he didn't know how to write one up, either.

"I looked at him, and I said, 'You're the broker, and you don't know how to write up a contract either? How did you ever become a broker?' 'Well,' he said, 'I just had the educational requirements, so I took the test and became a broker.' (In California a person must have taken six required courses and have a college degree, *or* two years of full-time real estate experience to qualify for the broker's exam. Therefore, a college graduate can become a broker and open his or her own office without any experience at all.)

"So that meant I had to learn how to do it myself. It also got me thinking that if *he* could become a broker, so could I. All I had to do was get some experience and get those educational requirements behind me.

"I decided when I sold that first house that real estate was a lot easier than everybody said it was, and I went on to prove it. In my first six months, I sold seventy-seven houses, and I was just getting warmed up. In the following year, I sold three hundred and thirty-three. Then a funny thing happened.

The Tax Man Cometh

"While I was busy selling all those houses, another man in the office was buying houses, thirty-five of them in one year. I had sold him seventeen of them, and my wife was all nervous about it. 'Oh,' she told me, 'I just know he's going to be unhappy with those houses and decide that he's made a mistake, and then he's going to be mad at you, and we're going to have to leave town.' But I looked at that man, and I thought about how much those houses had gone up in value in just one year, and I realized he had made almost as much money in appreciation by buying only 35 houses as I had made by selling over three hundred of them. And he didn't have to pay a dime in taxes on that money, while I had to pay over $50,000 to the government.

"So that got me thinking, and after that, I decided to start buying houses instead of only selling them, so I could save some money on taxes, but I really didn't know anything about it. I knew all about selling houses by then, but I really didn't know anything about buying them. So the first book I read was *The Monopoly Game*, by Dave Glubetich, and just five lines in that book—all about lease options—really got me going.

"I went out and bought 73 houses over the next several months, and then turned around and sold them all on one year lease options for about $10,000 more than I paid for them, and I figured that after all expenses, I would make about $7,000 on each one. The only problem was the negative cash flow. By the end of the first year, it was running about $3,500 a month, but I was able to cover it pretty easily, because each month I would sell off one or two houses that I'd optioned the year before, and pick up my $7,000 or so profit on those.

"In January, 1979, I also started a flat fee brokerage company called Homeowner's Showroom, and by August, we had 11 sales people and 105 houses in escrow. I still didn't have a broker's license at that point, so I was paying someone else 10 percent of the money we took in just to front the operation.

"In September, 1979, the *Modesto Bee*, a local newspaper, ran an article on us, and we began selling franchises. We sold 17 of them before the state stepped in and told us we didn't have the proper permit, and made us stop. We kept applying and reapplying... we must have spent about $150,000 on lawyer's fees before we finally gave up... and getting turned down on all kinds of technicalities. Finally we decided someone was deliberately blocking the idea, so we just took the 17 offices back as branch offices.

"I hired a general manager, who was a friend of the broker. He had been the West Coast manager for a large savings and loan association, so he seemed like a good prospect, but he got the urge to go on to other things, and he left after a short while.

"About this time, in the summer of 1980, the bottom also fell out of our business. My houses weren't selling any more because people were no longer exercising their options, and my expenses were up to $8,500 a month. For a while, things got a little tight. Then I saw an article about Advance Mortgage Company in New Jersey. They had a special program where they only charged people 12 percent for second mortgage loans instead of the usual 18 percent, in exchange for getting a one-third equity interest in the property. It said the delinquency rate on this program was running about one-tenth of one percent, as opposed to seven percent on their regular loans, and that gave me an idea.

No Money Down and No Negative Cash Flow

"Earlier in the year (1980), I had seen an ad for Robert Allen's seminar on how to buy real estate with nothing down, and signed up for that, just to see if he knew anything I didn't already know about. Well, there wasn't too much that was new to me, but it was a great seminar anyway. I had been buying a lot of property without putting any money down, and I knew that worked, so now I decided to add a little twist to it: equity sharing. The Multiple Listing Book was full of good homes I could buy with no money down, but most of them carried negative cash flow—the rents wouldn't match the payments. So I decided to find people who wanted to own a home and could afford the monthly payments, but didn't have any down payment money, and offer them half interest in a house if they would live there and cover all the maintenance and expenses.

"I ran an ad in the *Modesto Bee* saying, 'Why rent when you can own?' and I got over 400 phone calls. People were calling in and saying, 'Have you got anything in a nice two-bedroom on the north side of town?' and I'd say, 'Hang on a minute,' and I'd look through the Multiple Listings to see if there was anything like that which looked as if it would sell with nothing down.

"Now, of course, most of these 'No Money Down' deals involved some cash. It just wasn't coming out of my pocket. Most of the time I would just get a house with an old, low-interest assumable loan, get a purchase money second from a mortgage company so the seller could get some cash out of the deal, and then have the seller carry back a third mortgage for the balance. That's why there was usually at least some negative cash flow involved, but the equity sharing program solved that problem.

"I would offer people half interest in the house if they would live in it and be responsible for the entire payment and all the maintenance. That way, I was giving away half of something which hadn't cost me anything in the first place, and I had no maintenance or negative cash flow problems to worry about, so I could buy as many houses as I could find. My only rule was to try and stay under $60,000, because when you get above that price range, the payments get too high for the average family to afford.

"So I started taking people's names and just putting them on a waiting list if I couldn't find anything for them right away. The response was just fantastic. I wound up buying over $4.5 million worth of houses in one year. I made up a contract with my co-owners, obligating them to keep up all payments and maintenance for a three- to five-year period, depending on how long the seller was willing to carry the third, and stating that the agreement will be cancelled automatically if they miss any payments or do not keep on top of the maintenance as they promised to do.

"At the end of the three- to five-year period, the agreement calls for the property to be appraised, and then my co-owner has the option to buy me out if he/she wants to go on living there. If he/she doesn't want to buy me out, then I have the option to buy him/her out, otherwise, we put the house on the market and split the profits.

A Star Is Born

"So I was doing this for a few months, and then in November, 1980, I got a phone call from Robert Allen offering me a free trip to the Bahamas at Christmas. If you are a graduate of his seminars, and you buy and hold a million dollars' or more worth of property in one year, you are invited to join. He had heard about me and the fact I had bought over $4 million in one year, and he wanted to know how I did it.

"So I went to the Bahamas, and I spoke to the people there about equity participation, and they went crazy over the idea. Robert Allen came to me afterwards and said several people had told him I would make a good speaker, so he offered me a job doing seminars for him. I told him I had been working for myself for too long to suddenly start working for someone else, but that got me thinking.

"On January 10, 1981, I held my own seminar, my first one, in Fresno, California. I got fourteen people—including Robert Allen—at $195 a piece, to hear me talk about equity participation.

"Then I went up to Sacramento, California, the state capital, and did seven free previews to try and stir up people's interest, and then did a seminar on equity participation for 50 people on January 26, two weeks later.

"My third seminar was in Concord, California, at the local junior college. I drew eight people, including my general manager and my partner in Sacramento, and they were both ready to quit.

"Then we got a contract to train all the agents in all the Century 21 real estate offices in Northern California about equity participation, but we went our separate ways.

"I went on to Cleveland, where a man named Paul Dieter set everything up for me and arranged it all, the hotel, the advertising, all that, and I had 73 people. Then I went on to Columbus, Ohio, and sold out. The room was packed. I went back to Cleveland and had 200 people this time. Then I went on to Florida, and back to California, and I've been selling out ever since. Right now (September, 1981), I'm booked solid until Christmas.

"I'm also working on a book for Impact Publishing Company, called *A License to Steal*, all about the various ways I know of to buy property without any money. And I'm writing a monthly column for Impact's *Update Newsletter*. Each month I'll go into a different trick deal which people can use to make money in real estate. I can go on with that forever. I know a million of them, and I'm thinking up new ones all the time.

"Just the equity participation alone can be worked so many different ways. For instance, I sold my house, and now I live there rent free, and I even have a $25-a-month positive cash flow.

"I found a doctor who was looking for a legitimate tax shelter, and I said to him, 'Look, my house payments are $1,300 a month. If you will pay half of that, I'll give you half interest in the house.' Well, he liked that idea, because he could write off all the money he paid out each month and depreciation on half the house, so it really wasn't costing him anything, and he was getting half the appreciation on a $150,000 house which was going up in value by at least 10 percent a year.

"Well, he liked the idea so much that he brought another doctor around, and wanted to know if I could work out the same sort of arrangement for him. So I said, 'Sure,' and sold this other doctor the other half of the house, provided I could live there rent free as long as I wanted to.

"Well, they didn't care. They were just so happy to be doing it this way, with no down payment, so they're each paying $675 a month, for a total of $1,350. But my payment is only $1,325, so I actually *make* $25 a month.

"Plus, I figured I had thirty thousand dollars' equity in the house, so I'm charging them 10 percent interest on that. There are no payments until the house is sold, but it's just building up.

"I also picked up a trick at that Millionaire's Club meeting in the Bahamas. John Schaub, of the Miller/Schaub seminars, made a joke. He talked about buying a house on a lease option, and then selling it again on a contract of sale. At a higher price, of course. That way, you wouldn't have to transfer title to the property, and so no one would have to know you didn't even own it.

"Well, he just said it as if it was funny, but I figured out a way to make it work. I agree to buy a house for, say, $60,000 on a lease option for one year or longer, and talk the seller into renting it to me for $400 a month for that year. Then I sell it to someone else, also on a lease option, for $70,000, and I charge them $600 a month, with $200 of that credited towards the down payment if they actually buy the house.

"So I'm getting $200 a month positive cash flow, and if they buy the house, I get $7,600 cash, minus my selling expenses, closing costs, etc.

"Equity Participation is the only way to go, though, if you're buying property out of your own area, because it eliminates the maintenance. I've been buying houses all across the country. Wherever I go, I buy houses, and I give some of them to people in my seminars, and I keep some for myself.

Today Not Tomorrow

"The company we formed to run the seminars is called 'T.N.T. Productions—Today, Not Tomorrow,' and we have a man who travels ahead of me to the different cities where I go. He finds deals both for the corporation to buy and for me to give away at the seminars for $2,000 to people who really want to get started and try equity participation themselves to see how easily it works.

"There's just nothing but good buys out there, all across the country. In Dallas, we're buying 90 houses in one batch, and we're not having any trouble finding people to move in there on an equity participation basis. But better than that, we're getting them so cheap I'm pretty sure I can slap new loans on them and crank $5,000 cash out of each one right away. That will be $450,000, just for buying them and taking them off the seller's hands. Plus, we'll have half equity in all of them, and get half the appreciation when they're sold in a few years.

"In Florida, we put an ad in the newspaper, saying 'T.N.T. Corporation is looking for houses to lease option for its employees.' We got a call from one man who had a house he wanted $650 a month for. We told him we were sorry, but that was too much money and we couldn't go above $450. 'Well, $650 is not that much when you consider that it's a $120,000 house,' he said. So we went and looked at it, myself and

Jim, the man who books all my seminars for me. He lives in that area. It turned out to be a beautiful four-bedroom house with an indoor swimming pool.

"Jim and I looked at each other, and then he said to the seller, 'We like it. It's a nice house. But we can't afford $650 a month. We'll give you $550.' Well, that guy had obviously been trying to sell that house, or rent it, for a while, and he just couldn't get $650 for it, because he finally accepted $550 a month. He wanted a two-year lease; Jim talked him into going three years.

"Then came the clincher. Jim told him he wanted the whole $550 a month credited towards the down payment when we bought the place in three years, and the seller agreed to it. So we're really buying that place for $100,000 three years from now, because the seller's going to be crediting $19,800 ($550 × 12 months = $6,600 per year × 3 years = $19,800) towards the $120,000 purchase price, and it will be worth almost $160,000 by then, even if it only goes up ten percent a year. ($120,000 + $12,000 = $132,000 value at the end of one year; $132,000 + $13,200 = $145,200 value at the end of two years; $145,200 + $14,520 = $159,720 market value at the end of three years) In the meantime, Jim decided it was such a steal at $550-a-month rent that he moved in there himself.

Work Can Be Fun

"Of course, there are occasional problems in getting people to think creatively. In Dallas, for example, we had to go to three different brokers before we found one who would present an offer which was not on an official Texas state-approved form. They all said they wouldn't do it. Finally, we called the State Department of Real Estate and were told that brokers were bound by law to submit any and all offers. If *they* wrote the offer up, it did have to be on an approved form, but if we wrote it up ourselves, it could be on a roll of toilet paper and they still had to present it. So finally we found a broker willing to go along with what we wanted to do. He's got five offers accepted so far, and he'll make a lot of money if he gets all the rest accepted.

Then I was in Florida at a RAND (Robert Allen Nothing Down) group meeting, and there were a lot of agents and brokers there, and the Chairman asked, 'Who would like to be a buyer's broker?' Do you know, not one of them raised his hand. Why? Because they're too used to doing things the traditional way. I said, 'Heck, I'll do it, if no one else will. I'll even move to Florida.' With all the people in that group, you could make $250,000 a year that way, easily, but they'd rather go after listings, because that's the way they were trained. I don't even take listings any more. I either turn them down, or give them to someone in the office. You make a sale, you know you'll get paid. You get a listing, you're not guaranteed anything.

"For me, real estate's a lot of fun, though, and I enjoy every minute of it. My wife usually comes with me when I travel, and whenever I have any spare time we both love to go and look at houses. Our kids are not really involved with real estate at all, not at this point, anyway, but they're all busy on their own.

"Our son is 22, and he's always loved cars, so he's the manager of the Parts Department at a Chevy dealership, and he loves it. Our oldest daughter is 20, and I think she'll get into the real estate business some-day. Right now she is a manager of five or six departments for Payless Drug Stores and a buyer for them, and she just got married, so all of that's keeping her busy, but she's sort of interested in real estate, too.

Our youngest daughter got married when she was 15, and got preg-nant a year later, so she's 18 now and our granddaughter is almost two. We bought her and her husband a house when they got married. We even made the mistake of putting up a down payment—we didn't know any better at that time—and then a year later they broke up and sold the house.

"So now she lives in a rent-free house, just like we do. I also got a house for my father and one for my mother to live in rent-free. Then one day I found out my father had moved out and someone else was living in the house. He had just given it to them, and he was living in a one-bedroom apartment somewhere else. I went to see him, and he said, 'Son, you know I never wanted that big house.' So I bought the building he lives in, and now he's got his apartment rent free, instead. And now we're buying from one to fifteen houses a week, all across the country, all using equity participation. That way we don't even have any bookkeeping. We stopped counting how many we owned back in March, 1981, and we owned over 100 then. One of these days, we'll have to sit down and count them all.

"With equity sharing, it's all so simple that it's not even work. For instance, my wife's brother is a builder in San Antonio, Texas, and he called up and said he had thirty-five houses, and he couldn't sell them. So we went down there, and I got twenty-eight of them sold in a week and a half."

Definitions

AITD or   *All Inclusive Trust Deed* or

AIDT   *All Inclusive Deed of Trust* The same thing as a wrap-around. This term is frequently used in states like California, where deeds of trust are used instead of mortgages.

Amortized   A loan is amortized in 30 years if, at the end of that time, the borrower will have paid off the entire loan in regularly scheduled, equal payments, and will then own the property free and clear. To amortize is to kill. It takes 30 years to "kill" the debt to the lender.

Assume a Loan   To formally have the loan transferred to your name and agree to accept full responsibility for the payments, thereby relieving the seller of all liability. Not all loans can be assumed this way. Check with a local Realtor or attorney to see what the rules are in your area, and how they apply to the type of loan you are interested in.

Balloon Payment   Not all loans are amortized. Some loans are payable interest only for a specified period of time, with all the principal due in one big balloon payment at the end. Other times, borrower and lender will agree to a straight note, with no payments at all during the life of the note—say five years—and interest and principal all due in one really big balloon payment at the end. It is called a balloon because you go from small or no monthly payments to one big, inflated payment at the end. The final payment just blows up, like a balloon.

Carry Back   See *Take Back*.

Cash to Loan   This means the buyer is putting down cash to cover the difference between the existing loan, which the buyer wants to assume, and the purchase price. For example, a house is selling for $60,000. The buyer puts down $20,000 cash to the existing $40,000 loan and takes over the house and the loan payments. The seller walks away with $20,000, minus expenses, and everyone is happy.

Closing Costs or Settlement Costs   The fees charged whenever a property changes hands. Title insurance, escrow, or attorney's fees (depending on whether you are in a state where lawyers or title-escrow companies handle property transfers), state and/or local transfer taxes, loan fees, any or all of these, can be included as part of the closing or settlement costs, and can be charged to either the buyer or seller, or split between them, depending upon what the buyer and seller agree on.

Conventional Financing   Is through a bank, savings and loan, or mortgage company, as opposed to getting government-sponsored (FHA and VA) or owner financing, or just assuming an old loan. With high interest rates, it is no longer the "conventional" way to finance property sales in most areas of the country, but the name lingers on.

Don't Wanter   A seller who doesn't want the property. He/she has a problem and just wants to be rid of it as soon as possible, so he/she is likely to give a buyer a favorable price and/or terms.

Escrow   The time between acceptance of the buyer's offer and the formal transfer of title at the "close of escrow." Escrow also is used to refer to the sale and all related details, e.g., "I have five escrows going right now," or, "That was a difficult escrow."

FHA   *Federal Housing Administration* A division of the Department of Housing and Urban Development (HUD), a branch of the federal government. Loans are made to eligible homebuyers and investors with a relatively low down payment, and these loans are automatically assumable by a new buyer. This means that the new buyer saves loan fees, and does not have to worry about qualifying for the loan. He/she just pays a modest assumption fee and takes over the payments. (The same thing applies to VA loans.)

Finder's Fee   A fee paid to someone who finds a buyer for a particular piece of property or a piece of property for a buyer, or a loan for a borrower. It can be either a flat fee, or percentage arrangement.

FISBO or FSBO   *For Sale By Owner.* A house or other property which is not listed with a real estate agent.

Foreclose   When someone does not keep up payments on a note secured by property, the note holder can foreclose on the property—have it legally taken away from the borrower and sold at auction. The note holder then is paid off in cash for his note, and if there is any money left, it goes either to the borrower, or to anyone else who may have a lien against the property.

Gentrification   The movement by the middle class, usually young professionals, into ghetto and low income areas where they begin renovating buildings and driving rents and prices up, thus squeezing out the existing lower income residents.

Graduated Payment   Some new mortgages start with low payments which gradually increase each year, over a five- to seven-year period. For instance, a straight 30-year loan of $40,000 at 17½ percent interest would cost a borrower $586.54 a month. But let's say the borrower has just gotten a new job. Right now, he/she cannot afford $586.54 a month, but within five years, he/she should be able to comfortably afford that much and more, so a graduated mortgage seems perfect. The payment might start out at only $521.81 and then gradually—as the borrower's salary goes up—it will increase to about $625 a month, where it will remain for the life of the loan.

Lease Option   You are leasing a property with an option to buy it at a future time. Generally, the purchase price—if you decide to exercise your option and buy the property—is set in advance, and you are betting that the property will be worth more than that amount by the time the option runs out, while the seller is betting that it will be worth less. For instance, a house is worth $80,000, but you agree to buy it in three years for $100,000. If inflation drives prices up 10 percent a year for the next three years, the house will be worth $106,400, and you will be ahead. The seller, of course, is betting that housing prices will not go up that much over the next three years.

Lease options are a way to buy property if you have little or no cash. You tie up the property now, but you put up no down payment—except maybe a thousand dollars or so, as a deposit, or option fee—and the rent is bound to be cheaper than the payments would be if you owned the house. Quite often, the seller will even credit part of the rent towards the down payment if you do buy the house.

Leverage   The art of stretching your money so that you get the greatest return on the least amount of capital. If you have $100,000 in cash and you buy one house outright, you will be getting, let's say, $650 a month in rent, of which $150 a month will go to cover expenses (taxes, insurance, maintenance, etc.) and $500 a month or $6,000 a year will be a return on your $100,000 investment. If the house appreciates 10 percent over the next year, you have gotten a total return of 16 percent on your money. But if you took that $100,000 and bought 2 houses, each one rented at $650 a month, and had payments on each one of about $550 a month, you would get $200 a month, that's $2,400 a year, or a 2.4 percent return; plus $20,000 total appreciation on the two houses, or another 20 percent on your $100,000.

If you bought ten houses, putting only $10,000 down on each one, you would lose about $4,000 a month, because your payments would be much higher than your rents; but you will get $100,000 worth of appreciation, leaving you a net gain of $52,000, or a 52 percent return on your investment. Now, if you could get those 10 houses with nothing down, you would be leveraged to the maximum—about as far as you can go.

MLS   *Multiple Listing Service* A book put out each week by the local Board of Realtors which contains pictures and information about various properties listed with its members. This way, companies share information on their listings with each other and expose them to the maximum number of buyers.

Money Market Rate   The interest rate paid by "Money Market Accounts." It varies from day to day. Banks and savings and loans offer certificates of deposit, where the interest rate is fixed for several months, but the money market rate is constantly fluctuating.

Mortgage   A note secured by a lien on a piece of real property. A mortgage gives the note holder the right to take away the property if the borrower does not keep up the payments.

ORDT   *Over-Riding Deed of Trust* This is another term for a wraparound mortgage.

PITI   Stands for *Principal, Interest* (your basic mortgage payment), *Taxes and Insurance.*

Points   Loan fees. The money paid in advance for the privilege of borrowing money. Each point is one percent of the loan amount. If someone talks about paying 18 percent and 5 points to borrow $10,000, they are talking about paying $500 (5 × $100) in points or loan fees as soon as they get the loan, and then $1800 a year in interest, besides.

Redevelopment   When the government declares an area a Redevelopment Zone, and begins tearing down old buildings and building new ones—or occasionally renovating the old ones. This, too, frequently has the effect of driving out existing residents.

Refinancing   Getting a new first mortgage against a property you own, as a way of taking equity out. For instance, you own a house worth $100,000 which you bought five years ago for $50,000. The original $40,000 loan is paid down to around $38,000, so you have about $62,000 worth of equity in the property. You go to a bank and get a new $80,000 loan. You pay off the old $38,000 loan, and you still have $42,000 left over, plus $20,000 equity left in the property.

Rehab   To rehabilitate a building or an area, to fix it up.

Secondary Financing   An alternative to refinancing. Your house is worth $100,000, and you only owe $38,000. Instead of getting a new $80,000 loan at 17½ percent interest with 3 points and paying a $2,400 loan fee and $1,173.07 a month in principal and interest, you get a second mortgage for $42,000 at 18 percent with 5 points. This way, you pay a $2,100 loan fee and $632 a month principal and interest for the second mortgage, and keep your old first mortgage at 9 percent with payments of $321.85 per month. Your combined payment is $953 a month on $80,000 in loans, so you save $300 on the loan fee and $220 a month in payments.

Section 8   A government sponsored rent subsidy program in which tenants pay up to 25 percent of their income, or less, depending on their situation, and the local Housing Authority—using funds provided by HUD—makes up the balance. For instance, Mrs. Jones makes only $800 a month, but she has four children, and the rent for her three-bedroom home is $450 a month. She would pay no more than $200 and the Housing Authority would pay the balance. (Rents are set in advance by a city-wide formula which takes into account only the size and condition of the property itself, not the area.)

Settlement Costs   See *Closing Costs*.

Straight Note   A note on which no payments are made until the note is due and payable in full, at which time all principal and interest must be paid in one big balloon. Interest is usually compounded over the term of the note, but this, like most things in real estate, can be negotiated between the buyer and the seller.

Subject To   To take a property subject to the existing loan means you are taking over the payments, but not the formal responsibility for the loan. You are not formally assuming the loan, and so the seller's name will still be on the loan papers, and theoretically, his/her credit can suffer if you default.

T-Bills   Short and long term notes put out by the Treasury Department whenever the government needs to borrow money. They are auctioned weekly, and the interest rate varies, depending on how many billions are offered and how strong the demand is for T-Bills as an investment.

   The T-Bill rate affects real estate because banks and other mortgage lenders have to compete for the same funds people invest in T-Bills. Banks offer T-Bill-Plus accounts, etc. This drives up the lender's cost of borrowing money from savers, and so it drives up the cost of mortgage money.

Take Back (*as in take back a second*)   The practice of sellers taking back part of their equity in a property they are selling in the form of a note and deed of trust. For example: a seller gets an offer of $100,000 for his house. The existing loan is for $60,000, and the buyer has $20,000 cash for a down payment. The seller takes back the remaining $20,000 of the purchase price in the form of a note secured by the property he has just sold. Or maybe there already was a $20,000 second mortgage on the house, in addition to the $60,000 first mortgage; the seller could agree to carry back a third mortgage for $20,000, and the buyer would get in with no money down at all.

Trust Deed   The same as a mortgage, except that the deed to the property, which is the security for the loan, is held by a neutral third party between the borrower and the lender, the trustee. When the loan is paid off, the trustee reconveys formal title to the property. Until the loan is paid off, the borrower is still the owner of the property, and has the right to use the property, to borrow more money against it, to sell it, etc. But, the formal title rests with the trustee.

VA *Veteran's Administration*   Eligible veterans can get 100 percent financing up to $125,000 on owner-occupied housing. VA loans are automatically assumable by anyone, veteran or otherwise, so many investors look for properties with old, low interest VA loans which they can assume.

Variable Interest Rate   An interest rate that can go up or down with the cost of borrowing money. Old-fashioned variables—those in effect before 1981—could only go up ¼ percent every six months and a total of 2½ percent over the life of the loan, according to a formula set by the federal government, but there was no limit on how far or how fast the interest rate could go down. This year, a new type of variable interest rate loan was introduced. The interest on the new variable rate loans can go up an almost unlimited amount. Bankers are no longer willing to take a chance on getting squeezed by continuing inflation which forces them to pay out high interest on savings while taking in low interest on old long-term, fixed-rate loans.

Wrap-Around   Often referred to simply as a "wrap" or "wrapping" the existing mortgage, it is used frequently in situations where there is an existing first mortgage with a low interest rate which makes it difficult to assume. The seller keeps up the payments on this loan while offering the buyer a larger loan than he/she carries, usually at a higher interest rate. For example: A property with a $30,000 loan at 9 percent is sold for $80,000. The buyer puts down $20,000 and the seller carries a loan for $60,000 at 13½ percent interest. He/she keeps making payments on $30,000 at 9 percent, and pockets the difference. The buyer is happy, because new conventional loans (as of September 1981) are going at interest rates of 17½ percent or more, and the seller is happy because he/she is making 13½ percent on $30,000 and another 4½ percent on the bank's $30,000.

References

Several real estate investment books and authors are mentioned or recommended by one or more subjects of *Fortune Builders*. For your convenience, these are listed here.

Nothing Down by Robert G. Allen
Double Your Money in Real Estate Every 2 Years by Dave Glubetich
How to Grow a Moneytree by Dave Glubetich
The Monopoly Game by David Glubetich
Think Like a Tycoon by Bill "Tycoon" Greene
Win Your Personal Tax Revolt by Bill "Tycoon" Greene
How to Wake Up the Financial Genius Inside You
 by Mark O. Haroldsen
How to Make Money 24 Hours a Day by Elbert Lee
An Offer You Can't Refuse by Paul Simon

If you have trouble locating any of these books, please contact Impact Publishing Company, 1601 Oak Park Blvd., Pleasant Hill, CA 94523, or call (415) 935-4370.

For More Information

Many of the subjects of *Fortune Builders* mentioned that they were writing books of their own to help others achieve the kind of success they have found in real estate investing. Some are also available for lectures, seminars, or consultations. A list of all these successful investors and how to contact them is included here to aid readers who would like to benefit more personally from fortune building advice.

John Broadfoot
c/o Broadfoot Enterprises
1015 West 10th, Amarillo, TX 79101   Phone 806-373-2886
Attorney and author of *Creative Leverage Forms*. Mr. Broadfoot is available for legal work, consulting, lectures and seminars.

Charles Carrithers
c/o Carrithers Realty
12345 Warwick Blvd, Newport News, VA 23606
Phone 804-599-5555
Licensed broker, owner and manager of approximately 400 single family homes. Seminars on making money with notes; consulting.

David A. Chodack
2428 Oregon Street, Berkeley, CA 94705
Author of *Fortune Builders, Real Estate For Home or Profit*; available for seminars, lectures, consulting and ghostwriting.

Phil Drummond
Prosperity Productions
5151 Adamson Street, Suite 200, Orlando, FL 32804
Phone 305-628-5970
Mr. Drummond gives seminars, lectures and workshops on "Control Without Ownership" and puts out a newsletter.

Randy L. Green
P.O. Box 7343, Long Beach, CA 90807   Phone 213-330-1689
Licensed real estate agent and consultant; works primarily with investors interested in single family rental homes. Available for lectures and seminars.

Nick Koon
c/o Nick Koon Realty
460 South State Street, Westerville, OH 43081   Phone 614-882-1288
Licensed broker and owner of over 100 single family homes. Mr. Koon lectures, gives seminars on investing in single family houses, and is available for consulting.

Elbert Lee
P.O. Box 3872, Pinedale, CA 93650   Phone 209-435-3110
Mr. Lee is the author of two books, *How To Make Money 24 Hours a Day* (a real estate investment manual) and *Strive to Arrive* (motivational material). Available for seminars, lectures and consulting.

Wayne Phillips
c/o Phillips Brothers Seminars
28 Allegheny Avenue, Suite 2404, Towson, MD 21204
Phone 301-321-6992
Experts on larger units as well as small residential income properties. Both Phillips brothers are available for seminars, lectures and consulting.

Paul Simon
c/o T.N.T. (Today, Not Tomorrow) Inc.
P.O. Box 3481, Modesto, CA 95353   Phone 209-527-0940
Seminars and forthcoming book about equity participation; books, lectures and tapes about creative real estate investing.

Jennifer Steves
c/o University City Victorian Homes
4730 Warrington Avenue, First Floor, Philadelphia, PA 19143
Ms. Steves works with investors interested in single family homes, as well as large renovation projects. Also available for consulting, and conducts lectures and seminars.

Matthew and Marion Toller
c/o Impact Publishing Co.
1601 Oak Park Blvd., Pleasant Hill, CA 94523
Attention: Judy Moretz, Senior Editor   Phone 415-935-4370

About the Author

David A. Chodack is a real estate agent and investor who works primarily with single family houses and small income properties. He has taught seminars for home buyers, sellers and beginning investors, and in addition to *Fortune Builders*, he is the author of *Real Estate For Home and Profit*, and three novels. He currently lives with his wife and two children in Berkeley, California, where he is working on making his first million.